GOVERNING THE POOR

Governing the Poor

Exercises of Poverty Reduction, Practices of Global Aid

SUZAN ILCAN AND ANITA LACEY

McGill-Queen's University Press
Montreal & Kingston • London • Ithaca

© McGill-Queen's University Press 2011
ISBN 978-0-7735-3797-2 (cloth)
ISBN 978-0-7735-3805-4 (paper)

Legal deposit first quarter 2011
Bibliothèque nationale du Québec

Printed in Canada on acid-free paper that is 100% ancient forest free
(100% post-consumer recycled), processed chlorine free

This book has been published with the help of a grant from the
Canadian Federation for the Humanities and Social Sciences, through
the Aid to Scholarly Publications Programme, using funds provided
by the Social Sciences and Humanities Research Council of Canada.
Funding has also been received from the Social Sciences and Humanities
Research Council of Canada, Canada Research Chairs Program.

McGill-Queen's University Press acknowledges the support of the
Canada Council for the Arts for our publishing program. We also
acknowledge the financial support of the Government of Canada
through the Canada Book Fund for our publishing activities.

Library and Archives Canada Cataloguing in Publication

Ilcan, Suzan, 1960–
    Governing the poor: exercises of poverty reduction, practices of
    global aid / Suzan Ilcan and Anita Lacey.

Includes bibliographical references and index.

ISBN 978-0-7735-3797-2 (bound). – ISBN 978-0-7735-3805-4 (pbk.)

1. Poor – Developing countries. 2. Poverty – Developing countries.
3. Neoliberalism. 4. International agencies – Developing countries. 5. Non-governmental organizations – Developing countries.
6. Poverty – Government policy. I. Lacey, Anita, 1974– II. Title.

HC59.72.P6I53 2011   362.5'526   C2010-905686-8

This book was typeset by Interscript in 10.5/13 Sabon.

Contents

Figures

Acknowledgments

Our work has drawn from much collaboration, which has made this book possible. We would like to recognize the participation of and the inspiration that we gained from the many generous individuals who were willing to discuss issues of development aid and poverty reduction from varying historical, contemporary, and policy viewpoints. We are especially thankful to those who spoke with us as members of local community groups, nongovernmental organizations, private-sector enterprises, development agencies, and international aid and development organizations in the field sites in Namibia and Solomon Islands. We are grateful for the program, policy, and historical documents that we received from research and policy personnel working for development organizations in Ottawa, Canada, and from the United Nations agencies in Namibia, New York, and Solomon Islands. We would also like to express our appreciation for the tremendous help of archivists and librarian assistants at the United Nations Archives in New York and the National Archives of Namibia in Windhoek. We owe a particular debt for the assistance of Ms Casini and Ms Lulukikeni, at the United Nations Archives in New York, and of Mr Hillebrecht, at the National Archives of Namibia, for their time and generosity.

Various sections of this book required the invaluable help of our research assistants. We appreciate the superb work of Pauline Barbou, Cyril Blondel, Jason Byrnes, Frances Cachon, Selma Eren, Marie Fuki, Heather Graydon, Christopher Heron, Heike Lacey, Shaun Metcalfe, Natalie Redstone, Minerva Saddler, and Lauren Tooker, and we are grateful to them all. We would like to acknowledge the exceptional and dedicated work of Steven Richter, data archivist of the Social Justice and Globalization Data Archive at the University of Windsor, for his enhancement of the photographic images that we took at the United Nations Archives and elsewhere and for his conducting library research and providing us with policy and internet materials throughout our research and writing of this book.

Globalizations has kindly given us permission to reproduce paragraphs from S. Ilcan and A. Lacy (2006) in chapter 3. Artist Dudley has kindly given us permission to reproduce Figure 4.3.

It would be impossible to list all the people from whose comments and criticism we have benefited at professional meetings and invited talks where we have individually or jointly presented ideas of this book over recent years. We would like to acknowledge comments from audiences at the Institute on Globalization and the Human Condition (McMaster University, 2004), the Pacific Sociological Association (2005), the International Sociology Association (2006), the Citizenship, Identity, and Social Justice Conference (University of Windsor, 2007), the Gender and Social Politics in an Era of Globalisation Conference (Carleton University, 2007), the University of Saskatchewan (2007), the Canadian Political Studies Association/International Studies Association (2008, 2009), the Security and Exclusion Conference (University of Windsor, 2008), the University of Auckland (2008), the Humanitarianism, Politics, and Culture Conference (Carleton University, 2009), the Society for the Advancement of Socio-Economics (2009), the University of Adelaide (2009), and the Oceanic Conference on International Studies (2010). We also received critical feedback on ideas that we presented at these gatherings or in draft chapters from Rob Aitken, Pat Armstrong, Tanya Basok, Janine Brodie, William Coleman, Alan Cumming, Dia Da Costa, Rianne Mahon, Peter Nyers, Daniel O'Connor, Cristina Rojas, Daiva Stasiulis, Yvonne Underhill-Sem, and William Walters. We alone, however, are responsible for the views the book expresses and for whatever errors or omissions it contains.

Our research received generous support from the Social Sciences and Humanities Research Council of Canada (SSHRCC), Canada Research Chairs program, in which Suzan holds a Tier II Research Chair, and SSHRCC awarded us a three-year grant. This funding made possible all our field, archival, and policy research, our participation in conferences, seminars, and workshops, and our writing of the book. We are most grateful to the SSHRCC for its support of the research and to the University of Auckland and the University of

Windsor for their support. Anita would particularly like to acknowledge the memory of Beverley Cornish, who was a tremendous inspiration to her. Suzan would like to thank Maureen Irish, Anna Lanoszka, Myra Tawfik, and Marcia Valiante for their friendship and intellectual support.

We have benefited enormously from a fine editorial process at McGill-Queen's University Press. Our sponsoring editor, Jonathan Crago, waited patiently for this manuscript and steered it knowledgeably through evaluation and publication. We are very thankful for his dedication to this project. We thank John Parry for his careful and diligent preparation of the manuscript and Joan McGilvray for her suggestions and assistance. We acknowledge with great appreciation the intellectual generosity of the anonymous reviewers who provided invaluable comments and suggestions, and we express our gratitude for their time and efforts during the constructive process of peer review.

Collaborating as we have across distance brings with it some challenges, as well as exciting stimuli, and we would like to thank each other for the persistence this sometimes required and for our friendship.

GOVERNING THE POOR

Introduction

We encounter the poor virtually and physically each day. Beseeching voiceovers on television sets across the affluent global North claim that "fourteen thousand children will die of hunger today" (World Vision 2008). In cities throughout the world, people sleep 'rough' and homelessness increases. Newspapers report the latest local- and national-government initiatives to assist the urban poor through such solutions as the "urban poverty eradication programme" that registers the number of "urban poor" (*The Star* 2008). Finite descriptions jockey with superlatives in the 'everyday' narratives of the plight of the poor, with the poor "hit hardest" or affected "the most."[1] Academe, government, and media collectivize and universalize the poor, with the term covering a vast range of people who lead very different lives in vastly different circumstances. It conjures up such images as people begging on sidewalks, development-aid workers delivering sacks of branded food to victims of famine, and simultaneous Live8 concerts to help the needy in venues across the globe. Such everyday images belie complexity and diversity, as do common reflexive synonyms such as deprivation, destitution, idleness, inferiority, and waywardness. Yet these ideas and their promotion can shape governance of the poor, providing meaning and validation for diverse rationalities and techniques.

Notions of helping the poor drive policies and philanthropic campaigns and act as a framework for reforming them. Assisting the poor has long constituted a powerful political and social imperative, emerging as early as the time of England/Britain's fourteenth–nineteenth-century Poor Laws and their medieval antecedents and debates on the 'right to assistance' for the needy that followed

France's 1848 revolution. More recently, the same desire inspired the War on Poverty in the 1960s' United States and subsequent variants in many advanced liberal states including 'workfare' and 'timed-out' welfare. Barbara Cruikshank shows how the U.S. War on Poverty and the Community Action Programmes effectively welded together the notions of helping the poor and facilitating their own 'self-help' (Cruikshank 1999).

Helping the poor also facilitates a totalizing depiction of the social problems that the poor supposedly face and the desire to remedy them by a range of governmental authorities. This holistic approach directly associates all the generalized characteristics of these people – their diet, dress, employment status, epidemiological risk, gender, housing, hygiene, and race – to their poverty, their state of being very poor. For example, a recent bipartisan commission in the United States led at least fifteen states and the District of Columbia to launch "comprehensive campaigns to help the poor, the majority of whom are women," and to "help low-income people find stable jobs with liveable wages" (Women's e-News 2008). Concurrently, United Nations (UN) officials report: "Rising food prices around the world are likely to drive poor women to trade sex for basic goods like fish and cooking oil, raising the risk of new AIDS infections" (Reuters 2008). Overall, many experts seem to assume that such maladies require reforming the poor as a collective population and thereby transforming their lives.

Central to such totalizing depictions is a trend to quantify the poor. Debates abound regarding the accuracies of such measures as the human development index, country rankings by gross domestic product, and narrower, income-related measures of poverty and concerning the ways in which these comparisons reveal the 'truth' about the poor, their distribution and national rankings, and their relative distress vis-à-vis each other. In this book, however, we do not seek to depict the poor in general or quantify their difficulties. Such simplifications, we contend, only further marginalize them and their experiences. Generalizations about them also enable a plurality of players – national governments, private enterprises, international organizations, and some nongovernmental organizations – to act on populations of them via 'one-size-fits-all' remedies. We aim, in contrast, to explore the ways in which reform efforts affect them by grouping them and treating them as a generalized and singular population. Of central concern to us are the ways in which governmental authorities construct this heterogeneous group as a problematic population in need of aid. Our examination reveals the ways in which the poor are assembled to be cohesive populations for reform. We seek to uncover how these efforts target such heterogeneous people as a single population. Despite their varying encounters with poverty – socially, ethnographically, and at the policy level – various influential groups, organizations, and national governments depict and understand them as a singular population so they can address their poverty via techniques, rationalities, and programs of poverty reduction.

A consideration of these programs enables us to analyse their spread around the world, stressing powerful actors' global solutions to poverty. We show how this response at the global level demands new sites of governance – local, regional, national, and international. These sites differ widely yet apply common modes of reform. Considering the poor as a population needing targeted reform has brought about systematic attempts to solve their problems through rationalities and technologies of global governance. We argue throughout this study that such examples as the rationality of 'responsibilization,' diverse programs of poverty reduction that emphasize empowerment and the market, partnership initiatives, the racial biopolitics of populations, and the securitization of the poor aim to transform their conduct. These rationalities and technologies inform a framework we refer to as the 'new global-aid regime.'

The new global aid regime, we argue, is a form of government that shapes ways of thinking about, problematizing, and reforming the poor. It engages in various aid programs and practices that involve private enterprises, local agencies, national governments, and international organizations, and it operates within, across, and beyond the nation state. The development-aid arrangements involving programs and practices of development and change supported by a wide range of development experts, actors, and participants that have emerged over the last two decades – especially their scope and density – profoundly affect this regime. International organizations, including both intergovernmental organizations and nongovernmental organizations (NGOs), expanded during this time to meet longer-term development goals rather than to provide emergency relief. An assemblage of such bodies – and their poverty specialists, analysts, and advisers – aim to provide long-standing development assistance. Their emphasis on such aid and the growth in their numbers coincided with the debt crises of the 1980s, retrenchment of the welfare state, development of advanced-liberal 'benchmark' goals, and escalating initiatives to promote social and economic change on a global scale. Partnership arrangements now abound between private philanthropic foundations, nongovernmental aid organizations, local, state, and regional governments, international development organizations, and international financial organizations, such as the World Bank. These partnerships contribute to a complex reflexivity of programs and practices in development aid. This arrangement is integral to the new global-aid regime.

We employ a governmentality framework to examine this new regime. This framework allows us to identify diverse schemes and programs that seek to shape the actions of individuals and members of communities that they target as poor. Governmentality both requires and facilitates an analysis of particular regimes or practices of government. This analysis concerns not only "liberalism, conservatism, authoritarianism, managerialism, and so on" but also "liberal, conservative and authoritarian ways of government," features that Dean (2007: 83) more generally refers to as an 'analytics of government.'

In this regard, rather than analysing government in terms only of state activities that laws or policies legitimate, we follow the literature on governmentality and understand government as also involving diverse programs and practices that seek to direct the action of others. These may govern the social and economic conduct of a variety of individuals and groups within and across agencies, organizations, and authorities, including participatory efforts that aim to create more efficient and performance-oriented individuals and organizations.[2] For example, Miller and Rose show how useful it can be to identify and explore the ways in which governance is multifarious, despite key patterns or connections (2008: 21). Thus, while the meaning of governance has expanded, it increasingly involves an array of agents and organizations both within and beyond the state apparatus (Morison 2000: 100; Mosse 2005b: 1–3).

This kind of government, often described as 'advanced liberalism' consists of an assemblage of initiatives that various authorities use to act on particular populations – in this case, the poor – to ensure effective governance. It fosters new ways of configuring problems and finding solutions and underscores approaches and practices that give rise to unpredictable consequences and outcomes. A governmentality approach allows us to recognize what Larner describes as the abilities of advanced liberal rule to govern such populations as the poor from a distance and in diverse ways (2000: 6). Such an analysis of the governmentalities of rule reveals advanced liberalism as varying and having multiple effects, rather than being a singular program or ideology. Further, as we expand on below in our delineation of a genealogical approach and ideas of dis/continuities of rule, it recognizes the effects and influences of earlier, historical rationalities of rule.

In our study, we emphasize the ways in which contemporary approaches to governing the poor and to poverty consist of an assemblage of ways of thinking about and acting on 'the poor' as a problematic and singular population. As a contribution to governmentality studies, our research brings new insight to the dynamic flows of partnerships, programs, and policies that aim to transform the lives of the poor and that impinge on wider social and political processes. Further, it builds on ideas relating to diffusion of governmental activities among a network of international and non-state organizations, or what Larner and Walters (2004a) call 'global governmentalities.' It suggests that a new regime of global aid, as an element of global governmentality, consists of flows (of capital, governmental rule, ideas, information, and people) that move within and across borders and that a range of local, national, and international players enact for a wide variety of purposes and ends.

Our framework facilitates an examination of wide-ranging programs and practices of poverty reduction within that new regime. This regime operates at multiple sites and levels with common approaches, despite clear differences facing poor individuals and communities. We see it as being advanced liberal in orientation: it frames development goals in terms of facilitating development aid recipients' participation in global markets, supports efforts at self-responsibility as a way to serve the interests of government broadly understood, employs the rationality of race and security to govern the poor biopolitically, and endorses various governing practices to influence international organizations to seek partners via policy dialogue, consultation, and participation. These broad-ranging techniques express themselves as initiatives to reduce poverty.

The poor are the locus of socio-political organization and control and are the objects of programs and policies that aim to ease their impoverishment. The resulting poverty-reduction initiatives emphasize aspects of advanced liberal agendas, rather than reducing poverty and facilitating development as a form of social justice. From our perspective, social justice refers to a more equitable distribution of social and economic resources, inclusive political participation, and recognition of the diverse cultural expressions of various groups, including the poor. While academic, policy, and public discussions support, contest, or redefine the concept, it has been a useful term to interrogate the effects of social, economic, and cultural processes on human lives and conditions and to shape legislation, public policy, and the governance of diverse populations. Discourses of social justice are not static repositories of particular forms of knowledge, but rather modes of action and practices that can facilitate and enable other practices as well as being ways of attempting to bring about transformations at many different levels and scales.

In this regard, and like other concepts, social justice is never unitary, as it forms a mixture of contrasting elements that produce various effects, events, and actions. Rather than striving for a politics of recognition where minority groups seek affirmation in public life, we see social justice as a way of changing everyday life worlds via actions that move through and beyond individuals, groups, and organizations. We refer to this kind of transformation and politics as a social-justice life-politics. This orientation seeks actions, belongings, and new forms of knowledge that can engender transformations by linking everyday actors to forces which in turn can generate a network of change and interchange. It resembles Tsing's view about making a difference that changes the world, a view that moves beyond cultural specificity and focuses on the knowledge that makes a difference, which for her "travels and mobilizes, shifting and creating new forces and agents of history in its path" (2005: 8).

Operating within the new global-aid regime, poverty-reduction initiatives present themselves as a remedy for the global poor and as pro-poor solutions, yet we demonstrate throughout this volume that these advanced-liberal problematics of rule in fact do not address the challenges facing the poor. We examine how such a regime gives rise to and depends on particular forms of knowledge and how, as a consequence, it initiates various programs of social transformation that focus on poverty reduction. This study sheds new light on the governance of the poor, precisely in its examination of their global governance. A central theme is that arrangements between communities themselves, local NGOs, states, regional organizations, and international organizations act to govern the poor. This examination of the global governance of the poor shows increasing recognition of the world's poor as a concern. Governmental authorities problematize them in order to seek a solution and consider them a population suitable for remediation and repair.

We employ a range of methods to examine how, and to what extent, international organizations and their partners engage in various rationalities and techniques of governing poverty and the poor. They include a discourse-analytic approach to poverty-related policies, documents, and programs; in-depth, semi-structured interviews of personnel active at local, regional, national, and international levels of poverty expertise; and field research in key program field sites, such as Namibia and Solomon Islands, as well as at international organization sites. Like other qualitative 'triangulation' research (for example, Denzin and Lincoln 2005), this method facilitates formulation of mid-range concepts in such fields as development, governmentality, and international studies.

In light of our in-depth interviewing,[3] our interviews have formed a vital component of our project, allowing us to generate new information to clarify or substantiate organizations' published programs and policies and to confirm our interpretations of relevant discourses and documents. These interviews have also given us an opportunity to hear additional details of poverty-reduction initiatives from those people and institutions charged with implementing them – for example, information that is alternate or supplementary to the organizations' public discourses. In this regard, they have shown us how individual organizations participate in the practices that govern global poverty.

Furthermore, and like other field and ethnographic research in international development aid (see, for example, Ferguson 2006; Goldman 2005a; Gould 2005a; Mosse and Lewis 2005), our field research provided us with a contextual understanding of how, and the extent to which, governance of poverty operates 'on the ground,' links to specific pro-poor or self-responsibility relations, and connects with local aid and NGOs and the governing regimes of international organizations. More specifically, we used it to illuminate extensive documentation on poverty-reduction plans, initiatives, and policies since the 1980s, covering a wide range of countries in the 'North' and select developing countries in the 'South,' particularly Namibia and Solomon Islands. Our policy and archival research allowed us to collect documents on poverty and poverty-related programs and initiatives from international bodies and organizations (namely, the International

Monetary Fund, Oxfam Canada and Oxfam International, the United Nations, USAID, and the World Bank) and to assemble reports from local and national archival sources and websites and secondary source materials. In this context, our archival research at the United Nations Archives in New York and at the National Archives of Namibia in Windhoek proved invaluable.

We also conducted in-depth interviews with policy and program personnel from international organizations and from local and international NGOs working in Namibia and in Solomon Islands. We undertook field research in Namibia in 2006 and 2008 and in Solomon Islands in 2007. During this process, we visited international and nongovernmental organizations and the sites of their programs and met with relevant personnel. Multi-site ethnographic research helped us understand how these bodies work to reduce poverty and how the people most affected by their efforts perceive their strengths and weaknesses.

Indeed, the impetus for this study emerged from initial discussions during field research in Namibia in 2006, when we recognized that programs and policies that we were examining in one site found echoes and replication in other development and non-development contexts. We have since examined the globalizing aspects of governance of the poor and the constitution of the poor into a singular population to act on and reform. Our work here builds on what Gibson-Graham refers to as an ethics of change (2006: xxvii), seeking to bring awareness of governance of the poor to spur change of both advanced liberal governance of impoverished peoples and the rates and experiences of global poverty. Lakshman Yapa articulates the potential role of academics: "'My solution' [to poverty] is aimed at fellow academics who, like myself, are deeply implicated in the problem and whose power lies primarily in our capacity to engage the discourse critically" (1996: 723).

SUMMARY OF THE BOOK

Two central themes – the globalizing aspects of advanced-liberal governance of the poor and formation of the poor into a singular population – shape this study. Each chapter considers both the globalized and the localized, and the rationalities and technologies of governing the poor. While we consider how globalized policies and programs of poverty reduction broadly aim to shape the poor's

experiences of poverty and reduce poverty, important local particularities exist. Further, governance occurs at the individual level, and
the governmentalities that transform the lives of the poor rely on
relations of power that go beyond, as Dean contends (2002: 135),
the "direction of conduct and the shaping of choice."

In order to highlight the relationships between the ways programs
target the poor as singular populations in various places and through
global governmentalities, this book features several case studies. These
cases are diverse, as we intended, and make clear the scale and inten-
sity of global governances of the poor. Further, they speak to local
particularities and remind us of both the disparate and the analogous
ways in which the new global-aid regime affects the poor. We explore
programs to reduce poverty in Namibia (chapter 4), in Katutura (chapter 5), and in Solomon Islands (chapter 7) in order to reveal the application of various technologies of governing the poor in diverse
locales – to shape the poor according to ideas of responsibilization, to
entangle them in new biopolitical relations and in new partnerships,
and to promote market-based solutions to their poverty.

These case studies are perhaps less well-known sites of the new
global-aid regime and of the ways in which international organizations are working with networks of private partners, NGOs, and national governments to govern the poor, yet they represent both the
exceptional and the extensive character of advanced liberal rule. The
three case studies – Namibia, Katutura, and Solomon Islands – speak
to the convergence between contemporary development practices
and poverty reduction and highlight the intersections between advanced liberal rule and authoritarian and colonial rule. All three are
postcolonial sites, and all of them display a range of programs and
policies of the new regime. Yet, as we see below, they reveal that this
regime manifests itself in different ways, and people respond to
globalized solutions to poverty in different ways as well.

We offer additional case studies to emphasize the non-place-based
locales of global governances of the poor: Oxfam International
(chapter 3) and USAID (chapter 6). These two case studies, as well as
the genealogy of poverty reduction (chapter 1), which explores the
mandate of the United Nations Relief and Rehabilitation Agency
and later, advanced liberal rationalities of rule of the poor, emphasize the scope of the new regime of global aid. This regime affects
not only commonly constituted populations of the poor in distinctly
defined local communities but also global organizational practices,

which help shape the poor in new sites of governance, at local, mezzo, national, regional, and international levels. These case studies of
international organizations extend and support our argument that
sites of governance vary yet display common methods of reforming
the poor.

Chapter 1 maps a genealogy of efforts to reduce poverty and
establishes their increasing globalizing tendencies since 1945, particularly since the 1980s. These endeavours commonly treat the poor
– at local, mezzo, national, regional, and international levels – despite their great diversity, as singular populations. The chapter examines a key moment in a genealogy of globalizing solutions to poverty
– the creation in 1943 of the United Nations Relief and Rehabilitation
Administration (UNRRA). This wartime and postwar relief agency
was a precursor to the contemporary UN organizations.

The chapter explores liberal rationalities of governing the poor,
and in UNRRA's case the victims of war, and compares them with
today's advanced liberal rationalities. This analysis reveals influential flows of governmental rule by constructing a genealogy of governances of the poor. It also demonstrates, however, that, from the
1980s on, advanced liberal rationalities have altered governance of
the poor and that these differences, as we see in this chapter and in
the book's case studies, have helped shape the current global-aid regime. We develop a genealogy to explore flows of rationalities of rule
and to reveal discontinuities or shifts in rule of the poor.

The new global-aid regime emphasizes the market, partnerships,
responsiblilization of the poor, and development itself, rather than
relief. Chapter 1 uses ethnographic accounts and international and
local examples to examine how these recent rationalities differ from
earlier, liberal approaches. We argue that a new global method is
emerging as more and more businesses, NGOs, national governments,
and international organizations practise global solutions to poverty,
which belie the diversity of experiences facing the poor and provoke
resistance from them. Larner argues that resistance and contestation
are the inevitable result of advanced liberal rule. Challenges – by, for
example, the poor against the programs and policies of the new
global-aid regime – occur within relations of power that they contest. In formulating challenges as inherent to regimes of power,
Larner shows the poor to be not victims but active subjects of power
relations (2000: 17). Their resistance can also reflect their thirst for
social justice, which their lived experiences inspire them to seek.

Chapter 2 explores the ways in which the new mode of governance encourages diverse populations to take on greater responsibilities. This inquiry augments our analysis of the complexity and multifariousness of governance of the poor. Volunteers, parents, and the unemployed and under-employed are examples of groups who are being encouraged to take on greater responsibilities. Volunteers, for instance, receive training to care for others – the poor, the disadvantaged, and the vulnerable – in ways that reorient and emphasize their roles in administering and providing key aspects of social welfare.

Chapter 2 poses a central question: are new solutions to global poverty emerging that rely on modes of responsibilization? We think so. We argue that the new global-aid regime stresses responsibilization, giving the poor increasing levels of responsibility for their states of and solutions to impoverishment. In this analysis, we consider how international organizations, and increasingly privatized initiatives within and across nation states, apply this approach to poverty. Social justice approaches, in contrast, might stress equitable distribution and redistribution of resources, political participation, and diversity. The new schema of global aid, which we show to be fluid and far-reaching, we also reveal as being antithetical to various notions of and demands for social justice.

Practices of responsibility by individuals, private and state institutions, and international organizations occur today within a responsibilizing ethos. This ethos is a new kind of cultural mentality of rule that is central to advanced liberal agendas. Of key concern to this chapter are the connections between these main developments and the ways in which this ethos fosters emergence of new, responsibilized citizenship groups, such as the poor, and their governance by private solutions to poverty. The chapter examines a range of initiatives, such as international aid and microcredit and microfinance programs, to demonstrate how privatization of national and international programs generates new responsibilities for the poor.

Within the context of global governmentality studies, chapter 3 analyses Oxfam International's initiatives to reduce global poverty as a form of governmental practice. In light of Cruickshank's insights on the will to empower, we argue that this organization has tirelessly advanced self-management, self-empowerment, and the pursuit of free trade as a development tool as solutions to poverty. The chapter shows how it bases trade and development campaigns on advanced liberal programs of empowerment, which aim to shape poverty relations and the conduct of the poor in the 'developing' world. We view the new politics of empowerment as most deeply targeting and affecting communities and thus manifesting itself as community-targeted empowerment.

Chapter 3 presents an inquiry into Oxfam International as an empirical site of investigation in order to ascertain the many ways of devising strategies to reduce poverty and the extent to which their deployment shapes and targets particular communities. Further, an investigation of its key campaigns and programs lets us figure out how they relate to practices of empowerment. This analysis of governmental practices reveals Oxfam's ability to champion poverty alleviation and global social justice while campaigning for liberal trade and market-based initiatives that necessarily evoke self-management and empowerment to lessen poverty. This study derives from the authors' ongoing investigation into the relationship between aid and empowerment and its connection to wider advanced-liberal efforts to govern the poor.

A probe of the interrelations within the new global-aid regime requires attention to its particular local, national, and international bodies. Such a focus shapes chapter 4 – a case study of post-apartheid Namibia, which considers both forms of advanced liberal governance and poverty-reduction initiatives as part of the practices and programs of international development aid and the synergies between them. The chapter outlines Namibia's colonial and apartheid pasts in order to explain contemporary practices of development aid involving private enterprises, local participants, the state, and international organizations. Our study then turns to key features of the new global aid in the country.

The chapter examines the complex relationship between the many private and local participants, NGOs, and international organizations that are engaging in development aid practices in Namibia. It shows these practices to be contingent with the rationalities that characterize the new regime of global aid. The regime renders aid subject to recipients' participation in the market, rather than offering it as relief. We demonstrate that the activities and rationale of aid also employ ideas relating to the poor, foster distinct plans to reduce poverty and 'solve' the poverty of many Namibians, and demand complex forms of global co-ordination that often exclude equitable and democratic considerations of marginalized groups. Our analysis reveals an 'authoritarian liberalism' (Dean 2007: 108–29), an advanced liberal government of civil society, and authoritarian measures by the state and, increasingly, by international organizations to administer diverse local communities in Namibia.

Chapter 5 deals with local manifestations and experiences of the new global-aid regime. It explores a key example of social and political segregation in Namibia – the settlement of Katutura on the outskirts of Windhoek, the capital. We examine the mobilization of Katutura by first the colonial and apartheid-era government and by later a host of national and international governance actors. We argue that Katutura is both a governable and a governed space, rather than a space that is bound or self-enclosed. Our analysis reveals it as the object and target of governmental action, biopolitics, and sovereign decisions and as a site where a range of actors participate in the new global-aid regime. One means of locating Katutura within this regime is to identify the complex assemblage of international development-aid actors at work there.

The chapter first outlines Katutura's colonial and apartheid relations of ruling, including their racialized biopolitical dimensions, to show how contemporary resettling practices overlay these ruling relations. This genealogy demonstrates the many forms of racialized biopolitics, ranging from administration of towns, cities, and particular human bodies to attempts to manage the life-worlds of certain populations. The chapter then critically analyses the ways in which contemporary Katutura, including its populations and individuals, becomes the target of anti-poverty, pro-poor, and aid initiatives of this complex assemblage of new global aid regime actors. We show that these initiatives are antithetical to calls both within and beyond Katutura for social justice for the poor. The poor of Katutura are in the thrall of dynamics that manifest themselves locally, but also nationally and internationally. They also participate in these networked relations, in key aspects of the new global-aid regime that require a change in conduct in return for development aid and poverty reduction. The local and international NGOs are in turn the product of their own practices of partnership and the new global aid regime's emphasis on partnerships.

Partnerships are increasingly delivering development aid and poverty reduction to the poor. Chapter 6 identifies these arrangements as a major rationality of the new regime of global aid. It also relates them to a vast range of ventures and locales and shows them to be crucial to advanced liberal governance. The chapter first relates partnerships to long-standing practices of reform and transformation of the poor. It then shows how they collectively constitute and guide populations of the poor. It demonstrates how a 'partnering mentality' acts to collectively reform the poor, responsibilizing individuals as a route for them out of poverty.

The second half of chapter 6 offers a case study of the partnership arrangements of USAID. USAID is an increasingly prominent donor of and actor in international development aid, and here, as we did in chapter 3 vis-à-vis Oxfam International, we apply understandings of global governmentalities to examine USAID's practices. We reveal that the organization employs practices of partnership to assemble the poor as a homogeneous population in need of transformation by means of its development aid. Further, we contend that it engages the poor in programs of responsibilization and emphasizes market solutions to their poverty while making use of pro-poor and social-justice discourses. Through its governing initiatives, USAID leads the poor to market. Finally, the chapter focuses on the means by which it governs the poor via a series of reflexive, networked partnerships. We argue that these partnerships self-reference each other and mobilize notions of security that regulate the poor and derive from USAID's own security imperatives.

Rationalities of security and securing the poor are principal points of inquiry in the final chapter of our study. In chapter 7, we again explore a particular space of the governance of the poor. We do this to analyse the ways in which such governance in one locale – Solomon Islands – is at once particular and exemplary of the practices of the new global aid. Like Namibia and Katutura, Solomon Islands is a postcolonial space, a site of policy spaces that a wide range of international development-aid actors and organizations govern. It is also a post-conflict environment, and we argue that this status confers on this state and its peoples exercises of governance that are the result of discourses of security. The governance of the poor, we determine, explicitly links their poverty to their insecurity. As Dean (2007: 191), after Neocleous, contends, "security is a component of a rationality of government which is viewed as an ontological feature of contemporary human existence and which is germane to all domains that are conditions of human existence." Security, as a rationality of advanced liberal governance, acts to enmesh vulnerable populations such as the poor into diverse power relations, including those that emerge within the new regime of global aid.

Chapter 7 further considers how certain types of security discourses reveal different ways of being. It demonstrates the concurrent emphases on territorial security and human security and how these discourses and their related practices target populations and individuals in Solomon Islands. As with people in widely diverse 'governance states' (Duffield 2008) and Western advanced liberal states, global biopolitical governmentalities shape the lives of Solomon Islanders. These governmentalities, however, differ starkly from public rationalities of security, as we show in chapter 7. The rationality of biopolitical governance allows us to examine the constitution of the poor, through their corporeality and individual subjectivities, as a population and their governance at the individual level. Local, regional, and international development-aid organizations govern through the biopolitical. Global biopolitical governmentalities, as we argue, accentuate Solomon Islanders' individual capabilities and responsibilities and present solutions to their poverty and insecurity as lying within, rather than grounding solutions in discursively and popularly mediated notions of social justice.

The Conclusion synthesises the central contribution of our work: the ways in which the new global-aid regime brings diverse forms of global co-ordination into being – involving private enterprise, NGOs, national governments, and international development-aid organizations – and the governmentalities that these new forms enact. It affirms advanced liberal governance of the poor through such technologies as empowerment, responsibilization, market-oriented poverty solutions, and partnership schemes. These governmentalities, including the racial biopolitics of populations and biopolitical securitization, are deployed across wide-ranging, increasingly globalized policy and physical spaces. The study ends not with a final statement regarding governance of the poor, or with a solution; instead, it raises issues regarding new governmentalities of poverty and of the poor. Governance states are promoting tourism as a pro-poor solution to poverty – that is, as a means of lifting the poor from their impoverishment and allowing them to determine their own futures. As we demonstrate, such approaches are not in fact working for the poor and are habitually at odds with social-justice approaches to reduction of poverty.

On a broader scale, throughout the study we explore solutions to poverty in the new global-aid regime. It is a regime of rule that we demonstrate diffusely seeks to help the poor to bring themselves out of poverty and employs governmentalities of responsibilization, market-based governance, partnership arrangements, and biopolitics in order to govern them. We show these so-called solutions to be partial only and not to represent the lived experiences of poverty or the poor's own solutions to their predicament. We emphasize social justice and pro-poor approaches to poverty to challenge dominant practices and accounts of poverty reduction in the new regime, thus extending the range of governmentality analyses of power to focus also on contestations and a social-justice life-politics as intrinsic to relations of power. We thereby open the account of the governances of the poor to the possibilities of thinking of the poor not as victims of poverty but as agents of critical mobilizations and transformations.

1 Towards a Genealogy of Poverty Reduction: From Relief to the New Global-Aid Regime?

In Washington the world's hunger and pain were written down in neat columns of figures.

Time (1945a)

The poor existed in the Government reports; they were percentages and numbers in long, close columns, but they were not part of my experience.

Michael Harrington (1962: 191)

INTRODUCTION

This chapter establishes a genealogy of efforts to lessen poverty by mapping the ways in which local, national, mezzo, regional, and global entities have targeted it. It focuses on the years from about 1900 to the present day and argues that this period, particularly the time since 1945, has seen globalization of poverty-reduction efforts. Using a governmentality mode of analysis, it demonstrates that these efforts constitute the poor, despite their great diversity, as a collective, albeit in various locales. This approach emerged, as this chapter shows, with the experiences of the Second World War and the subsequent international relief and rebuilding, which engaged in globalized solutions to poverty. We trace these globalized solutions back to the creation of the United Nations Relief and Rehabilitation Administration (UNRRA) in 1943. The chapter contrasts the pre-1939 and the postwar articulations of the poor as singular communities.

This chapter depicts the shift from local to global solutions in its discussion of the new global-aid regime, which, it argues, has shaped responses to poverty since the 1980s. It presents this regime as possessing both flows and shifts from postwar modalities. It contrasts a genealogical approach and ethnographic accounts of poverty with the ways in which similar ideas of the poor are now shaping global solutions to poverty. Just as this chapter seeks to trace dominant ways of thinking and acting on poverty and governing the poor, so too does it seek to establish diverse ways of thinking about the poor themselves.

The chapter demonstrates major continuities and discontinuities between earlier liberal rationalities, such as UNRRA's efforts to alleviate poverty, and advanced liberal ones, which have come to typify the new regime of global aid. The genealogy of poverty reduction illuminates the relationship between early, postwar efforts and those since the 1980s and reveals both flows and ruptures. Particularly since the 1980s, efforts have stressed advanced liberal modes of poverty reduction, centring on the market, on partnerships, and on development itself rather than relief. The new regime of global aid has strong links, as we hint at here and explore in later chapters, to colonialism, authoritarianism, and liberalism. Here, we work with ideas of global governmentalities, which entail governing efforts and representational practices that aim to shape the social, economic, and political understandings and problems of the poor as well as offering global solutions to these problems. In doing so, this chapter also outlines how the book's local examples and case studies speak to the globalizing dimensions of poverty-reduction programs and policies, and vice versa – there is a symbiotic relationship inherent in the new regime between local and global ideas of the poor and solutions to their poverty.

The chapter ends with consideration of challenges and resistance to liberal modes of poverty reduction. It acknowledges and briefly explores everyday contestation by the world's widespread and highly diverse poor. These practices of life-politics, it shows, derive from ideas of social justice.

GENEALOGIES OF POVERTY

A genealogy of efforts to reduce global poverty is complex yet revealing. Central to the presentation of this genealogy is a desire to work with the difficulty, rather than against it, which involves presenting global poverty as simultaneously reflexive and rhyzomatic. Poverty-reduction efforts are global in reach, but their programs and practices vary among local, national, mezzo, regional, and global settings. This complexity necessitates a telling of how this situation came to be.

Our understanding of 'the global' in the new aid regime derives substantially from our critical engagement with notions of globalization. Rather than seeing a common global era, as Tsing claims most theories of globalization do (2005: 3), we observe local, national, mezze, regional, and global processes, which occur both concurrently and in a complex, intersecting manner. Globalization is a highly contentious notion, and researchers disagree about its significance, age, and impact – as a structure, a process, or an epoch. Despite their differences in emphasis and theoretical orientations, most agree that it involves a shift in contemporary social, cultural, and economic relations that is evident within, across, and beyond the nation state. Popular definitions see it as the increasing predominance of world communication, world markets (Chase-Dunn et al. 2000; Jameson and Miyoshi 1998; Ong 2006b), the network of dependencies (Bauman 2001; Sassen 2003), and the transcontinental flows of activity, interactions, and exercises of power (for example, Appadurai 2001b; Castells 1996). As production becomes more transportable, economic activity more digital, communication more instantaneous, and people more migratory, integration and connectivity increase. We remain cautious, however: this view of the world can lend itself to uniform accounts of globalization for all societies and a massive range of outcomes (see, for example, Sklair 1999) and to a linear and evolutionary image of the present (Larner and Walters 2002: 392; Walby 2003: 230).

We prefer to think of globalization as the product of multiple and discontinuous practices that aim to transnationalize and transform social and economic relations (Ilcan 2006: 854–5) in ways that create diverse ties, interconnections, and networks among people, populations, places, institutions, and organizations within, across, and beyond nation states. Processes of globalization, for example, have incited national governments to think up new ways of governing, which contribute to their valuing different categories of their populations. Ong sees the emergence of 'graduated sovereignty,' whereby the state, even as it maintains control over its territory, can permit some corporate entities to set the terms for constituting and regulating some domains (1999: 217). Our orientation to processes of globalization encourages specificity in our analytical accounts and in turn shapes our notion of the global. The global does not to us indicate homogeneity, or a single scale, or a high point. Tsing reflects our own view: "The term 'global' here is not a claim to explain everything in the world at once. Instead, it introduces a way of thinking about social projects ... First, such projects grow from spatially far-flung collaborations and interconnections. Second, cultural diversity is not banished from these interconnections; it is what makes them – and their particularities – possible" (2005: ix). Her elucidation of the global as connoting diverse interconnections and simultaneous local particularities meshes with the central concept of this book, that of the new global-aid regime.

From our perspective, the new regime of global aid is a form of government that shapes ways of thinking about, problematizing, and reforming the poor, engages in diverse aid programs and practices that involve local agencies, national governments, and international organizations, and operates within, across, and beyond the nation state. More specifically, it displays an advanced liberal orientation that frames poverty-reduction goals in terms of establishing conditions for successful participation in global markets; supports efforts by the poor at self-responsibility as a way to serve the interests of 'government' broadly understood; and endorses various governing practices to influence a wide range of international organizations to engage in partnership arrangements, such as policy dialogue, consultation, and participation. It is an aid regime that is 'new' and 'global' because of its transnational use of these advanced liberal rationalities in far-flung configurations that connect distant peoples through rationalities and technologies of rule in simultaneous locales, albeit with often-differing consequences and effects. This regime has a distinguishing capacity for decontextualization, recontextualization, and movement across various social, cultural, and political situations and spaces.

In what follows in this chapter, we demonstrate the novelty of this regime of global aid in terms of its development since the 1980s, in contrast to, for example, the liberal rationalities of poverty reduction in the years after 1945. We show that dis/continuities of rule both shifted and flowed between the post-1945 era and the period since the 1980s. We use the idea of dis/continuities to demonstrate simultaneous connections and disjunctures, evident in the shifts from emergence of liberal rationalities of governance at a global level after the Second World War to those of the new era of global aid. The initial global approaches emerged in order to rebuild devastated physical environments and rehabilitate populations in the name of reconstruction and development. In this context, there are certainly continuities with governances of populations through, for example, the Bretton Woods organizations of the International Monetary Fund, the World Bank, and the broad United Nations agencies, which are still prominent today; there are also stark disjunctures or differences between these initial global approaches and those of the more dense and extensive global governing rationalities of the new global-aid regime.

As we show in the sections below, features of the global coincide with earlier liberal rationalities as well as with advanced liberal rationalities, and they prompt new risks, inequalities, and responsibilities; further, they also introduce forms of exclusion by marginalizing certain kinds of social and economic activities. The new global-aid regime, dense and vast in scope but not homogeneous in effect, expresses itself through advanced liberal rationalities of poverty reduction as development. It involves a novel assemblage of participants, ranging from nongovernmental, state-level, and international organizations to the poor themselves. These actors have coalesced since the 1980s and have formulated solutions to poverty that respond to ideas of development, rather than to the earlier, liberal rationality of short-term emergency relief. The new global-aid regime is the product of this new grouping of actors and of their common, though heterogeneous, employment of advanced liberal rationalities, such as the use of partnerships as a mode of delivering social and economic reform and market-oriented solutions to poverty.

A genealogical approach allows us to unearth these multifaceted relationships and treat them not as progressively or lineally connected, but rather as interwoven in a series of complex relationships. Nietzsche proposes the same in his genealogical approach, which involves studying a complex range of aspects, components, actors, and problems in relation to questions of morality. Such a method permits the unknown to emerge and perhaps submerge and re-emerge. "Out of the answers grew new questions, investigations, hypotheses, probabilities: until finally I had a land of my own, a soil of my own, a completely unknown, burgeoning, flourishing world, like a secret garden, whose existence no one had been allowed to suspect" (Nietzsche 1999: 5). This analogy resembles Foucault's approach: "Genealogy is gray, meticulous, and patiently documentary. It operates on a field of entangled and confused parchments, on documents that have been scratched over and recopied many times ... Genealogy ... rejects the metahistorical deployment of ideal significations and indefinite teleologies. It opposes itself to the search for 'origins'" (Foucault 1994: 351–2).

Our necessarily partial genealogy of poverty reduction, particularly at the global level, follows Nietzsche and Foucault's desires to scratch at muddied surfaces and reflects our desire to decentralize or defocus locations of power. James Ferguson argues that Foucault's genealogical analysis "avoids giving a central place to any actor or entity conceived as a 'powerful' subject" (1994: 19). In using such a method to unearth the new global-aid regime, we are not suggesting that power is top-down; rather, we demonstrate that power exists in many locations and practices. We return to this idea at the close of the chapter when we discuss poor peoples' resistance.

THE POOR AS OBJECTS OF POVERTY?

A key shift or flow from liberal conceptualizations of and actions on the poor to advanced liberal ones is the articulation of the poor in and on differing scales. Throughout much of the twentieth century, social and economic reform of the poor occurred at a local level. This view shifted drastically from the 1980s on, with the conception of the poor at a global level, as well as locally. The new regime of global aid envisions a singular group that it can govern and act on globally. This view of course belies the diverse experiences of poverty and lives of the poor, even locally, let alone globally. Here we both describe the constitution of the poor as a single global population and problematize this depiction, which Foucault (2007: 21) asserts is essential to liberal rationalities of rule from the eighteenth to the twentieth centuries and which, we argue, continues under advanced liberalism.

The issue of representation is central to our discussion of the new global aid regime's ideas of the poor as well as its simplistic and totalizing depiction of the poor. Images and ideas of the poor that occur in literature, in the media, in the many ways that capture popular imaginations, or derive from them present the poor as a homogeneous grouping commonly in need of assistance. The poor are vagabonds, they live precariously, on the margins of another, more secure and mainstream life. This inhabiting of the edges is a characterization that has affected both social spaces and policy spaces, as we can see in spatial demarcation of zones for the poor, in the racialized groups that colonial, apartheid, and post-colonial authorities set up in Namibia (see chapters 4 and 5), and in the poor of the Solomon Islands (see chapter 7), which local, national, regional, and international players act on in the name of security policy. These latter two cases are unique, representing local particularities, yet typical of the myriad ways in which the new global-aid regime has simplified the experiences of the poor in order to act on them.

The poor, collectively and individually, have long been the subject of ethnographic studies. Jacob Riis's *How the Other Half Lives* ([1891] 1997) is one example – an early ethnographic, rather than fictional, account of poverty in New York in the 1870s and 1880s. Riis, originally an immigrant from Denmark, became a newspaper photographer. He was keen to record the extremes of poverty he saw around him in his job and used these images and text as part of a travelling speaking program to bring attention to the ways in which 'the other half lived.' These images highlighted the plight of thousands of new immigrants and non-immigrants in the city, and he later incorporated them into a book, which appeared in 1891. Riis's text and images convey ideas that correspond to liberal rationalities of rule. These rationalities are steering ones, directing the lives of people – in this case, the poor – in all-inclusive ways, from the manner in which they receive assistance to its desired outcomes (Dean 2002: 42–3). Riis, reflecting liberal authoritarian rationalities of rule, takes a welfarist approach, which views the poor as needing fundamental alteration via assistance. He seems to be implying that welfare can solve all their ills, directing them to productive lives and work.

Many of Riis's images and much of his text, mixing philanthropic notions of care and reformism, would seem at home in the U.S. War on Poverty of the 1960s: "Perhaps of all the disheartening experiences of those who have devoted lives of unselfish thought and effort, and their number is not so small as often supposed, to lifting this great load, the indifference of those they would help is the most puzzling. They will not be helped. Dragged by main force out of their misery, they slip back again on the first opportunity, seemingly content only in the old rut" (Riis 1891:130).

This combined sympathy and responsibilization of the poor – a key rationality of liberal rule and of future advanced liberal rule – appears in so many accounts of the lives of the poor.[1] This claim is not in any way to downplay the magnitude of benevolence of Riis and others. And not all ethnographic accounts of poverty or the lives of the poor, nor Riis's in totality, is merely reformist in representation or intent. Nevertheless, a liberal rationality of rule of reform is discernible. Barry Hindess refers to this stance as subjection to improvement and as part of the government of unfreedom (2001). According to his analysis, such attitudes towards populations – both 'hopeless cases' in 'civilized' societies (such as Riis's poor) and subjects in colonial settings – assumed that they possessed capacity for autonomous conduct but required compulsion – "imposition of more or less extended periods of discipline" (2001: 101).

Duneier's method of participant observation in *Sidewalk* (1999) offers a different vantage point vis-à-vis New York's poor. Rather than focusing on their living conditions, his 'diagnostic' (1999: 342–3) ethnographic study of sidewalk vendors in Greenwich Village attempts to relay their life stories. He seeks not only to reveal their circumstances, but also to reflect those "constraints and opportunities" that shaped their lives (1999: 343). It is highly specific, not speaking of the poor as an entirety, as a population, but instead focusing on some twenty women and men who make a living on the sidewalks at the corner of Greenwich Avenue and the Avenue of the Americas in a five-year period during the 1990s.

How does Duneier's sociology-style text differ from policy documents, from such sources as City Hall in New York, the United Nations Development Programme or its indirect predecessor, the UNRRA, and international NGOs and governmental aid agencies? A key difference is the attempt to personalize the poor; they are not, for Duneier, or for Riis for that matter, a nameless mass. A search through UN documents, for example, reveals no specific accounts of who the poor are in any one place. Instead, they seem a demographic entity whose individual identities and experiences give way to such collective labels as 'the community,' 'the villagers,' 'the rural poor,' and 'the urban poor.' Estimates of daily earnings – perhaps the most common way of collectivizing the poor today – replace the diversity of their lives.

Two points are essential here. First, ethnographic work à la Duneier and Riis, which looks into and conveys the lives of poor people, continues to this day and is not specific to any period. Second, there is a distinct difference between liberal governance of the poor and advanced liberal rule since the 1980s. These are differing rationalities,

though not without connections – both govern a singularly conceived population. UNRRA conceived of and acted on war-affected
people as singular populations and applied common technologies of
rule in order to reform them to active and contributing economic
citizens in diverse locations; hence our claim that we see an emerging, globalizing dimension to the governance of poverty. UNRRA
depicted their poverty as temporary or transitory and a direct result
of war, soluble by an international, representative institution – itself.
Its intervention embodies liberal technologies of economic rule, of
governing through the economy, of law, of security, of representation, and of governing the social (see Dean 1999: 114–20).

UNRRA was a precursor to contemporary international bodies
under the vast UN umbrella, including the Food and Agriculture
Organization (FAO), the International Bank for Reconstruction and
Development (now part of the World Bank) and the International
Monetary Fund (IMF), the United Nations Development Programme
(UNDP), the World Food Programme (WFP), and the World Health
Organization (WHO). UNRRA's efforts covered the mandates now in
the purview of these organizations, and much of its work addressed
poverty reduction through emergency relief, especially in response to
the devastation of war. Notions of emergency relief evolved into
ideas of economic participation, which firmly embed the activities
and practices of the UNRRA in a liberal rationality. A link thus emerges between postwar rationalities of poverty reduction – arguably
the first global-oriented solutions to poverty – and contemporary
development aid, which articulates and enacts similarly styled solutions to poverty. The shift occurred during the 1980s. The key point
of association is the global orientation of these solutions. The global
has become a locus for the governance of the poor, and the advent of
UNRRA and its programs is a founding moment.

Technologies of liberal governance are evident in photographic
documentation, for example, of UNRRA's work (see Figs. 1.1, 1.2, 1.3).
In photos from such diverse locations as Indonesia, the Philippines,
Sweden, and Yugoslavia, UNRRA is ordering the lives of these varied
populations. These people, collectively conceived of as a population
by their affectations, are determined to be in need of rationed economic assistance and order, with their existence and activities – from
food intake to shelter, clothing, and healthcare - also under UNRRA's
auspices. Relief and rehabilitation in effect become a form of
biopolitical liberal governance – Dean's "therapeutic governance"

Figure 1.1 UNRRA's biopolitical governance, Shanghai, China, 1946.
Courtesy of United Nations Archives, New York.
The original caption reads: "No. 19. Shanghai – 29 April – 1946 –
Guarding China's health. At Woosung, crew members of a junk arriving
from Foochow are sprayed with DDT powder by officers of the Shanghai
Quarantine Service in their effort to prevent the spread of bubonic plague.
UNRRA public health experts are supplying the DDT chemical and work
closely with Chinese health officials." UNRRA photo by Rothschild.

(2007: 118–19). Such rationalities of governance have links to both
authoritarian and colonial governmentalities. The continuum of
governance at work in these UNRRA practices demonstrates the close
relationship – the flows[2] – between liberal, authoritarian, and colonial rationalities of rule, particularly governing through freedom,
as distinct from governing through authoritarian methods. We explore these broad rationalities of rule in case studies in Namibia
(chapters 4 and 5) and Solomon Islands (chapter 7).

This genealogy presents governance of the poor as being shaped
by flows, and we argue that rationalities of governance are flows
rather than discrete disjunctures between rationalities of governance. Yet advanced liberal rationalities of governance have shaped
the regime of global aid and rendered it both novel and global.
Again, Dean's work informs our own understanding: he identifies
four features of new regimes of government that have emerged
since the 1980s – the "new prudentialism," technologies of agency,

Figure 1.2 UNRRA's global efforts to aid the war affected, Canada. Courtesy of United Nations Archives, New York. The original caption reads: "Canadian manufacturers co-operated with Mutual Aid to prepare a shipment of millions of pounds of laundry powder to go to Europe through UNRRA. This picture, taken in the Colgate-Palmolive-Peet factory at Toronto, shows the final stages of packing – putting the Mutual Aid export insignia on a carton." National Film Board photograph, UNRRA 740.

Figure 1.3 UNRRA's efforts to help the poor help themselves, Albania. Courtesy of United Nations Archives, New York. The original caption reads: "Mr. Frank Woodard, Director of the Agricultural Division of the UNRRA, Albania, explains to Albanians working on one of the State Farms the workings of the UNRRA grain drills which have recently been brought on to the farm." UNRRA 1263/Albania Photo 4146 by Ristani.

technologies of performance, and a new form of pluralism (1999: 166). These features shape the regime of global aid: the new prudentialism sees managing of risk as responsibilizing the poor for their own ways out of poverty; technologies of agency target the poor with programs of self-empowerment and community orientation yet also generate resistance; technologies of performance lead to diverse partnerships for and with the poor; and a new kind of pluralism has generated many new actors now governing poverty and consequently shaping the lives of the poor – all this in the name of a global community of actors for the poor.

The shift from liberal governance of those populations that UNRRA deemed to be the most affected by war and hence in need of rehabilitation to advanced liberal governance of the poor becomes manifest in new ways of quantifying the poor. The UN benchmark for the first Millennium Development Goal (MDG) – eradication of extreme hunger and poverty – depicts the poor as people whose income is less than $1 a day (UNDP 2009a). Thomas Pogge terms that severe poverty and its sufferers the very poor, unlike the people in Duneier's New York, whom he considers relatively poor (2007). Pogge does not dismiss the difficulties of the relatively poor; rather he looks especially at severe poverty, which he finds so extreme that it demands a different type of political, social, and ethical focus (2007: 2–3). The distinction is blurry, however, and may lead observers to ignore the ways in which 'experts' may see the poor as populations in need of reform, regardless of their level of poverty. We return to this point in other sections of the book in our delineation of the new global-aid regime, which moves easily and with great fluidity between local and globalized populations and employs common methods regardless of extent and degree of hardship, relying on simplistic quantifications.

Duneier looks at people whom Pogge would call relatively poor.[3] Yet Pogge's description of poverty could be more widely applicable and is more useful than quantification: "Severe poverty and the powerlessness it entails are all but impossible for us affluent to imagine. Such poverty involves continuous and acute vulnerability to events over which one has no control: job loss, poor weather, illness, funeral expenses, theft, an accident, a police fine, an increase in taxes or food prices, and a wage reduction – any such event, and many more, can cut very poor persons or families off from basic necessities" (2007: 2).

Is there a way to describe impoverishment while maintaining the agency of the poor, which Pogge's description above effectively negates? While we do not seek an all-purpose definition of poverty or an all-encompassing description of the global poor, we think it possible to think of the poor in widely different circumstances, in different locales, and recognize their agency as individuals and communities. This view corresponds with poststructural encounters with the subject – in this case, an individual *living* poverty, rather than a composite or generalized and abstract poor person. Drawing on Braidotti's (1994) notion of living subjectivities, which she elaborates in *Transpositions* (2006: 123) as a 'model' of subjectivit(ies) that is porous, fluid, and consisting of multiple interconnections and symbolic interrelations, we argue that the poor live their poverty in many ways and that this living does not totally shape their subjectivities.

UNNRA AND ITS POSTWAR POVERTY-REDUCTION INITIATIVES

Ideas of the global and a globalizing dimension to poverty reduction are not new, as we showed in the book's Introduction. The advent of UNRRA in 1943 was a key continuance in the globalizing of efforts to reduce poverty. We can see earlier transnational endeavours, but UNRRA represented a transformation. There were both shifts and flows between transnational and global-oriented approaches, and isolating them is central to our genealogy. UNRRA governed the poor – a governable population because of constituents' experiences of wartime devastation - through liberal rationalities of rule. Dean describes these rationalities as manifesting "the recurrent emergence of illiberal practices and rationalities which occur in the name of liberalism and in defence of its values ..., that the authoritarian side of liberal governing is intrinsic to liberalism itself" (2007: 200).

UNRRA acted via authoritarian aspects of liberal rule, determining whole swaths of people as needing therapeutic reform via emergency relief aid. It governed these diverse peoples according to their exceptionalisms as needy, as poor, as disposed, via its programs and policies not as the autonomous individuals of liberal ideals, but according to the concurrent liberal rationality of governing populations in their best interests. Dean lists exceptions to the autonomous individual that require authoritarian aspects of liberal rule. These exceptions flow through UNRRA's descriptions of its population: "insufficient education, poor character, welfare dependency, statelessness, under-developed human capital, absence of spirit of improvement, lack of social capital, absence of citizenship of civilized state, inadequate methods of labour and cultivation, and so on" (Dean 2007: 121). Such exceptionalisms warrant rationing of essential supplies, of physical-wellness programs, of workfare education, and of agricultural reform, for example – all typical UNRRA technologies of governance (see, for example, UN 1947).

UNRRA was a deliberative attempt to avoid the postwar chaos of the years immediately following 1918, when "nation was allowed to compete with nation for food and necessities" (Wilson, quoted in Shephard 2008: 405). In the midst of a world war, it was to be an international agency that would represent the interests of a broad range of Allied nations for this purpose. Representatives of forty-four Allied nations set it up at the White House on 9 November 1943.[4] Canadian Mary McGeachy, its director of welfare (and its only woman executive), described the mandate as being "to blunt the sharp edge of need" (McGeachy, cited in Thomas 2006: 206).

The emphasis on relief aid is apparent in the original agreement of 1943: "based on a preamble in which the United Nations declare that they are: 'determined that immediately upon the liberation of any area ... the population thereof shall receive aid and relief from their sufferings, food, clothing and shelter, aid in the prevention of pestilence and in the recovery of the health of the people, and that preparation and arrangements shall be made for the return of prisoners and exiles to their homes and for assistance in the resumption of urgently needed agricultural and industrial production and the restoration of essential services'" (cited in address by Franklin Roosevelt, 1943). These broad goals speak to the fervent desire to rebuild as quickly as possible at war's end and to avert a repeat of, for example, the crises of post-Versailles Germany.

Shifts and flows between liberal and advanced liberal rationalities of rule of the poor are manifest in the framing of post-conflict aid in both this period and today's UN policies. A recent example from Guinea-Bissau – the WFP's Post-conflict Relief and Rehabilitation Programme – illustrates the ways in which programs target aid and support relief. The UN planned immediate and longer-term emergency relief after the 1998 internal civil conflict and intended it to "assist rural vulnerable groups in a post-conflict environment, targeting regions with the highest vulnerability to food insecurity, the highest acute malnutrition rates and the lowest primary school enrolment rates as identified by the recent vulnerability analysis and mapping study" (World Food Programme 2009b). It thus targets relief aid in terms of dominant ideas of poverty reduction and measures of poverty according to the human development index.[5] These specific targets, which it codified into five more detailed Strategic Objectives for Guinea-Bissau,[6] emphasize reconstruction and relief and echo the sentiments that Franklin Roosevelt expressed in 1943 (see World Food Programme 2009a). Michael Dillon and Julian Reid call on Foucault's *Security, Territory, Population* (2007) to demonstrate the replication today of these 1940s' ideas of rebuilding and their resonance with liberal biopolitics from the eighteenth century on. The emphasis on rebuilding, particularly physically, was not a moral impetus, but instead a desire to "avoid riot and sedition," while also strengthening the state apparatus and rule, and to improve the functioning of capital in the pursuit of trade and hence profit (Dillon and Reid 2009: 134).

The juxtaposition between promoting broad goals and narrowing practices, of both relief and rehabilitation, is clear in the rapid reconfiguration of UNRRA's remit in the postwar period. This juxtaposition is captured by Walters in his discussion of performative political rationality (2002: 385–6). Walters sees social capital as largely performative rather than ideological, following Robert Putnam: contemporary social politics requires a social meaning of the citizenry. Citizens engage socially in political life and in performing their political participation and association. In turn, they confer authority on political leaders, who in turn expect the authority to rule (Walters 2002: 385–6). This authority relies not on ideological narrative but on a mutually constituted performative rationality, as with UNRRA. UNRRA constituted and targeted populations and asked them to participate actively in their own recovery from war, which in turn gave it authority. Its field of authority narrowed almost immediately. While it remained "the first sharing of a major task which has both military and post-combat implications – the first sharing on a really international basis" (Jessup 1944: 367), early enthusiasm for its wide scope faltered soon after the war ended. There were concerns about its ability to garner enough contributions, and signatories worried about their own resources in the face of severe shortages at home (see Reinisch 2008: 457–60; Sumberg 1945: 698–9). Nevertheless, the agency continued as an international effort for postwar reconstruction.

The agency itself recognized its international nature: "UNRRA is the first postwar international body to function on a worldwide basis" (UNRRA European Regional Office 1946: 3). Its initial 'international' reach extended to countries it deemed, "after thorough investigation," to lack foreign exchange to purchase goods and services for relief and rehabilitation (ibid.: 4). In 1946, for example, it ran operations in Albania, Austria (when requested by the Austrian government), Byelo Russian Soviet Socialist Republics, China, Czechoslovakia, Finland, Formosa, Germany (vis-à-vis 'displaced persons of United Nations nationality'), Greece, Hungary, Italy, Korea, Philippines (to a certain extent), Ukrainian Soviet Socialist Republic, and Yugoslavia. Only 'uninvaded countries' financed its operations (ibid.: 4), which were to "aid in the relief and rehabilitation of the 'victims of war'" (Sumberg 1945: 698), rather than in long-term reconstruction projects. It considered immediate relief imperative to ensure that societies could "get back into production for their own needs – the period when quick help will check the sapping of men, women and children from hunger, exhaustion and despair" (Fay 1944: 11). This 1944 description offers portents of how UN organizations today conceive of poverty – like wartime devastation, as something to act on.

FROM RELIEF TO REDUCTION EFFORTS

UNRRA's relief activities did not garner universal applause, and great scepticism persisted about its rebuilding efforts. Less than two years after its inception, and before the bulk of its undertakings started, an article in *Time* was scathing: "With victory in Europe, men turned their eyes to UNRRA. What had this unwieldy, $2,000,000,000 United Nations Relief and Rehabilitation Administration accomplished to date? ... not much" (1945b). This commentary found broad echoes, with concerns that this "humanitarian community chest" (Fay 1944: 8) would result in reliance and dependence on aid, ideas that continue in debate and public discourse today.[7]

This contestation played out in discursive shifts of UN organizations' aid practices. These bodies present aid as relief, when they actually intend it to trigger markets: "It is, in general terms, the purpose of UNRRA to deliver basic supplies – food, clothing, and so on – in quantities sufficient to raise consumption to a reasonable minimum standard" (UNRRA European Regional Office 1946: 6). A la Foucault's continuities and discontinuities of rule (1972), we see the volley between relief and market-led recovery throughout today's global aid, as seems clear in this chapter.[8] It is a rationality of rule itself that 'the poor's' participation in the market will lead them out of poverty. The market continues to relieve and consequently rehabilitate the subject.

These dis/continuities of rule take on a periodic dimension when in the language of UN Year Books. From its inception, the UN has documented its work – the work of all of its agencies – in annual publications. In his Foreword to the 1960 volume, Acting Secretary General U Thant wrote: "Progress in international co-operation for world peace and the well-being of nations and peoples depends to a considerable degree upon informed understanding of the many problems involved. Like its predecessors, this fourteenth edition of the Yearbook of the United Nations is intended to help provide such understanding. It gives, within a single volume, a compact, authoritative account of the vast variety of activities, proceedings and decisions of the various United Nations organs" (UN 1960: 1).

These yearbooks provide insight into UN bodies' implementation of policies and programs to reduce poverty as rationalities of rule, stressing the market, community empowerment, complex interdependent aid actors, and responsibilization of the poor – all features of the new global-aid regime. Yet the yearbooks also make evident the shifts and flows from liberal to advanced liberal governing rationalities. Ideas of development aid for poverty reduction, rather than relief as poverty reduction,[9] are evident, representing dis/continuities of rule – the new regime of global aid continues some elements of liberal rationalities of rule, but advanced liberalism has been formative.

One commonality between yearbooks of 1946 (the first), 1950, 1960, 1970, 1980, 1990, 2000, and 2009 is the framing of poverty reduction as simply an aspect of development. While commentators often describe development as a recent, ahistorical discourse (Crush 1995: 9), it dates back to the UNRRA period and places discourses of development, and consequently of poverty reduction, firmly in a nonlinear trajectory that constantly reinvents itself. Arturo Escobar argues that "development has functioned as an all-powerful mechanism for the production and management of the Third World in the

post-1945 period" (1995a: 213). Perceived needs served as a rationale to generate a vast institutional network and strategies and programs to implement development (Escobar 1995a: 214) and to
govern the poor. Certainly, the yearbooks' strategies and programs
– simply one manifestation of this immense international network
– are neither constant nor fixed, hence dis/continuities and flows.
These are not smooth or uniform flows and beginning in the 1980s
shift back and forth between liberal and advanced liberal rationalities in shaping notions of poverty and the poor.

In the inaugural yearbook (1946–7), the broad goals of the new
UN family have shifted from reconstruction and rehabilitation to
promoting "(a) higher standards of living, full employment, and
conditions of economic and social progress and development;
(b) solutions of international economic, social, health and related
problems" (UN 1947: 28). The 1950 volume reports as a highlight of
the previous five years the launch of the United Nations Expanded
Programme of Technical Assistance for Under-Developed Areas for
"improving economic conditions" (1950:10), especially in the Third
World, via statistical and technical interventions, such as professional forms of expert knowledge used to define populations according
to types of labour, land holdings, goods, and industry; to compile
central registrars of comparable nation-based statistics and census-
es; and to produce the need for so-called less developed countries to
transform their outlook as well as their conduct. These and other similar interventions were made in the name of development (Escobar
1995b: 94–101; Ilcan and Phillips 2003: 442–3), and they continue
today. In 2000, we see oblique reference to poverty as an issue of development in "the role of the United Nations in promoting a new
global human order": "the well-being of people and the full development of their potential is the overall goal of sustainable development"
(UN 2000: 782).

The years 1960–2000 were Development Decades for the UN organizations, with adoption of successive, co-ordinated International
Development Strategies for each decade (UN 1960; 1970; 1980;
1990). Poverty reduction receives scant mention, except as an inevitable outcome of development. The emphasis continues on economic
growth; for example, "the principal aim of the Strategy" for the
1990s was "accelerated development in the developing countries
and that policies and measures were proposed to support and realize
that goal" (UN 1990: 335). Qualitative references to development
refer to overall global output and economic growth (UN 1990: 335)

and display the advanced liberal technology of audit as a means of structuring expectations (Larner and Le Heron after Strathern 2004: 214). In the same 1990 yearbook, a report of General Assembly Resolution S-18/3 – Declaration on International Economic Co-operation in particular the Revitalization of Economic Growth and Development of the Developing Countries – uses loose, technocratic, very impersonal language to describe the effect of lack of development: "The eradication of poverty and hunger, greater equity in income distribution and the development of human resources remain major challenges everywhere. Economic and social progress requires that growth be broadly based, offering equal opportunities to all people, both women and men, to participate fully in economic, social and political activities" (UN 1990: 338). As with earlier UNRRA mandates, the General Assembly aims to make people active in their own development and hence solvers of their own problems.

The first United Nations Decade for the Eradication of Poverty (1997–2006) came more than thirty years after the first Development Decade yet ignores the poor as potential active subjects of global solutions. The establishing resolution for the decade (55/210) recognizes that poverty is increasing: "The General Assembly ... expressing its deep concern that the number of people living in extreme poverty continues to increase." It suggests a solution, which demonstrates the continuities of rule: "Also recognizing that for the poverty eradication strategy to be effective it is imperative for developing countries to be integrated into the world economy and equitably share the benefits of globalization" (UN 2000: 796).

Walters argues in his genealogy of unemployment that singular, unitary designation or definition of the unemployed can have myriad consequences. A governmentality analysis exposes excavations of power, and hence description of 'the poor' as a population facilitates both their governance and their resistance: "If the generation of an official definition of unemployment intensified the regulation of the poor..., it also opened up the possibility of new forms of subversive personal re-invention on the part of those same subjects" (Walters 2000: 72). We next explore these subversive reinventions.

CONTESTING SINGULARITIES: POOR PEOPLES' RESISTANCES

While the new global-aid regime acts to govern the poor in the name of solutions to poverty, our analysis does not offer a comprehensive account of their lives. This is deliberate; we hope to expose advanced liberal rationalities of rule and locate them in scales of power at multiple levels. Governance of poverty employs an immense range of developmental techniques, and each of these attempts to shape the lives of the poor – a vast, diverse, and disparate group. We cannot capture such plurality of experiences and hopes and instead locate some peoples' lived experiences of poverty in the context of governing programs and policies, such as some people in Katutura, in Namibia, and in Solomon Islands. Our analysis implies that the governing of the poor is neither myopic nor one-dimensional. Instead, the subjects of poverty reduction are also active agents, who contest, resist, and divert the will of the reformer or the developer in greater or lesser ways (see Crush 1995: 22).

If the yearbooks suggest the dis/continuities and flows between liberal and advanced liberal rationalities and the ways in which they constitute the poor as a singular population and govern them accordingly, one can also imagine the multiple ways in which the poor resist these rationalities. Power is diffuse, and the poor can exercise their own governmentalities, both in response to the new regime of global aid and in reaction to their own circumstances and desires. Contrary to agents of the new regime and their ideas of poverty reduction and the targeted population, the diverse 'poor' are active participants and determine their own lives.

We seek to 'excavate' the many ways in which the new regime operates in order to better explain the terrains in which the poor can displace and transform these terrains (see Foucault 2002: 4). We do not see the poor as a singular whole. We cannot possibly offer a comprehensive ethnographic account of some peoples' experiences of poverty and their efforts to live it, manage it, and potentially overcome it. We wish instead to excavate one aspect of the new regime of global aid from one vantage point. Along with considering the rationalities of governance, we explore subversions and contestations of development and poverty reduction in case studies of sites and practices of poverty reduction. We acknowledge, for example, practices of everyday resistance by numbers of the world's poor, such as the adapting of the basic income grant in Namibia to suit individuals' needs and the challenges to large-scale market initiatives by subsistence farmers in Solomon Islands.

In these practices of resistance we demonstrate Gibson-Graham's 'ethics of change' – an "ontology of a politics of possibility, and the theoretical commitment to such an ontology is an ethical act of enabling such a politics" (2006: xxvii).[10] This ontology – the philosophical analysis of what exists, of what is and what will be – facilitates a clear articulation of the dimensions of autonomy that the poor, individually or collectively conceived, claim over their own lives. An ethics of change allows for recognition of the everyday nature of politics and therefore the myriad ways in which people shape their own lives and exercise power and agency in doing so. Benedict Kerkvliet argues that this form of change is indeed the power of everyday politics and that it is here – in the everyday – that one can see struggles and resistance take place. He writes of the experiences of Vietnamese peasant farmers and the struggles manifest in their everyday lives: "Everyday politics occurs where people live and work and involves people embracing, adjusting to, or contesting norms and rules regarding authority over, production of, or allocation of resources. It includes quiet, mundane, and subtle expressions and acts that indirectly and for the most part privately endorse, modify, or resist prevailing procedures, rules, regulations, or order. Everyday politics involves little or no organization. It features the activities of individuals and small groups as they make a living, raise their families, wrestle with daily problems, and deal with others like themselves who are relatively powerless and with powerful superiors and others" (2005: 22). Such everyday social and political activities can have multiple effects and embody orientations of a social-justice life-politics.

Recognition of the ability of the poor to exercise power and endorse, modify, or resist advanced liberal governmentalities of rule in their daily lives follows from a Foucauldian reading of power itself, that it is diversely constituted and acted on and occurs within a locus of power, not external to it. Within populations of the poor, even as actors in the new global-aid regime constitute them, the poor themselves exercise power. They can participate in programs and policies, subvert them, or avoid them. One can identify or locate such resistance and challenges in local initiatives and in how they work with exercises of power by the poor themselves.

Sally Matthews writes about the responsibility of relatively privileged people, including academics, vis-à-vis such people struggling against poverty (2008). She, like Gibson-Graham, calls for academics and more direct practitioners to respond to cues from the poor themselves and thus subvert long-standing development notions of reform. She cites an example from a Senegalese NGO, Enda Graf Sahel: "After years of trying to get several income-generation and community-development projects off the ground, the NGO workers realized that it was more effective to support already existing local initiatives than to impose their ideas and projects upon poor communities. Commenting on their change of direction, one of the NGO workers said: 'we need to redefine our role as development workers. We cannot blindly seek to make people take on our ideas, but we must rather learn from them ... We must constantly interrogate ourselves, bringing into question the kind of relations we have with the population ...'" (2008: 1044). This insight illustrates the possibilities of pro-poor solutions emerging from the experiences of the poor themselves.

Arjun Appadurai explores collective acts of resistance in his account of urban poor groups in Mumbai, India (2001b). In doing so, he tells much of the everyday politics of poor people, not only of formal groupings. His account recognizes the flows between Kerkvleit's (2005) notion of everyday politics and organized collective action. It also articulates a social-justice life-politics and suggests that poor peoples' resistance represents solutions to poverty: "The official world of multilateral agencies, Northern funders and Southern governments can be persuaded that the poor are the best drivers of shared solutions to the problems of poverty. What is at stake here is all the energy that has been invested in setting precedents for partnership at all levels, from the ward to the world. The hoped-for payoff is that, once mobilized and empowered by such partnerships, the poor themselves will prove more capable than the usual candidates – the market, the state or the world of development funding – of scaling up and speeding up their own disappearance as a global category" (2001: 41).

Optimism towards the ability of partnerships for and by the poor to generate pro-poor poverty reduction is evident here and runs counter to some experiences of the partnering rationality of the new global-aid regime as we show it in later chapters (nos. 2, 4, 5, and 6). We call Appadurai's counter-governmentality (2001b: 33) resistance. Such resistance, including contestation, challenges, or denials, is as diverse in scope and scale as the populations of the poor. Diana Mitlin, for example, follows Appadurai and looks into slum dwellers' collectives in Namibia and South Africa (2008) and their ability to exercise power in their relations with state governments in order to shape the lives of the poor.

Recognizing the poor's individual and collective power challenges the advanced liberal orthodoxy of social justice, which Brodie describes as promoting "its own vision of social justice – one which, following from economic doxa, brackets out the influence of structure and systemic barriers to citizen equality and social justice, revolving, instead, around the primacy of individual choices and open systems that empower people to make their own choices about how they will live their own lives" (2007: 103). This emphasis on individual responsibility is a key rationality of advanced liberal governance of the poor and runs counter to social justice. Giovanna Procacci warns that the simplification of integrating the poor into solutions to poverty – and responsibilization represents one technology of doing so – ignores the very processes that lead to both poverty and social vulnerabilities (2007: 30). Rather, pro-poor participation can change existing power relations and behaviour (Chambers 2007: 23) and offers an understanding of social justice vis-à-vis poverty that is reflexive and open to contestation, plurality, and collective action and decision-making (see Fraser 2009: 74).

We see such pro-poor solutions to poverty in resistance in Namibia and Solomon Islands. Resistance takes variable forms, which are locally contingent and the product of poor people themselves, in complete contrast to the homogenizing tendencies of new global-aid rationalities.[11]

CONCLUSION

This chapter has unearthed a broad contemporary genealogy of poverty reduction, which contrasts with the singular conceptions of the poor that underlie liberal and advanced liberal governance of the poor through distinctive and uniform populations. A genealogical approach can reveal rhyzomatic connections. By tracing the associations and the dis/connections between ideas of the poor as a population in need of reform and local, national, mezze, regional, and global governmentalities to reduce their poverty, we have provided a genealogy that informs both liberal and (since the 1980s) advanced liberal rule without falsely constructing a neat and singular picture of either 'the poor' or solutions for them.

A central theme has been flows between liberal and advanced liberal governances of the poor, while we also revealed the shifts that distinguish them. Ideas of who the poor are, as those who are in need of both help and reform, emerged from accounts of New York and in detail from the work of UNRRA. UNRRA represents a pivotal moment in the genealogy of poverty reduction, as it is the mandate, reach, and approach of this 'relief and rehabilitation' organization that brings an international and globalizing dimension to liberal governance of the poor. This globalizing dimension is, we showed, a new way of constituting the poor as a singular population across vast distance and difference and clearly informs the UN yearbooks.

A key node in the genealogical excavation of global solutions to poverty reduction, and consequently to the poor themselves, is the advent of advanced liberal rationalities of rule. This advent is not a disjuncture, but rather a series of fluid shifts and flows, marking both continuities from liberal governance but also novel governmentalities that have shaped what we term a new global-aid regime. This new regime constitutes the poor as singular populations in need of reform, and, as we demonstrate in the chapters that follow, responsibilizes them vis-à-vis their own solutions to poverty, encourages them to join in deep and far-reaching partnerships between private and public actors across diverse physical space, and subjects them to biopolitical and securitization techniques of their poverty, whereby their state of 'being' poor allows for extensive governance of their whole lives. Vitally, these rationalities do not eradicate subjectivities or power. The poor are continually shaping their own solutions to living poverty. These solutions constitute resistance to advanced liberal rule and to the rationalities and technologies of rule of the new global-aid regime.

2 Making the Poor Responsible

With the development of a form of rule animated by the ethos of the welfare state, the object of government becomes, in the first half of the twentieth century, the welfare of society.

Mitchell Dean, *Governing Societies* (2007: 88)

In the late twentieth century and early twenty-first century, we have witnessed the rise of new rationalities of government ... The primary focus has been to 're-engineer' the welfare state.

Engin Isin, 'Governing Cities without Government' (2000: 154)

INTRODUCTION

Various national governments, private enterprises, and international agencies are mobilizing many groups of people from diverse parts of the world to take on greater responsibilities. They are, for example, encouraging the unemployed and the under-employed to act responsibly by retraining themselves in order to acquire employment. New solutions to poverty are emphasizing the responsibility of certain individuals, private institutions, and international organizations to secure social and economic rights to poor citizens. These new relations of responsibility clarify the nature of the 'problems' that need solving, the objectives worth seeking, the targets for change, and new ways of shaping poor peoples' actions. Within the new global-aid regime, groups and citizens around the world are thinking in new ways about their responsibilities and changing their practices; they are responsibilizing themselves vis-à-vis their futures. This rationality affects the poor through the mediation of an array of unpredictable acts and actions, forms of resistance, and institutional constrictions that involve and implicate them.

This chapter explores this rationality of the new regime of global aid by asking if private actors, local agencies, states, and international organizations are reconceptualizing the poor and their level of responsibility for their own impoverishment. We examine current research on and about the poor in Canada, the United States, parts of Europe, Africa, and elsewhere, and we show how the privatization of national and international programs generates new responsibilities for the poor. Our analysis concentrates on some initiatives, including international aid, microcredit, and microfinance programs, that seek to make poor individuals and groups responsible for their own well-being and that of others. We consider this emphasis on self-responsibility to reflect neither a homogeneous or tightly knit structure or arrangement nor a model of cause and effect, but rather an advanced liberal style of thinking and acting on problems by 'privatizing responsibility.'[1] This approach problematizes liberal 'social' government and formulates solutions to such concerns. It comprises diverse elements, shapes forms of conduct, and takes part in various forms of governing. It coexists alongside governmental strategies, operates as a mobile assemblage that brings into play actors, groups, practices, and events, and manifests itself in different parts of the world (Ilcan 2009: 208), often to the detriment of lives and livelihoods. The kinds of conduct it aims to create, and the kinds of relations between people, resources, institutions, or organizations it intends to achieve, are diverse.

In what follows, we examine how privatizing responsibility manifests itself in familiar and new environments, spreads out across several sites, and facilitates a range of possibilities to mobilize citizens, such as the poor, to act responsibly. We argue that the relationship between privatizing responsibility and the poor relates to three main developments under advanced liberalism: reconsideration of the relations of public and private, mobilization of the poor as responsible participants, and formation of a new kind of cultural mentality of rule or responsibilizing ethos that works alongside these developments. We look at new responsible-citizenship groups, namely the poor, and the ways in which empowerment schemes shape their activities and relationships. In the examples we draw on, we demonstrate how national governments and international organizations aim to reduce poverty through advanced liberal programs, which encompass private solutions to address the lives of the poor and lessen their impoverishment through self-management efforts. The transformation from social to private responsibility changes the role of private enterprise vis-à-vis the poor and poverty reduction, and the regime of global aid today introduces new kinds of divisions, expectations, and private partnerships, as well as other arrangements, as the poor live and care for themselves and others.

THE 'SOCIAL' IN LIBERAL SOCIAL GOVERNMENT

We hear and read so much about 'our' new responsibilities. What kinds of decisions and events encourage us to think differently about responsibility? Who is crucial in resolving social, economic, or political problems in a responsible manner? While the posing of these questions results in part from the restructuring of liberal 'social' government, we must first examine the term 'social' and the transformations in liberal social government. These changes, we argue, invoke a new understanding of responsibility for certain individuals and groups. Although the social sciences offer many understandings of the term 'social' – ranging from its opposition to the natural, through its ability to act as a force on individual behaviour, to, more broadly, its capacity to shape the relations and associations that exist between people – we look at it from a Foucauldian perspective. This viewpoint views the social as a distinctive way of governing in many domains, including those of family, education, and prison; everyday practices of care and reproduction; and issues such as citizenship, unemployment, and poverty, all of which conceive of individuals as active participants in their own government (see, for example, Brodie 2008; Walters 2000).

For example, and in terms of the governmental aspects of the social, Brodie (2008) analyses the various ways of imagining and practising the social in 'social citizenship' in prevailing rationalities of liberal governance. She terms the process of incorporating the social way of thinking into modern liberal political rationalities "social governance" and draws specifically on the Canadian experience. Similarly, Walters (2000) examines the government of unemployment by focusing on the relationship of the social to the economic and on the labour market, the wage, and economic governance more generally. His genealogical account reveals the discursive dimension of the social and economic problems vis-à-vis unemployment and how the practices of government work alongside practices of self-government (2000: 25) for the unemployed. Thus, and for our purposes, studying the social requires conceiving it not only in governmental terms but also in terms that clarify its relationship to responsibility. In the following, we focus on some of the dimensions and tensions in the transformation from social responsibilities under liberal 'social' government to privatizing responsibility under advanced liberal government.

An emphasis on the social and on social responsibilities emerged in the twentieth century partly because of changes in one type of social government – the liberal state government of the industrial economies. This form of government conceived of its task in terms of the division between state and society and between the public sector and private sector. In doing so, it created a *social* domain, an order of collective being and collective responsibilities and obligations that, as Dean argues, a particular set of authorities assumed and which gave rise to forms of knowledge and disciplines, such as welfare economics and social statistics (2007: 88–9). Liberal social government sought to cushion the hardship of the worst-off people, fears of unemployment, and, as O'Malley suggests, the "potential harms delivered by an *uncertain* future" (2004: 55). To these ends, it established mass education, public housing, public policing, social insurance, national poor relief, national taxation systems, and so forth.[2] These programs would require state-centred networks of personnel and resources to maintain collective security, social protection, solidarity, and citizenship (Brodie 2007; Isin 2000). Ideally, this form of government would shape, organize, and administer the affairs of all sectors of 'society' – a cohesive domain with a national culture, population, territory, and government (Rose 2007: 62).

The social was in effect a single space that encompassed a nation but also included entitlements and social rights for citizens from the social welfare state, as sociologist T.H. Marshall (1983 [1950]) notes. The social welfare approach shifted harm and risk from individual citizens, groups, and firms to society (O'Malley 2004; Urry 2000). It supported and fostered an image of civil society that was consistent with Fordist production, which centred on the adult 'male bread-winner' and the notion of a 'family wage.' It assumed not only a gendered division of responsibilities, with women responsible for social reproduction, both daily and generationally, but also women's access, as Fudge and Vosko (2001) remind us, to subsistence through the male wage. Implementing this approach were the state and its agencies, directly or indirectly, via specific social, rather than individual, responsibilities and obligations. Furthermore, this stance grounded notions of citizenship in the universalistic aims of state-provided social security and social welfare.[3]

As Walters points out, social security supposed and encouraged "bonds of solidarity and income redistribution" between earning and non-earning sectors; it also fostered "lines of mutuality linking men and women, rich and poor, young and old, employed and un-employed" (2000: 129–30). Thus the social welfare model assumed that citizens would understand themselves to be members of a single, integrated national society. Separation of the public and the private would embed them, and they would depend on liberal social government and its programs to mitigate the insecurities of capitalism. While social policies and programs did, as Donzelot (1988: 397) contends, "compensate for the effects of poverty and reduce the effects of oppression," they also produced and regulated citizens and national populations through, for example, obligations of caring for and rearing children and techniques of security, punishment, internment, and disqualification. Brodie shows that development of social ways of representing and intervening was "tentative and uneven both within and across post-Second World War welfare regimes" (2008: 32).

During the late twentieth and early twenty-first centuries, in almost all advanced industrial countries, from Australia, Britain, and Canada to Sweden, and in many 'developing' countries, from Mexico, Namibia, Solomon Islands, and Uganda to Turkey, confidence in liberal social government, particularly its social welfare–state schemes, would come under challenge. Many governmental experts no longer thought that it worked efficiently or smoothly and could handle rapid change. Some worried that a 'society of commitments' would interfere with the growth and movement of free-market solutions, hinder entrepreneurialism, drain public resources (see, for example, Amin 2005; Lakoff 2005), and render certain individuals and groups too dependent on government, at the cost of their autonomy. Consequently, there has been a move away from the social dimension of liberal social government – from various rights, entitlements, obligations, and public-order and security practices of the welfare state.

Many new developments flowed from this sea change. These include privatization of public utilities, marketization of unemployment and health services and pension schemes, new contractual relations between government departments and agencies in the private and not-for profit sectors, and new emphasis on the personal responsibilities of individuals, their families, their neighbourhoods, and their communities for their own well-being. For example, and like many other liberal democratic states, Canada has been privatizing government ('crown') corporations, contracting out some public-service work to the for-profit sector, reducing the availability and accessibility of social programs, and producing greater responsibilities for non-profit agencies and certain kinds of communities to engage in service delivery.[4] Brodie stresses that "social programs are progressively abandoned as all nation states are forced to engage in a competitive race to the bottom, while citizens are released from social entitlements and obligations as they maximize their choice and capacities for self-sufficiency" (2008: 39). These and other changes in liberal social government have moved the basis of citizenship from collectively respected social rights (Lazar 2007; Molz 2005) – which provided language for the systemically disadvantaged to mandate the state to regulate and avert the structural undermining of individual and collective well-being (Brodie 2007) – to a focus on individual and citizenship-based entrepreneurial responsibilities.

Alterations in liberal social government and its social welfare schemes have re-emphasized the entrepreneurialism of individuals, such as poor individuals, and their ability to invest in themselves and to meet new kinds of obligations. This emphasis has been growing alongside other commercial appeals, such as those to business, which Walters (2000: 132–3) identifies in the popularization in Britain and North America since the early 1990s of such concepts as 'corporate citizenship,' 'the new corporate philanthropy,' and 'corporate social responsibility.' Vis-à-vis the history of the government of unemployment, Walters also reveals the growing number of networks, institutes, and centres that deliberate and transmit principles of corporate citizenship among business people and the public – for example, unemployment as "a 'blight', a 'waste', something potentially avoidable" (Walters 2000: 135).

Similarly, there are private initiatives to reduce poverty. Sustained efforts to mobilize the poor into entrepreneurial actors and have them meet new types of obligations and to harness the market to lessen poverty receive endorsement from many national governments, development agencies, and international organizations. The World Bank,[5] for example, has established a consortium of thirty-three public and private development agencies – the Consultative Group to

Assist the Poorest (CGAP) – to expand access to financial services for the poor. Its work is to implement international financial programs, such as microcredit, and to enable the poor in the developing world to act in entrepreneurial, responsible ways, which would connect them to the global market and lift them out of poverty. Such programs not only promote partnerships between poor citizens, government departments, international organizations, and NGOs but also emphasize new ways of governing the poor by privatizing responsibility.

The move away from liberal social government towards a focus on privatizing responsibility produces new kinds of governing strategies. In the analysis below, we demonstrate the ways in which privatizing responsibility aims to govern differently, to assemble new links between governance and the well-being of individuals, and to mobilize new forms of citizenship. Efforts of privatizing responsibility connect to advanced liberalism, as a strategy of governing others and oneself, and surface in diverse relations, ranging from social welfare reform, through devolution of state responsibilities, private–public partnership programs, biopolitical developments, and structural-adjustment lending, to free trade and programs to reduce poverty.[6] In this regard, privatizing responsibility, as we argue, comprises a field of contemporary power relations.

PRIVATIZING RESPONSIBILITY: ENTANGLING POVERTY UNDER ADVANCED LIBERAL GOVERNMENT

The withdrawal of liberal state governments from providing public services and the new emphasis on privatizing responsibility under advanced liberalism have reconfigured the categories of public and private, welfare, responsibility, and government. In this discussion, we focus on reform of the public sector in national and international fields and its ties to market solutions to poverty. Here, the analysis reveals how private agencies and international organizations encourage responsibility schemes for certain groups, such as the poor, which in the past the state largely performed.[7] It demonstrates, we believe, a noteworthy aspect of contemporary governmental relations that involves new ways in which the private sector and responsibility schemes relate to questions about poverty and the poor.

As a style of thinking and acting on problems of liberal social government, privatizing responsibility emphasizes individual competition and self-reliance, responsible citizenship, and consumer choice rather than dependence on public resources. In the light of the work of Rose and Foucault, we view privatizing responsibility as a style of thinking and acting on problems. Nikolas Rose argues that a 'style of thought' is a particular way of thinking, seeing, and practising that involves identifying problems, formulating statements, and questioning arguments that are possible and intelligible only within that way of thinking. It involves, as Rose suggests, a certain form of explanation that "shapes and establishes the very object of explanation, the set of problems, issues, and phenomena that an explanation is attempting to account for" (2007:12). In this regard, it has taken the work of a massive number of experts, advisers, and authorities for problems relating to poverty, the poor, health, education, crime, retirement, and so on to reach the agenda of national governments, private enterprises, and international organizations. These problems are not merely enticements to solutions but also inducements to action that is governable. As Foucault (1990, 2007) claims, in order for something to be governable, or for someone to imagine it as such, it needs to be made into a problem.

Privatizing responsibility operates as a highly mobile assemblage that knows no particular spaces, rigid boundaries, or stable entities. It produces, among other things, normative categories, solutions for proper conduct, and relations of power. It resembles Deleuze and Guattari's (1987) 'assemblage' (from the French *agencement*). Appearing in the wake of critiques and questions about structure and its grounding in a logic of stability and linear causality, assemblage is a collection of practices and things that one can associate together and that can denote an understanding of states of temporal instability.[8] As a mobile assemblage, privatizing responsibility targets groups – including the poor, single mothers, pensioners, consumers, and volunteers – who are to take on more responsibility for their own well-being and others'.

This assemblage, we argue, emphasizes the practical features of governing responsibility that can depend on and include collecting and disseminating information on poverty, developing obligations and plans for the poor, and formulating ways of categorizing and offering types of training for the poor. This mobile assemblage inhabits spaces and places within and beyond nation states and attaches itself to and transforms groups, events, campaigns, and organizations. As Olds and Thrift suggest, "assemblages will function quite differently, according to local circumstance, not because they are an overarching structure adapting its rules to the particular situation, but because these manifestations are what the assemblage consists of" (2005: 271). Indeed, responsibility for the self implicates 'active' participants, such as the poor, the homeless, and the unemployed.[9] These people have lived and still live with problems centring on poverty.

Certain forms of explanation shape the problems relating to poverty and the poor. For more than a quarter-century, many people have seen poverty as a problem with links to reform of social policy, unemployment, urbanization, international development, and global markets. The constitution of poverty and its conceptualization as a problem, and proposed solutions, have shifted, along with views on social reform and economic and political relations, since the end of the Cold War and production and dissemination of knowledge through global aid partnerships. These partnerships target the poor and involve private and not-for-profit agencies, national governments, and international organizations such as the Organization for Economic Co-operation and Development (OECD), the United Nations, and the World Bank. In some of these and other transformations, policy discourses can emerge and come to endorse political inclusion, promote participation of the poor in policy dialogues, and highlight the need for national strategies to reduce poverty. M. Green (2006: 1109) asserts that discourses of poverty are the consequences of a paradigm shift that has sought to focus international development on reduction of poverty.[10] Such discourses also connect, we believe, to advanced liberal governance and its entrepreneurial schemes.

Under advanced liberalism, various agencies, organizations, and nation states favour less governing through society and seek instead to govern through the "entrepreneurship of autonomous actors – individuals, families, firms and corporations" (Rose 1999:139).[11] In certain Western liberal states, because of outsourcing and administrative decentralization, citizen groups such as the poor are taking over duties from the state. They are becoming active, responsible individuals who are to make choices, pursue preferences (Isin 2000: 154; see also Isin and Nielsen 2008), care for others, and seek to improve their lives.[12] The state, including its for-profit and not-for-profit partners, and non-state actors shape their actions from afar.

Advanced liberal government tends to govern 'at a distance.' Authorities govern not through direct and immediate force but rather by establishing networks, links, or partnerships with state and non-state actors. Networks of various kinds aim to overcome the distance between the state and other actors, with this distance an a priori given and part of the problem that the state faces. From a governmentality perspective, the aim is to enable control at a distance and, as Rose and Miller suggest, "to create locales, entities and persons able to operate a regulated autonomy" (1992: 173). But, and as Rydin (2007: 611) stresses: "The trick within governmentality is that the creation of autonomy actually enables the goal of government to be achieved." Thus the emphasis on autonomy changes the subjectivities of actors or citizens so that they internalize the goals of government.

The altering of subjectivities permits government at a distance, which helps to responsibilize citizen subjects generally and poor citizens in particular. Some international organizations, for example, aim to influence 'poor citizens' to become more entrepreneurial. The World Bank's Operationalizing Pro-Poor Growth (OPPG) program, which it initiated in 2003, seeks to better understand policy-makers' options to increase the effect of growth on reducing poverty and how they vary, depending on policies and country conditions. Rather than providing a specific policy, the OPPG governs at a distance by encouraging the poor to take greater responsibility for and participate in pro-poor growth and thereby reduce poverty. Its poverty experts work on the assumption that "the pace of overall economic growth is the main factor that determines how quickly poverty declines" (World Bank 2005: 2).

The program emphasizes that a successful pro-poor growth strategy would have "measures to achieve rapid economic growth," which include macroeconomic stability, well-defined property rights, a good investment climate, an attractive incentive framework, well-functioning factor markets, and broad access to infrastructure and education (World Bank 2005: 2). Where there is concentration of poor households in rural areas and agriculture, as in Africa, the OPPG identifies the rural poor as largely responsible for achieving pro-poor growth and reducing poverty (41). Consequently, new forms of citizenship, such as the rural poor, emerge in a world emphasized by a style of thought that links to new types of knowledge and expertise and new entrepreneurial connections, obligations, and communities.

As we emphasize in the Introduction, some of the critical issues about poverty focus on understanding the ways in which people conceive of it, categorize it, and view it as a problem that requires certain solutions. The concept of poverty, as we argue, exposes relations and associations that culminate in varied analyses, reports, and practices. Poverty analyses encompass different measures and understandings of poverty and include national economic memoranda, studies of living standards, social development reports, poverty diagnostics, poverty consumption measures, and profiles and assessments of poverty. A 2006 discussion report, "Income Poverty and Inequality in Namibia" (Van Rooy et al. 2006), from the Multi-Disciplinary Research and Consultancy Centre at the University of Namibia in Windhoek exemplifies the measurement and simplification of poverty.

The document stresses the link between alleviation of poverty and the nation state: "In order to develop realistic policies for poverty alleviation in a given context, it is essential to understand the nature of poverty in that specific setting. A common component in almost all approaches to poverty analysis is the setting of a national poverty line. This is a line that separates the 'poor' from the 'non-poor'" (Van Rooy et al. 2006). This report can alert us to the functions of the national poverty line and to a range of relations, from policy through monitoring to profiling, that become part and parcel of the concept of poverty:

> The specification of a national poverty line serves a number of purposes. Of direct relevance to the previously mentioned national and international processes, it can be used to *monitor changes in poverty* through time and to make comparisons across groups or geographic regions. It can also facilitate the development of a *poverty profile* that describes the characteristics of those in poverty. For some countries, the national poverty line has been applied as a way of *defining entitlements*, such as being a benchmark for determining whether individuals are eligible for state transfers or other state provided benefits. A poverty line can also assist in making poverty a *focus of public debate*, by increasing discussion on the circumstances of the poor and how they are changing with time. (Van Rooy et al. 2006: n.p.)

In these and similar reports, simplification and quantification of poverty permit homogenization of poverty across time and space. Generalizing poverty authorizes construction of poverty rankings,

which compare the amount and depth of poverty. However, and as
we argue, generalizing poverty does not explain how historical and
social dimensions differentially contribute to poverty in places around
the globe and how people come to understand the poor as a problem
in need of a global remedy.

Over the past three decades, many liberal states have been freeing
themselves of some of the responsibilities they acquired during the
late twentieth and early twenty-first centuries. They continue to reduce social welfare and social security and to advance enterprising
and responsibility initiatives for various groups such as the poor.
Beginning in the 1980s, many of them moved away from provision
of social services to promotion and promise of safety – a promise
that fitted well with the rise of 'law and order' campaigns, particularly in Australia, Britain, and the United States (Wilson 2006: 88).[13]
Here, Wacquant alerts our attention to "governments of the right"
that make law-and-order campaigns the basis of their hierarchical
conception of society. But, something new today, "politicians of the
left, or pretending to be left," have elevated "security" to a fundamental right by pretending (like Tony Blair in Britain or Lionel
Jospin in France) to "discover" that "the poor are the first victims of
street crime (which has always been the case, in all times and in all
countries) the better to justify its canonization as priority of public
action under the pretext of 'social justice'" (2003: 202).

This latter statement evokes other, reflexive views of social justice.
Nancy Fraser, in her current work on 'abnormal justice' and a call
for reflexive justice, argues that claims for socioeconomic redistribution, legal or cultural recognition, and political representation – the
three major families of social-justice claims – are increasingly subject
to "counterclaims whose underlying assumptions they do not share"
(2008: 396). While we do not prescribe a normative set of social
justice–style solutions to marginal and marginalized populations,
such as the poor, we value an understanding that can "reveal contemporary injustices for the moral outrages they surely are" and,
paraphrasing Fraser further, insist on reconstitution of the grammar
of solutions to poverty that enables the poor to speak authoritatively
(Fraser 2008: 422). We place this insistence within the broader ontology of change that informs this book, which seeks to unearth
dominant practices of advanced liberalism such as public-sector reform and responsibilization to create spaces of dialogue and change
for and by marginalized populations themselves.

Since the late 1980s and early 1990s, Australia, Canada, the United States, and parts of Europe, Africa, Asia, and Latin America have sought to reduce and reform the public sector. Such changes are broad and range from decentralizing state activities, through remaking public and private, to devolving national responsibilities to regional and local governments (Aretzaga 2003; Fuller 2005) and to voluntary and nongovernmental organizations (Lacey and Ilcan 2006; S. Phillips 2006).[14] They also include privatizing and outsourcing public services, such as airport security, education, health, home care, pensions, postal services, transportation, and water services.[15]

In health, for example, reforms continue to facilitate higher user fees, private health clinics, for-profit surgery, and more private health insurance. Privatizing health responsibility has devastating effects on some groups, especially people unable to afford such care. According to Rose, the private health insurance industry forces individuals and families to further monitor and oversee their own health. It encourages citizens, including the poor, to secure their own well-being and organizations and communities to secure the health of their employees and members, in what Rose refers to as the "new will to health" (2007: 63–4).

Many groups today are learning at first hand how public-sector reforms encourage a rethinking of responsibility and whom they identify as crucial in resolving social, economic, or political problems in a responsible manner. Responsibilities for welfare, care, and well-being, for example, increasingly devolve on households. In the welfare states of northern and western Europe, provision of public welfare has declined, so that families are increasingly resorting to private solutions to resolve previously public issues (see Ungerson and Yeandle 2007). According to Raghuram, Madge, and Noxolo. (2009), in the United Kingdom the mode of public provisioning has also altered. People in need of care now must make their own arrangements, for which the national government then repays them directly. Such reform positions people who require care as responsible, active citizens while altering the relationship between the parties by making recipients the entrepreneurial employers of the state. Changing notions of responsibility follow from the restructuring of liberal social government but also connect to a growing insistence that certain groups, such as people in need of care, meet new forms of entrepreneurial obligations.

Privatizing responsibility often means that advanced liberal governments must stop regulating aspects of production, trade, and investment, both domestically and across borders, and transfer as many assets and responsibilities as possible to private actors. Britain's Department for International Development, for example, invests heavily in privatizing public services. It encourages privatization of responsibility within and across the developing world through its enterprising initiatives, such as the Emerging Africa Infrastructure Fund (EAIF), the Private Infrastructure Donors Group, and the Public–Private Infrastructure Advisory Facility.[16] The EAIF provides pro-poor funds while privatizing the public sector and compelling the poor to behave as entrepreneurs.

The EAIF started as the Private Infrastructure Development Group's first initiative in 2002. It is a public–private partnership that provides long-term U.S.-dollar or Euro debt on commercial terms to finance construction and development of private infrastructure in 45 countries across sub-Saharan Africa. It grants long-term debt to pro-poor private-sector projects for infrastructure service that privatize energy, telecommunications, transportation, and water. It aims to "support projects that promote economic growth and poverty reduction" (EAIF 2007), which in turn encourages local populations, such as the poor, to participate in enterprising and responsible solutions to poverty. Such reforms under advanced liberal agendas promote competition and introduce market, quasi-market, and new responsibility arrangements, which facilitate public–private partnering and operate in similar ways through international organizations and initiatives. For example, Goldman shows how World Bank policy makers press project managers to promote privatization and sustainability of "common lands and resources" to bring about economic and ecological prosperity for the "Third World Poor" (1998: 25).

International organizations, such as the International Monetary Fund (IMF), the United Nations (UN), and the World Bank, and some NGOs, are restructuring relations[17] and launching responsibility projects to deepen market relations and influence pro-poor growth, development, and citizenship. These efforts form part of the new global-aid regime and reflect lack of opposition between public and private sectors. An example of this convergence is the OECD – a forum "where the governments of 30 democracies work together to address the economic, social and environmental challenges of globalization" (OECD 2007).[18] It promotes and identifies ways to restructure public services in industrial and 'developing' countries. OECD reform plans include devolution of administrative responsibilities to lower levels of the government, transfer of public organizations into private hands, introduction of market-like mechanisms of governance into provision of public services, and inclusion of private-sector management practices to increase efficiency (Capoor 2005; Dell'Aringa 2001).

Many countries that OECD reform plans target must promote greater consumer choice and the market as part of the effort to reduce poverty. As the OECD states: "Poverty in all its forms is the greatest challenge to the international community. One billion people live on less than $1/day. Renewed impetus has emerged to reduce by half those living in extreme poverty by 2015 and achieve the first goal of the [Millennium Development Goals]. To help donors sharpen their focus on poverty reduction efforts, the OECD's Development Cooperation Directorate Network on Poverty Reduction has produced guidance on how they can promote pro-poor growth in areas such as agriculture, infrastructure and private sector development. It has also focused on the cross-cutting themes of ex-ante poverty impact assessment and risk and vulnerability" (OECD 2006). International organizations such as the OECD view poverty as taking shape in an age of susceptibility or risk and regard the poor as 'at risk' and worthy of embrace in new interventions and reform efforts that involve expertise, global solutions to reducing poverty, and new categorizations of and forms of protection for the poor.

Reducing poverty has become the priority of many international organizations and development agencies and the target of reform efforts. The World Bank, a key player in international development, has been and remains a leader in defining and problematizing poverty and offering global solutions to remedy poverty. It has made clear its position on matters of poverty by promoting academic research on the subject and by publishing influential annual World Development Reports, such as the volume for 2000–1: *Attacking Poverty*.[19] And, more recently, it has introduced national poverty-reduction strategies (PRSs). The PRS increasingly influences the relationship between donor agencies and governments of developing countries that have fulfilled the macroeconomic and regulatory requirements. In the World Bank's international projects on privatization and development, poverty serves as a category of analysis. It is also an object of transformation and government, where the World Bank brings together specific countries, programs, and citizen groups in new ways that assemble and categorize the poor.

Countries subject to the IMF and World Bank's reform programs are witnessing privatization of social goods (affordable housing, transportation, utilities, water, and so on), which, as Hilary (2005) stresses, gives private enterprise greater control over crucial resources. More specifically, the IMF and World Bank endorse reform of the public sector by attaching strings to financial assistance. Several developing countries must reduce social welfare, such as health care and education, and privatize other state functions (Aronowitz and Gautney 2003; Goldman 2006). For example, the *Multinational Monitor* tracked twenty-six countries in receipt of loans from the IMF and the World Bank.[20] Conditions for the loans included downsizing the civil service, privatizing government enterprises, promoting labour flexibility by removing restrictions on the ability of government and private employers to fire or lay off workers, mandating wage reductions, and cutting social security for workers and making them more responsible for their own well-being.[21] Reduction of welfare and privatization of state activities hurt the unemployed, the under-employed, and people living at subsistence level. 'Spatial restructuring of citizenship' intermingles with privatization and marketization, which, according to Stasiulis, widens "the citizenship gap between those with financial means and those who are deprived of the basic means for economic and human security, both in poorer countries and in so-called advanced liberal democracies" (2008:139).

International organizations and their advanced liberal initiatives encourage national governments to restructure themselves so that their operations privatize formerly state responsibilities and follow the agendas and practices of private enterprise more closely. Development and implementation of microcredit and microfinance programs, as we see below, are critical examples of the effects of downsizing and restructuring national government. Their development makes it clear why Dean maintains that the liberal state is no longer "a government of society" – it no longer conceives its task in terms of "a division between state and society or of a public sector opposed to a private one." Rather, its aim now is to "bridge these older divisions so that the structures and values of the market are folded back onto what were formally areas of public provision and to reconfigure the latter as a series of quasi-markets in services and expertise" (1999: 172). Such reconfiguration has, among other things, made the poor into responsible citizens under a particular kind of cultural mentality of rule.

Their emergence as such is one of many links between some groups and a kind of cultural mentality of rule or a responsibilizing ethos. Resembling Dean's (2007: 62–9) critical discussion of attempts to govern the individual through ethical culture, or "culture-governance,"[22] this ethos is cultural in that it connects to the qualities and capacities of individuals and groups and their ability to transform themselves. It contains a ruling capacity as it has attachments to authorities and programs that responsibilize some individuals and groups so that they can be more agreeable to being ruled. Thus a responsibilizing ethos has links to relations of power, programs of rule, and practices of government.

A responsibilizing ethos manifests itself through programs, organizations, and governments that aim to make some groups more responsible for transforming their conduct. It derives substantially from enterprising and citizenship practices in Western and colonial governments and authoritarian regimes. Such sovereign powers, now dispersed as governmental powers, continue to shape the administration of the poor and unemployed and dictate to the latter what shall encompass freedom (Dean 2007: 71). We can also think of other practices that foster 'enterprising' individuals, such as the 'enterprise culture' of Britain's government under Margaret Thatcher, John Major, and Tony Blair, the United States's under George W. Bush, Australia's under John Howard, and Canada's under Stephen Harper.

Such a culture develops programs of rule that empower certain groups, such as 'the poor.' For example, the Howard government targeted long-term unemployed by making them responsible for their idleness by integrating them into compulsory work-for-the-dole schemes. It was only through their own participation and monitoring that citizens gained social security. And the U.S. Community Actions Programs in the 1960s, under President Johnson's War on Poverty, made poverty a national problem, which required development of certain solutions even in the face of opposing views (see Figure 2.1).

The War on Poverty sought to constitute the poor as an integrated group, 'empower' them, and – as choice makers – transform their subjectivity from powerlessness to active citizenship. Barbara Cruikshank (1999) referred to this process as a 'technology of citizenship.' The U.S. government encouraged the poor to participate voluntarily in anti-poverty programs, which in turn made them more responsible for their impoverishment. The War on Poverty set into motion a series of acts, including such initiatives as food stamps,

President Johnson's "unconditional war on poverty" is a small beginning toward what could become the most ambitious social venture undertaken in the United States since World War II.

·The antipoverty bill passed by Congress is, of course, no promise of achieving a goal that has eluded man through all the ages. It is too limited in means, too timid in ideas, even as a jumping-off point. Yet, the contrasting attitudes Mr. Johnson and Senator Goldwater have exhibited toward this program provide one of the reasons for our belief that the country's interests will benefit from a Johnson victory.

The President has shown an awareness that the onsurge of new technology will in coming years make it realistic, for the first time, to envision the elimination of basic economic distress in the United States. Paradoxically, this same technology closes to large numbers of people direct participation in its fruits through the mass displacement of men by machines in farms, factories and other fields. Poverty has become so ingrained in some areas that one generation succeeds another on the relief rolls.

The antipoverty program is based on the proposition that an America enjoying its greatest prosperity has an obligation to restore hope to the distressed and disinherited. This is a matter not solely of compassion but also of recognition that the nation's economic health is menaced when one-fifth of its citizens live in families with an annual income of $3,000 or less. The program's accent is not on handouts, but on work training and work experience for youth.

Mr. Goldwater loses no opportunity to emphasize that he has a "deep concern" about poverty, but almost everything else he says on the subject makes it plain that he believes most of the poor are poor because they are too stupid or too lacking in ambition to make anything of themselves. He regards the antipoverty program as a "worthless nostrum," and he insists that the country must choose between "Santa Claus dreams and rolled-up sleeves."

The Johnson program, in its present dimensions, is far short of measuring up to the President's assurance that "the days of the dole in our country are numbered." But, for all its limitations, the compound of idealism and realism it embodies is much more reflective of the American spirit than the lack of understanding that makes Mr. Goldwater blame the poor for so much of their own poverty.

Figure 2.1 "The Issue – Poverty," *New York Times*, 19 October 1964. Courtesy of United Nations Archives, New York.

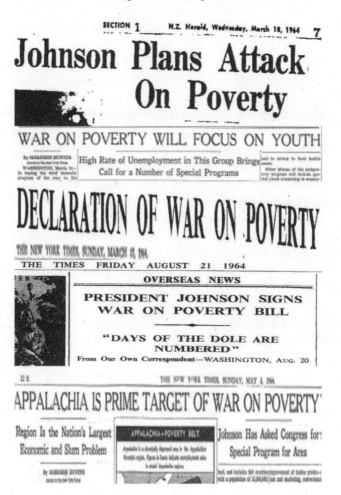

Figure 2.2 The War on Poverty – headlines, *New York Times* 1964. Authors' own media montage.

Head Start, Medicaid, Medicare, and work study, to reduce poverty and improve conditions for the poor (see Figure 2.2). As Dean (2007: 69) observes, such enterprising practices no longer simply occur through traditional and modern endorsed identities and forms of legitimation.

Governmental technologies can enable recasting of the poor and construction of them as objects of government. These technologies comprise strategies and techniques that can range from practices of calculation and standardization (Rose and Miller 1992; Murdoch

2004), through modes of 'being political' that implicate beings in solidaristic, agonistic, and alienating orientations (Isin 2002), to ways of monitoring subjects (Appadurai 2001b), including the poor's own participation in a responsibilizing ethos. For example, the OECD, through its pro-poor growth and empowerment initiatives, targets the poor as an object of government. It stresses that pro-poor growth can emerge through a 'successful interplay' between market development and dialogue. It cites emergence of a commercial radio market in Uganda, where, in 2004, 19 commercial radio stations were broadcasting to 7 million regular listeners. It claims that commercial radio enhances pro-poor growth by allowing poor citizens to "participate in debates on how to improve and bring about reforms of the local business climate" (OECD 2006: 38).

"For pro-poor growth policies to emerge, the poor need to be informed and empowered to influence a policy making process that is accountable to their interests" (OECD 2006: 35). Here, the OECD's view is that inhabitants holding a particular status and occupying a certain place, such as the poor, are not only ripe for change but are susceptible to empowerment via programs that regenerate their economic and business climate. Implementation of these sorts of programs clearly reflects an emphasis on seeing the subjects of government, such as the poor, in new ways that focus on their capacities of self-responsibility and on seeing new strategies for governing economic life and ways of life as beneficial to the poor. More broadly, these programs emerge within a responsibilizing ethos that involves diverse actors engaging with the poor and makes the poor more responsible for their conduct and compels them to meet new forms of entrepreneurial obligations.

RESPONSIBILITY PROJECTS AND ENTREPRENEURIAL AID

A responsibilizing ethos cultivates support for individuals and groups working to advance themselves socially and economically so they can seize opportunities to do so and engage in 'responsibility projects.' Such endeavours mobilize groups, such as those labelled as poor, to work on themselves and take charge of their life choices and conditions. Aihwa Ong claims, for example, that certain citizen groups are increasingly acting as 'free agents' to confront insecurities by making calculations and investments in their lives (2006a: 501).

In this regard, a responsibilizing ethos demands action.

This ethos is producing a new kind of responsible citizenship. It is taking on a new urgency of late, with private agencies, national governments, international organizations, and some NGOs supporting more and more people seeking to act responsibly. Several responsibility efforts introduced by governmental actors within and beyond the nation state are in place to produce responsible and knowledgeable participants, groups, citizens, and communities. These include programs to uphold the best practices of 'responsible communities,' advocate the enterprising features of responsible living and caring, and encourage solutions to the problem of 'risky' citizens. Britain's Blair government, for instance, promoted a kind of 'technological citizenship' that educated groups technologically so they could engage in social life (Ong 2005: 339).[23] Here, these and other citizens are to avoid risk (risk of poverty, unemployment, illness, crime) and protect themselves against risk by seizing all possible chances to 'improve' and secure their own and other peoples' lives. Isin emphasizes: "Just as avoiding risk becomes the responsibility of individuals as authors of their own destiny, ill-fate and misfortune also become the responsibility of individuals: the unemployed, the homeless, and the poor are constituted as responsible for their own condition" (2002: 248).

In the following, we discuss how new responsible groups, such as poor citizens, are establishing links to new private and public partnerships and to other enterprising programs. We focus on international responsibility projects for the poor, such as international aid and microcredit and microfinance, and on how they relate to public-sector reform. Our analysis reveals the replacing of the social logics of social welfare by new logics of market initiatives and development aid and shows that governing the poor can be profitable.

While many liberal states rely on business, voluntary initiatives, and government to provide services to the public, numerous organizations around the globe are supporting privatization and devolution of public services. In this process, they are mobilizing groups of people to deliver humanitarian and other services. These groups work through the values, attitudes, and ideals that strengthen their own well-being, solve personal problems, and care for others. International aid organizations, such as Food for the Hungry International (FHI), International Relief and Development (IRD),

USAID, and WFP, work to solve long-term social and economic problems, such as poverty. These solutions extend far beyond the borders of nation states.

A good illustration is international organizations' addressing long-term poverty in a style of government that encourages 'aid' through the training of 'poor' youth. USAID programs provide financial and technical 'assistance' to developing countries, while piloting development models that can expand over time. For example, USAID sends aid to Namibia and in 2003 found that country ranking 124th (of 175 countries) on the United Nations' Human Development Index Report, which measures income, literacy, and life expectancy (USAID 2007a). "The needs and expectations of a substantial portion of the population are not being met. With a continuing under- and unemployment rate of around 60 percent and only one-fifth of the 20,000 Namibian school-leavers each year finding jobs, the Government of the Republic of Namibia (GRN) is vigorously seeking ways to accelerate income growth and job creation" (USAID Namibia 2007). USAID provides funds to train mainly jobless male youth in construction and building (bricklaying, carpentry, plumbing, and welding). Such training enables the young men "to work as self-employed entrepreneurs and contribute to the growth of private sector" (USAID Namibia 2007). USAID also sponsors internships in the United States for students of the Hotel Management School (Polytechnic of Namibia) through a Global Development Alliance partnership with a consortium of three U.S. community colleges and the hotel-tourism industry in Florida and Hawaii (USAID Namibia 2007).

Under a responsibilizing ethos, USAID attempts to transform the relations of the poor by engaging in the ubiquitous language of enterprise and entrepreneurialism that it directs at the poor. Its indicators of poverty feature in the social and political life of nations such as Namibia, are a form of governing the poor, and include low income, low levels of job creation, and slow growth of the private sector. These poverty indicators are understood to be useful, rendering complex data simple and easy to understand, revealing compliance with obligations, and capturing advancement over time and across countries. They sit at the nexus of numerous administrative and governing apparatuses, of local, regional, and international development aid initiatives, and of expert forms of knowledge that standardize notions of poverty and measures to eradicate poverty.[24]

From our perspective, poverty indicators can identify and provide information about the poor, which in turn facilitates calculation, evaluation, and intervention vis-à-vis poverty. Calculation enables us to see links between the subjects of calculation and their quantification. Rydin observes: "Calculation is at the heart of indicators since their purpose is to provide a means of comparing performance over time or space. In so doing they define the object of their calculation that is, the performance being monitored" (2007: 612).[25] Calculations about the poor by international aid organizations, such as USAID, are never simply technical solutions to the 'problems' of the poor. They are also ways of linking the poor and poverty to 'technologies of performance' (Dean 1999: 169) or to technologies of government that subsume domains of expertise about the poor to 'calculative regimes' (Miller 1992) that, for example, set performance indicators, create benchmarks, and privatize public services. As such, calculations do indeed produce knowledge about the poor and make them transparent as well as controllable.

International aid organizations in many parts of the world are increasingly managing the more vulnerable members of society instead of campaigning for social justice and change for the disadvantaged and the marginal. These organizations, which form part of the new global-aid regime, often consider their 'aid' activities as laudable attempts to solve the problems of poverty. However, the problems of poverty have themselves operated as relations of power that can enable and control development and formulation of many issues and practices. Microcredit and microfinance programs provide a good example of these relations, especially as they link to the expansive restructuring demands of the public service and serve as a technology of government aiming to reduce poverty and make the poor responsible for their well-being. Technologies of government are not simply mechanical devices; they assemble, according to Rose (1999: 52), forms of practical knowledge, with practices of calculation and types of authority and judgments that rule the conduct of the governed.

ON 'SMART' CONSUMERS AND ENTREPRENEURS

The 1980s brought about new solutions to the problems of poverty. States curtailed public-sector provision of health care, education, transport, and food subsidies. Along with the IMF and World Bank's imposition of structural adjustment to deal with the developing global debt crisis, poverty experts, advanced liberal governments, and international organizations – perhaps governmental actors that Tsing would view as those with a "singular vision" (2005: 81) – came to view 'market failure' as a major impediment to alleviation of poverty. Markets had in effect failed to provide incentives for the poor to improve their conditions – perhaps short-term 'catch-up' initiatives could help (Lucarelli 2005)?

Two financial programs – microcredit and microfinance – became possible panaceas. The generic term 'microcredit' covers a range of credit programs, including small loans to poor people for initiating or expanding a business. 'Microfinance' includes banking services (for example, cell-phone banking, debit cards, and savings accounts), loans (for example, consumer, home mortgage, and small business), and insurance policies (for example, health, home, and life). The lending organizations can be NGOs, savings and loan co-operatives, credit unions, government banks, commercial banks, or non-bank financial institutions (Corsi et al. 2006).

For Latin America, for example, the Inter-American Development Bank (IDB) launched microcredit and microfinance initiatives at a gathering of key members of the Washington Consensus in June 2006 in Washington, DC. IDB President Luis Alberto Moreno commented that in Latin America roughly 360 million poor people do not have access to financial services (IDB 2007). While most of these people live on less than $2 a day, their 'purchasing power' exceeds $510 billion per year. Moreno commented on their potential to become "smart consumers and entrepreneurs": "These people are not passive recipients of charity and government handouts. They are smart consumers and entrepreneurs who constantly look for goods and services that improve their quality of life at an attractive price. And the tragedy is that those goods and services are either not available or too expensive" (IDB 2007). These programs liberalize the financial sector and expand financial services – particularly noteworthy with the reappearance of structural adjustment. Proponents speak in terms of an 'enabling environment' necessary to permit the poor to act as entrepreneurs. Here, and according to H. Weber (2004: 362), liberalization of the financial sector gives poor people greater access to credit.

Since the early 1990s, private financial institutions, development agencies, NGOs, the IMF and World Bank, and UN organizations have emphasized microcredit for the poor and expansion of microfinance in the fight against poverty. In 1995 the World Bank introduced market initiatives to fund microcredit at the Consultative Group to Assist the Poorest (CGAP). In advancing the idea of 'banking the unbanked' (Flynn 2007), the CGAP sees the 3 billion global poor – half the world's population – who live on less than U.S.$2 a day as beneficiaries of microfinance (CGAP 2006). The CGAP seeks to promote 'best practices' in microcredit and act as the central funding channel for small projects. As Basok and Ilcan (2006) stress, the CGAP works towards this goal by contributing services to microfinance industry, donors, and NGOs and by offering technical advice, providing training in market skills, and facilitating diverse forms of economic development.

In support of the CGAP's goal, several UN agencies promote microcredit and microfinance programs, including the FAO, the International Labour Organization (ILO), the United Nations Educational, Scientific, and Cultural Organization (UNESCO), and the UNDP, which launched Microstart in 1997. Other organizations, such as the Canadian International Development Agency (CIDA), Britain's Department of International Development (DFID), the Norwegian Agency for Development Co-operation (NORAD), and USAID, support microcredit and microfinance programs around the world in their efforts to reduce poverty. For example, CIDA has long helped Développement International Desjardins implement its community finance projects in Africa, the Americas, Asia, and Europe. Currently, it is supporting efforts by the Aga Khan Foundation to set up the first microcredit bank in Tajikistan. It also supports World Relief Canada's projects to provide microcredit to the poor in Bangladesh, Cambodia, Mozambique, Rwanda, and Vietnam (CIDA 2007). According to CIDA, "Microfinance is helping people around the world to earn a living, to eat better, to receive better health care, and to enrol their children in school. Families are improving their access to clean water and safe sanitation. And women are achieving higher levels of autonomy" (2007).

In the last decade, numerous programs of microcredit and microfinance have emerged through the support of agencies, groups, and organizations around the world. In 2004, as part of its commitment to microcredit, the FAO launched the Rural Finance Learning Centre (RFLC) – an internet portal to a large variety of resources and online training materials for rural finance. Donors, field practitioners, policy-makers, trainers, and universities use it. It makes financial services available in rural areas and aims to help people living there to improve their livelihoods. The director of the FAO's Agricultural Support Systems Division, Geoffrey Mrema, stated: "The challenges in rural areas are characterized by long distances, poor infrastructure, highly seasonal incomes and widespread poverty. Rural finance is about providing a range of financial services for people in these areas, including savings accounts, loans, insurance products and money transfers" (FAO 2007b).

An FAO news article – "Entrepreneurs Don't Grow on Trees" – introduced a new approach to help "poor people around the world turn trees into cash income – without felling the trees." Use of renewable resources in new ways can help "fight hunger and poverty." Sophie Grouwels of FAO's Forestry Department commented: "It's not just timber companies that benefit from forests – about 1.6 billion people worldwide depend on them for all or part of their livelihoods. And they often do so in ways that don't always involve cutting down trees, but through harvesting of renewable, non-wood forest products." Grouwels suggests processing these resources "into a product that sells for more in local markets, or even marketed overseas. All of these things could help people produce more food or earn more money for their families" (FAO 2007a).

In the light of these financial initiatives for the rural poor, the UN started one of the most significant developments in microcredit. Its General Assembly designated 2005 as the International Year of Microcredit. Large financial institutions began entering the business of small-scale banking and credit services in emerging markets. The General Assembly asked the United Nations Capital Development Fund (UNCDF)[26] – which gives the UNDP policy advice and technical assistance for microfinance – to develop a program of action for the International Year with contributions from member states, UN agencies, and other interested participants. UNCDF Executive Secretary Richard Weingarten remarks: "Microfinance is becoming a very important tool for development. At the UN Capital Development Fund, we think microfinance is important as it encourages economic growth and employment, and reduces poverty. I expect that microfinance activities will increase over the next years and contribute to reducing poverty around the world" (UNCDF 2007b). The UN views the International Year of Microcredit and other such initiatives as making financial services more accessible to the poor and assisting in the international pledge of the Millennium Development Goals to cut poverty in half by 2015, ideas about which we explore below in chapters 4 and 5.

Businesses, national governments, and international organizations often frame microcredit programs in terms of reducing poverty, empowering people, and expanding financial markets. These programs increasingly aim to target and govern the conduct of poor citizens, making them responsible for their conditions and dependent on private enterprise. One grassroots program of microfinance that has become prominent is 'village banking' – small loans to the poor, especially in the global South. It has grown from a small program that started in the 1970s in Bangladesh to international microloans and its apparent success was recognized when the Nobel Peace Prize was awarded equally to Grameen Bank and its founder, Muhammad Unus, in 2006 for their efforts to foster economic and social development from below. Non-profit organizations, such as CARE and Freedom from Hunger, aim thereby to 'empower' poor households. According to Hiatt and Woodworth, over 3,600 microfinance organizations have emerged in Africa, Asia, and Latin America. They provide over $18 billion in loans to more than 67 million individuals, 79 per cent of them women. In recent years, and as part of its new global aid, the World Bank has provided over $1 billion to NGOs active in village banking. The UN, USAID, and other organizations have channeled microloan funds to NGOs (Hiatt and Woodworth 2006: 471–2) in an effort to transform the lives of the poor. NGOs are establishing critical relations with the poor within the new global-aid regime and are becoming what Trudeau and Veronis (2009) call 'strategic sites' for investigating the restructuring of relations among civil society, the private sector, and national government.

Other notable microcredit initiatives target and govern the conduct of the poor. The Microcredit Summit Campaign is a project of the RESULTS Educational Fund, a U.S. grassroots organization that works to end hunger and poverty. It links microcredit practitioners with advocates, donor agencies, educational institutions, NGOs, international financial institutions, and other participants. It aims to promote best practices in the field and to stimulate exchange of knowledge. At its Global Microcredit Summit 2006 in November in Halifax, more than 2,000 delegates from over 110 countries assessed progress towards the goal of reaching 100 million of the world's poorest people by the end of 2005 and launched the second phase with two new goals. The first goal is: "Working to ensure that 175 million of the world's poorest families, especially the women of those families, are receiving credit for self-employment and other financial and business services by the end of 2015." The second: "Working to ensure that 100 million families rise above the US$1 a day threshold adjusted for purchasing power parity (PPP), between 1990 and 2015" (Microcredit Summit Campaign 2007).

These and other advanced liberal initiatives suggest microcredit and microfinance as viable solutions to poverty. The UNDP observes: "Poor households often fail to secure the capital they need and miss opportunities for growth because they do not have access to financial resources, loans or a safe place to hold savings. Over 80 per cent of all households in developing countries do not have access to institutional banking services. This includes nearly all the poor people in the developing world. When there are no financial institutions to serve them, poor enterprises and households rely largely on informal sources such as family, friends, suppliers or moneylenders for their financial needs" (2007a). The UNDP acknowledges the growth of microcredit and microfinance for the very poor and asserts that "poor people need a variety of financial services, not just credit. Current microfinance has therefore moved towards providing a range of financial services, including credit, savings and insurance, to poor enterprises and households" (2007a).

NGOs and banks – for example, the Banco Solidario (BancoSol) (Bolivia), the Bank Rakyat Indonesia (BRI) Unit Desa (Indonesia), the Grameen Bank (Bangladesh), and the Kenyan Rural Enterprise Programme (Kenya) – engage in new lending methods for the poor. One such approach involves small loans, without collateral and at full-cost interest rates repayable in frequent instalments. According to the UNDP: "The poor majority, who are generally excluded from the formal financial sector, can, in fact, be a market niche for innovative banking services that are commercially sustainable" (2007a).

There are, however, many critical issues about banking services for the poor. The UNDP and other international organizations ignore the fact that microcredit and microfinance programs reflect a transition in development thinking. The transition is from a position that the state (and the commercial banks it regulates or owns) was once responsible for providing finance capital to the poor as a group with beneficiaries and social rights to one where individuals are clients responsible for their own well-being (see Lazar 2006; Rankin 2001).

As Rankin points out, "when poor women are constructed as responsible clients in this way, the onus for development falls squarely on their shoulders, and their citizenship manifests not through entitlement but through the 'free' exercise of individual choice" (2001: 29). The World Bank's former president, Paul Wolfowitz, illustrates a similar conception: "Microfinance is a powerful tool for reducing poverty. It enables people to increase their incomes, to save and to manage risk. It reduces vulnerability and it allows poor households to move from everyday survival to plan for the future" (UNCDF 2007a). According to the Grameen Foundation, microfinance can empower the poor and lift them out of poverty:

> Microfinance is an amazingly simple approach that has been proven to empower very poor people around the world to pull themselves out of poverty. Relying on their traditional skills and entrepreneurial instincts, very poor people, mostly women, use small loans (usually less than US$200), other financial services, and support from local organizations called microfinance institutions (MFIs) to start, establish, sustain, or expand very small, self-supporting businesses. A key to microfinance is the recycling of loan dollars. As each loan is repaid – usually within six months to a year – the money is recycled as another loan, thus multiplying the value of each dollar in defeating global poverty, and changing lives and communities. (2007a)

Because of this responsibilizing ethos, recipients are not passive holders of social rights that the state grants but active citizens taking responsibility for their own well-being. As Lazar emphasizes: "The state can no longer be responsible for social rights: where the market fails, the 'community' must step in, and 'social capital' takes over" (2006: 4).

Advanced liberalism tends to shift responsibility for social rights from the state to external agencies and to those operating in partnership with the state. Private businesses may become partners with international organizations and financial institutions in administering microcredit to the poor. The UNCDF, for example, argues for engagement of microfinance with private-sector development (UNCDF 2007b). In this regard, microcredit encourages poor citizens to rely on the market to provide for their social welfare. Under such programs, the poor become a client population governable through individual choice and freedom and able to make responsible market choices and thereby engage in the privatization of responsibility. This analysis bears similarity to a study on human and citizenship rights by Basok and Ilcan (2006), which demonstrates that freedom (such as the freedom of the poor to make choices, manage their own risks, and improve their own situations) is not a universal right but a technology of government that derives from entrepreneurial programs for the poor.

There is an ominous side to microcredit and microfinance that donor institutions rarely acknowledge. Individual recipients, many of them women, become responsible entrepreneurs through coercive interventions. The most common form of microfinance is the solidarity group, which creates group lending contracts and makes borrowers jointly liable for each partner's loan. Such group lending mitigates informational asymmetries through peer selection, peer monitoring, and social enforcement (Corsi et al. 2006; Guerin 2006). Thus, and following the Grameen model,[27] credit goes not to individual poor women but to self-regulating borrower groups, consisting of about five to ten women. Members learn how to establish a savings fund, examine one another's proposed microenterprises, and agree on a collective basis to guarantee each other's loans (Rankin 2001: 24).

These groups control membership by weeding out 'less reliable' women, policing non-payment, and punishing non-repayment (Lazar 2006). Some recipients face extreme indebtedness and poverty. In India, some individuals unable to pay interest in excess of 20 per cent or not sure they can repay their loans have committed suicide (*Economist* 2006). Isabelle Guerin (2006) alerts us to such limitations: microfinance can contribute to under-employment and excessive debt and fail to mitigate inequalities and level gender hierarchies. Despite use of the language of empowerment to explain why women 'benefit' predominantly from these programs, international and nongovernmental organizations consider female borrowers more likely to repay loans. Some researchers have argued that microcredit does not empower women but instead depoliticizes their activities by co-opting them and directing them towards financial institutions' goals. As Lazar (2006: 27) states: "It is probable that the targeting at women is less about female empowerment than about ensuring repayment of loans, because of greater reliability on the part of women borrowers."

In recognizing the debates about the effectiveness and ineffectiveness of microcredit in the alleviation of poverty, we propose more critical consideration of the ways in which microcredit and microfinance target the poor, particularly women, make them responsible citizens and connect them to global market economies, and force them into new obligations vis-à-vis the market. Further research can usefully expand critical discussions of the particular ways in which marginal groups are financed by international organizations, the social and cultural implications of the finance process on the everyday lives of the poor, and, as Aitken (2010) suggests, of decentred and heterogeneous accounts of finance and its generation of uneven effects.

CONCLUSION

With all the critical concerns that surfaced about liberal social government over the years, many governmental experts concluded that it no longer worked efficiently or smoothly. Its interference in markets and entrepreneurialism, its encouragement to citizens to depend on government for their security and well-being, and its costs are key explanations for its ineffectiveness. As this chapter stresses, emphasis has shifted from social to private responsibilities. This sea change involves a new style of thinking and acting on problems and development of ideas on government and solutions to these issues. We have shown how withdrawal of liberal state governments from provision of public services has gone hand in hand with new ideas of citizenship, responsibility, and government and new programs to mobilize the poor and impose entrepreneurial obligations on them. Our analysis reveals that the social logics of social welfare evaporated in the face of new logics of market initiatives and development aid and that governing the poor can be profitable.

An enormous focus on governing poverty has been linked to initiatives on privatizing responsibility. We have demonstrated how poverty increasingly serves as a category in domains ranging from education and social policy to international development. Poverty is in fact a social and political construct that emerges from processes of assemblage. Throughout this chapter we argue that private-sector agencies, advanced liberal governments, and international organizations view poverty as a problem. This problem seeks not so much solutions as endorsement and negotiation, and so certain social-reform initiatives aim to transform and govern the poor.

Viewing poverty as a problem, however, diverts attention from the social and political relations that generate it. Very often it is not among the poor that we should be looking for those relations that have contributed most to the poverty of others. Robert Chambers (2001: 303) reminds us that the only asset that most marginal people possess is their own bodies. While the able-bodied can sell their labour finitely, inadequate access to health services and high risk of accidents render many destitute. In order to survive, some must engage in a body-politics that involves prostitution, bondage, slavery, or sale of human organs. Although many national governments dealing with the poor focus on the threats that they may pose, it is, as M. Green (2006: 1124) stresses, threats to the poor themselves that should concern more and more people, including pro-poor groups and anti-poverty activists.

Within the context of advanced liberalism and restructuring of the public sector, we have demonstrated the relationship between privatizing responsibility and the poor in terms of three dimensions: reconsideration of the relations of public and private, mobilization of the poor as responsible participants, and formation of a responsibilizing ethos that accompanies these developments. We have revealed how national governments and international organizations link solutions to poverty to a responsibilizing ethos and depend on advanced liberal programs of empowerment, which encompass private solutions to poverty. This ethos, we have shown, attaches to authorities and programs of rule that encourage 'the poor' to become more responsible for their choices. Marginalized citizens are thereby taking charge of their own choices, and this process is open to the forces of private enterprise. It is also open to diverse situations, including social inequities, gender and ethnic discrimination, deteriorating health and living standards, inadequate access to clean and safe water, and other unjust conditions.

A central task facing educators, activists, intellectuals, and other groups is overcoming the privatizing of responsibilities and the resulting practices and ethos. This might involve promoting development of more social, cultural, and political spaces for fostering dialogue and alliances across many domains and for encouraging participants to communicate and strive for more equitable change that does not involve or reproduce governing relations. Such changes would help to rectify the social injustices inherent in current responsibility plans for the poor. This is not an easy undertaking, as many anti-poverty groups, citizenship-rights and social-justice activists, and anti-privatization coalitions are challenging privatization of responsibility and struggling to publicize their views and to make a difference in the lives of the poor. Such collective forces nevertheless could establish further links to broader struggles over the responsibilities of public bodies and private corporations. They could also demand social justice in new forms of contestation that challenge advanced liberal forms of empowerment. It is to issues of empowerment than we turn next.

The following chapter focuses on governmental initiatives that assemble territories in the name of community and as sites of empowerment. Under the guise of empowerment, various Western liberal states, and international aid and development organizations, attempt to transform the poor, the homeless, and the unemployed. Within this context, the chapter analyses Oxfam International and its ties to the poor. It reveals how Oxfam's advanced liberal programs of empowerment target marginal populations on the assumption that they lack the skills of self-management to become active community members.

3 Empowering the Poor: Oxfam's Poverty-Reduction Initiatives

Whether inspired by the market or by the promise of self-government and autonomy, the object of empowerment is to act upon another's interests and desires in order to conduct their actions toward an appropriate end; thus 'empowerment' is itself a power relationship and one deserving of careful scrutiny.

Barbara Cruikshank, *The Will to Empower* (1999)

INTRODUCTION

Governmental actors' increasing role in shaping the lives of the poor involves far more than the technical aspects of reducing poverty. That is, 'what?' questions are inadequate in addressing poverty-reduction efforts across the globe. The less noticeable but more salient question is 'how?': how these strategies come to be and how they modulate behaviour, target communities as sites of governmental control, relate to practices of empowerment, and form part of the new global-aid regime. In this analysis, we focus on Oxfam International as an empirical site of investigation.[1]

Akin to the way numerous international governing organizations initiated new plans and programs to remedy wartime hunger and poverty, Oxfam emerged in response to famine in Europe during the Second World War. Since its inception, it has been active in liberal trade campaigns and market initiatives to lessen poverty and influence the poor around the globe. While Oxfam proclaims that it works globally to alleviate poverty and injustice (Oxfam International 2008a),[2] we argue that it actually operates in conflict with this broad aim. Two key policy areas – its emphasis on self-management and empowerment and its pursuit of free trade as a development tool – challenge its ability to uphold the voices of the poor, rather than supporting advanced liberal initiatives to govern individuals and groups in particular ways. The detailed analyses here of the politics of its initiatives to reduce poverty will, we hope, inspire the reader to think about the relationship between aid and empowerment, Oxfam's impingement on social and political processes, and its ties to governing relations on a global scale.

As a contribution to governmentality studies at the international level, our analysis examines Oxfam International's efforts against poverty as a governmental practice that has received scant critical attention. The organization's work depends on advanced liberal programs of empowerment at the community level, which we call 'community-targeted empowerment' – programs and practices of government that use trade-market solutions to social problems, such as poverty, and that emphasize improvement through self-management.

Our argument is not so much about the rise of a new community or new developing locales (see, for example, Amin 2005).[3] Rather, we claim that governmental techniques vis-à-vis community not only illustrate the complexities of administering but also foster new conceptions of community and poverty, as well as new ideas about governance that reflect views of global markets and trade. This chapter looks first at global governance of poverty under advanced liberalism and at how governance of community operates at this scale. Second, it considers which subjects are part of community-targeted empowerment and how governmental processes shape their implementation and relate to the new regime of global aid. Third, it examines what governing through community tells us about advanced liberalism. Our analysis draws on published, policy, and institutional documents on poverty and poverty-reduction efforts; Oxfam's statements, reports, and programs; and our interviews with key personnel from international aid organizations, such as Oxfam Canada.

ASSEMBLING ACTIVE INDIVIDUALS

In the industrial world of the twentieth century, reducing social and economic risks and distributing their costs was a primary concern of liberal state governments.[4] The resulting 'social welfare state' shifted risks from individuals, groups, firms, and communities to society (Simon 2002). The rationality of welfarism after 1945 emerged in relation to problems such as poverty, unemployment, the declining birthrate, anti-social behaviour, and the social consequences of ill-health (see also Brodie 2007; Isin 2000; Rose and Miller 1992; Walters 2000). Such an approach took place through the state and its agencies, directly or indirectly, as we saw above in chapter 2.

With the decline since the 1980s of social welfare in many Western liberal states, a new rationality of government – 'advanced liberalism' – is moving away from a focus on society and emphasizes instead the link between governance and individual well-being. According to Dean, this stance encompasses different types of government that are assembled from similar elements and resources. These approaches to ruling contrive markets, regulate indirectly, disperse and individualize management of risk, and construct multiple forms of agency. Consumer and community are their key forms of agency (1999: 207). As such, advanced liberalism encourages particular individuals, groups, and communities to take greater responsibility for their lives and livelihoods through 'empowering' methods of self-management (Brinkerhoff 2002; Ong 2006b). Political and administrative decentralization, privatization, and out-sourcing spur these efforts, thereby shifting national government responsibilities (such as public services) to citizens, private-sector organizations, NGOs, communities, regions, and international organizations. Development and poverty-reduction initiatives form part of this governance.

Advanced liberal efforts reframe the more than fifty years of 'development' initiatives and programs that grounded relations between the West and its 'others' (Mosse 2005b: 1). They also emphasize global governance of many issues, ranging from health and human rights to human security, empowerment, and poverty reduction. Despite decades of development planning, aid projects and programs, grants, loans, and structural adjustment, demand for poverty reduction became noticeable in the 1990s and suggests a new way of governing initiatives began to take place 'at a distance' and under the aegis of international organizations such as the OECD, the UNDP, and the World Bank, with endorsement following from a multitude of donors and from the IMF through its Poverty Reduction Strategy Papers of 1999 (Scheyvens 2007: 123).

Today, exercises of poverty reduction remain at centre stage in many development-based and international organizations. A plethora of international bodies are working with private- and public-sector organizations to advance new strategies to lessen poverty by empowering the poor and making them, as choice-makers, more accountable for their circumstances. This public–private empowerment framework treats the poor as potential recipients of stability, able to meet their basic needs and prospective beneficiaries of prosperity and consequently of human security.

Many current strategies to challenge poverty, such as those of UN agencies and the World Bank, constitute the poor as active participants responsible for their own condition and subject to market discipline. Expansion of tourism in poor communities has, for example, generated interest in that field as a route to prosperity. The United Nations World Tourism Organization (UNWTO) sees such 'pro-poor' development as a valuable instrument. The connection between tourism and poverty reduction received momentum in the early 1990s from efforts by the World Bank[5] and similar plans from multilateral development banks and bilateral aid agencies. Advocates of pro-poor tourism view it as a way to create human security and sustainable jobs for the poor.

As with other methods to reduce poverty, pro-poor tourism has critics. The focus on employing the under-employed, unemployed, or working poor is an advanced liberal strategy unable to address the injustices of the North–South divide, social and economic divisions within developing countries (M. Hall 2007: 2), and the privatized form of security known as development that Duffield calls 'securitization of development' (2001b: 310). Such advanced liberal rationalities are emerging not only in Western liberal countries and some developing states but in numerous international bodies and organizations, such as the IMF, Oxfam, UN agencies, USAID, and the World Bank.[6]

Such rationalities encourage practices of community and empowerment that seek to transform subjectivity and emphasize self-management. From our perspective, this connection implies that government, as one field of power relations, centres on programs, schemes, and practices that attempt to direct the actions of others, including the governing efforts of international organizations. Government entails any endeavour to shape with some degree of deliberation "aspects of our behaviour according to particular sets of norms and for a variety of ends" (Dean 1999: 10). It allows one to recognize a plurality of governing agencies and authorities and to focus on complex relationships, across political institutions, agencies, and communities (Folke and Nielsen 2006; Isin 2002), and at national, regional, and global levels (Aitken 2010; Ferguson 2006; Ong 2006a).

As a broad concept, government includes the deliberate shaping of the way people act in different sites and relations and under different authorities. For Foucault, government comprises not only "the legitimately constituted forms of political or economic subjection but also modes of action, more or less considered and calculated, that were designed to act upon the possibilities of action of other people" (2001a: 341). While these modes of action are diverse, they alert us to methods that animate community and link to forms of inclusion and exclusion, types of expertise, and styles of responsibility and accomplishment. Reflecting the workings of an assemblage, various methods and technologies of government can target communities and hold them together.

COMMUNITY AS A NEW AGENT

Government is said to occur 'at a distance' from formal centres of power precisely because regulation works by harnessing the duties and responsibilities, and forms of practical know-how, which families, firms, individuals, communities, and all manner of agents come to assume.

William Walters, *Unemployment and Government* (2000: 6)

For diverse interest groups, national and international agencies, many national governments, and international governing bodies, the community is a potential site for the promise of safety, individual salvation, and belonging and security. Diana Brydon and William Coleman remind us that "communities remain important forms of collectivity for generating trust and feelings of belonging and for enabling humans to engage in collective action toward chosen goals" (2007: 5). And when members face constraints on their self-determination, they can, as Nyers argues, organize themselves, advocate for change, and engage in public mobilization. Communities of non-status immigrants in Canada, for example, are reframing their political relations with the state and the city by constituting themselves as 'political subjects' and thereby challenging notions of political community and citizenship (Nyers 2007: 132) and governmental control.

In our current times of public-sector downsizing and outsourcing, authorities, advisers, and community experts look to the community for answers to 'problems' of governmental control, which is on the rise. There are new developments relating to community – new discourses and images about it: community housing, community groups, and community employment services; distinct associations with it: community health, community banking, and enterprise community; and new terms for managing it: community action programs, community development, community policing, and community consultation. This growing emphasis dynamically disengages the features of 'the social' that we outlined above in chapter 2. As Dean observes, "The social indicates a form of governmental territorialisation delimiting a nation and the conditions of its solidarity," and "community is a symptom of its 'detotalization.'" He stresses that the social is "displaced by the self-responsible subject tied to others by bonds of affinity" (2007: 89). Thus assembling community involves a trajectory of governing efforts, community experts, and self-responsible actors that are not tied to the disregarded domain of the social.

In the light of this rising focus, we analyse how some communities have become the aim of governmental efforts, expert authorities, particular kinds of knowledge, and demand for self-management and self-empowerment. Our analysis explores the political rationalities and discursive articulations of governmentality in relation to such areas as social and economic development, poverty and hunger, risk, and security.[7] This research examines critically the relationship between governmentality and community. Compelling perspectives are emerging on how advanced liberal forms of government work through the community, including the community of the poor, the community of the unemployed, the community of trade, and community policing.[8]

Especially since the mid-1960s and in attempts to address problems of government in Western liberal societies, community has become the locus for crime control, economic development, psychiatric services, punishment, and social welfare (Cruikshank 1999; O'Malley 2004) and given rise to new administrative policies and programs, ideas, organizational vocabularies, risks, and subjects. Some families, neighbourhoods, groups, and geographical zones have emerged as types of communities. Here, the notion of community seems an antidote to top–down technocratic approaches and, for the poor, a route to unlocking the power of development. Some researchers find the language of community superficial; Mosse, for example, sees it as a product of modernity, "trailing colonial histories of bureaucratically invented custom and tradition" (2005b: 5). From our perspective, however, its language and practices are increasingly developing connections to politics and to self-responsible actors and serve as a site of government.

The concept of community exists within a network of governing practices, ranging from professional bodies and expert forms of knowledge to political sites. Thus, to administer the community – however diverse this notion may be to specialists and commentators – it has become necessary to know, to plan, to assess, and to calculate community. This knowledge has been more than an exploratory issue and more than a question of the rhetorical structure of discourses on community and economic livelihoods.[9] For Rose, community has become a site through which political subjects surface as the state comes to rely on ways of shaping subjects whose lives it does not manage directly. It becomes a terrain for building trust, not only among citizens but also by private enterprises, national governments, and international organizations to encourage citizens to manage themselves. For example, a state's reliance on community as a new field of governing that produces responsible citizen-subjects goes hand in hand with a new political discourse about it and a new relation between it and governing that allows authorities and experts to govern through it. This field of governing has manifested itself amid a proliferation of communities claiming cultural and political autonomy. As Rose notes, communitarians must ask: "How can *virtue* be governed in a multi-cultural society in accordance with the liberal presuppositions of individual freedom and personal autonomy?" (1999: 183).

Community's link with government is most apparent when it becomes the object and target for the exercise of political power while remaining ostensibly external to politics (Rose 1999: 168). While the political attraction to it derives from its non- or pre-political status, any notion of it requires distinctions about it and ordering, mapping, or visualizing of its spaces. In this transformative process, invention of community allows a takeover of its responsibilities for governing certain types of risks and risky populations (O'Malley 2004: 175) and targeting of it as a site of transformation and control. Such a community, however, is not characterized by the traditional bonds of small-scale human associations, such as that of the village; rather, and according to Dean, it is more about the "the transitory, overlapping, multiple relations of affinity and identifications felt by self-responsible subjects" (1999: 192).

Writers, commentators, and experts have sought to understand individuals in 'communities' better in order to govern them more effectively. On the one hand, all kinds of concerns of community

– birthrates, crime, disorder, poverty, unemployment, unrest, and a great deal more – have become viewed as a problem in terms of the individual. There have been attempts to solve these problems by acting on the individual and the group. On the other hand, the organization of the community has become problematic in relation to a wider set of socio-political concerns, including access to global markets, citizenship responsibility, democracy, freedom, and peace. Responses have again focused on the individual and the group.

Concerns of community have been affiliated with the emergence of professional experts, such as those on poverty, and involving notions of empowerment.[10] In a *New York Times* bestseller, *The End of Poverty*, Jeffery Sachs (2005: 242) offers a common portrayal of and approach to ending poverty:

> The end of poverty must start in the villages of Souri and the slums of Mumbai, and millions of places like them. The key to ending poverty is to create a global network of connections that reach from impoverished communities to the very centers of world power and wealth and back again. Looking at the conditions in Sauri, we can see how far $70 per person can go in changing lives – not as a welfare handout, but as an investment in sustained economic growth. Looking at the conditions in Mumbai, we can see how a stable and safe physical environment for a community can enable its households to get a foothold in the urban economy, one that is already linked to global markets. For a sum similar to that in Sauri, it will be possible to establish that foothold.

He outlines how the poor should improve their own conditions:

> The starting points of that chain are the poor themselves. They are ready to act, both individually and collectively. They are already hard working, prepared to struggle to stay afloat and to get ahead. They have a very realistic idea about their conditions and how to improve them, not a mystical acceptance of their fate. They are also ready to govern themselves responsibly, ensuring that any help that they receive is used for the benefits of the group …
>
> In short, we need a strategy for scaling up the investments that will end poverty, including a system of governance that empowers the poor while holding them accountable. In each low-income

country, it is time to design a poverty reduction strategy that can meet this challenge.

These and other populist prescriptions, and their emphasis on empowering the poor and making them responsible actors, resound through numerous policy reports on poverty reduction from government departments, aid agencies, and international development organizations. The prevailing populist element is the prominence of an indistinct and nebulous notion of 'empowerment' as the key to abolishing poverty. Our work offers a critical assessment of this type of populist variant of advanced liberalism, as we see it in Sachs's words above.

Rather than studying empowerment at the level of traditional culture or solely in terms of a focus on the self, we look at how it works under advanced liberalism. To explain current forms of governing the poor, we consider how practices of empowerment act on human beings and their conduct in specific domains. To that end, we focus on the ways in which individuals who belong to 'communities,' such as the poor, receive encouragement to discover who they are, what they can do for their community and for its members, and how their self-improvement can be thought of as 'empowering.'

Practices of empowerment entail ways to shape and reshape human conduct. Not only do they attempt to reorganize various kinds of activities, but they involve technologies that aim to transform subjectivity and broaden powers of self-government. They exist, as Dean (2007: 83) suggests, within a specific set of relations of power between agents, such as the poor, technocrats, administrators, and politicians. For example, and, as we saw above, Cruikshank (1994, 1999) assesses critically the Community Action Programs (CAPs) of Lyndon Johnson's War on Poverty and the period's wider anti-poverty movement. She shows how a program of empowerment underlay the CAP, wherein the U.S. government encouraged the poor to participate by legislating local power relations – evoking the notion of community – between the poor and bureaucrats, juvenile delinquents, professional reformers, service providers, and social scientists. It sought to transform the poor into "self-sufficient, active, productive, and participatory citizens," so that they would participate as a unified community responding to a program of empowerment (Cruikshank 1994: 35). The poor would thereby become responsible citizens who need transformation into rational decision-makers. Cruikshank's critical-discourse analysis reveals how regimes of government extend far beyond their formal apparatuses and institutions. It also demonstrates, as Dean points out, that governing seeks to "define, connect and coordinate relations between state agencies, legislatures, communities, neighbourhoods, professionals, individuals, and so on" (1999: 71–2).

No matter how governmental schemes construct and reshape communities and their form of empowerment, they are not limited to programs and practices that advanced liberal agendas favour. They operate in private, international, and nongovernmental organizations and may encourage self-management and self-empowerment.[11] For example, the World Tourism Organization endorses the approach to poverty reduction of the UNs' Millennial Development Goals and claims that increasing tourism will further the 'war on poverty.' In this context, international development efforts play a role. Mark Duffield suggests that "faith in self-reliance is the obscured heart of development – habituated to the senses, never problematized in theory but instrumental in practice" (2007: 218). Many governing agencies operate under the agendas of advanced liberalism, and certain international aid organizations introduce and campaign for programs of empowerment that aim to remedy poverty in the world. As we see below, Oxfam International's governmental technologies (routine programs and policy initiatives) target particular communities as sites of social change, self-empowerment, and self-management.

OXFAM: FROM WARTIME FAMINE TO HUMANITARIAN AID

A brief history of Oxfam reveals the broad span of activities it has undertaken, ranging from wartime famine to humanitarian aid. Its creation was a response to famine in Europe during the Second World War, and it was one of over 200 local groups in Britain that formed alongside the original national Famine Relief Committee in the early 1940s. These bodies pressed the British government to allow for relief supplies, through naval blockade lines, to feed starving populations in Nazi-occupied countries such as Belgium, Greece, Norway, and Poland. While most of these committees disbanded in 1945, the Oxford Famine Relief Committee remained operating and became simply Oxfam (Oxfam GB 2002a, 2002b). In March 1943, it had received registration as a charity and launched its first public appeal for food aid. With the encouragement of public compassion, by May 1944 it began its Greek humanitarian effort. By this time, the Canadian government had sent two shiploads of wheat to that land, and Oxfam contributed a cargo of dried milk from South Africa for the Greek Red Cross to distribute to poor women and children. Duffield notes that this endeavour drew support from the vice-chancellor of Oxford University, the city's mayor, its Anglican bishop, and both of its MPs (2007: 38).

With the liberation of Europe in 1945, tremendous concern emerged about a region facing hunger, poverty, and numerous social and political insecurities. Humanitarian appeals from Belgium, France, Germany, and Holland led to formation of numerous international aid organizations, including Catholic Relief Services (CRS), Christian Aid, Cooperative for Assistance and Relief Everywhere (CARE), the International Rescue Committee, and World Vision (Duffield 2007: 38). After the armistice, Oxfam enlarged its objective to include "relief of suffering in consequence of war," and in 1949 it broadened its mission to encompass "relief of suffering arising as a result of wars or of other causes in any part of the world" (Oxfam GB 2002b). In 1948, it launched one of the world's first chains of charity shops, starting with an outlet in Oxford. This fundraising endeavour attracted donations ranging from false teeth and stuffed animals to a houseboat (Oxfam GB 2002b).

In its diverse flows of expansion, Oxfam made its first grant to Africa in 1953, while virtually the entire continent was still under colonial rule. Colonial development regimes in Africa and elsewhere conjured, as Goldman suggests, the role of the "*colonial state* to produce a *civilized subject* and productive laborer who would produce better goods, value, markets, and labor power for the metropole" (2005b: 13). Until the mid-1960s Oxfam worked mainly with colonial administrations, such as the British High Commission territories in southern Africa: Basutoland (now Lesotho), Bechuanaland (now Botswana), and Swaziland. Its work coincided with the UN's launch of the Freedom from Hunger Campaign in 1960 and its designation of the 1960s as World Development Decade. In 1960 not only did Oxfam's annual public funding reach £1 million, but its cash income for the first time exceeded in-kind donations, with most of the money going to Africa and Asia rather than Europe.

However, by 1970 Oxfam was worrying about its ability to sustain expansion and attract committed professionals. Over the years, these concerns gave rise to an emerging mandate vis-à-vis global poverty that focused on public identity, advocacy, and educational work. Duffield notes that in 1975 Oxfam's governing council confirmed its objectives as "relieving poverty and suffering" in any part of the world (2007: 43–63).

With food aid no longer the solution to poverty and suffering (see Duffield 2007), the organization today calls for "appropriate aid that empowers people" in crisis. Such assistance ranges from direct cash transfers and productive inputs to infrastructure and market support (Oxfam International 2008b). Over the past couple of decades, Oxfam has developed initiatives to combat the causes of famine, to enable people to become self-supporting, and to open international markets where poorer regions can sell crafts and produce at a fair price to benefit the producer.

Oxfam's programs revolve around development work to "lift communities out of poverty with long-term, sustainable solutions based on their needs"; humanitarian work that assists people in areas of conflict and natural disaster; and lobbying, advocacy, and popular campaigning to shape policy on the causes of conflict at local, national, and international levels (Oxfam International 2008a). Additionally, it works on issues ranging from debt and aid, education, fair trade, health, gender equality, HIV/AIDS, livelihoods, and trade justice to climate change, conflict, democracy and human rights, natural disasters, and security. Such initiatives and activities have transformed it into a broad-based international aid organization "dedicated to fighting poverty and related injustice around the world," the mission of which is "a just world without poverty and our goal is to enable people to exercise their rights and manage their own lives" (Oxfam International 2007a). Reflecting its continuing activities and growth, in 2004 its annual budget stood at about £120 million – seven times what it was two decades earlier (Duffield 2007: 48).

Oxfam International (formed in 1995) is today a confederation, consisting of thirteen affiliated Oxfams in Australia, Belgium, Britain, Canada, France, Germany, Hong Kong, Ireland, the Netherlands, New Zealand, Quebec, Spain, and the United States (Oxfam International 2007a). Each affiliate has the ability under the constitution and rules of Stichting Oxfam International (its full name) to determine its own programs (Oxfam International 2001a, 2001b). All Oxfam affiliates are in the developed world, or the North, and 20–50 per cent of funding for each must derive from local sources, with a "significant proportion" going overseas (Oxfam International 2001a).

Affiliates establish their own working relationships with partner organizations, both locally and overseas. For example, Oxfam Canada operates an anti-sweatshop labour campaign, No Sweat, with local partners among manufacturers and labour groups in Canada and partners abroad such as the Maquila Solidarity Network (Oxfam Canada 2007a). In total, the thirteen affiliates work with more than 3,000 local partner organizations (Oxfam International 2007a), and this loose structure embodies Oxfam's confederation, which works with local organizations through advanced liberal programs that aim to empower communities. "Oxfams strive to work through local partner organizations simultaneously seeking to strengthening [sic] these organizations. We believe that the empowerment of local organizations is a vital aspect of sustainable poverty alleviation and an important dimension of the achievement of civil and political rights" (Oxfam International 2002b).

The enormous number of members, staffers, and projects certainly generates organizational challenges. As one Oxfam Canada adviser explains:

> In principle Oxfam is a volunteer-based organization, operating
> in a membership-based organizational model; the volunteers are
> members of local Oxfam committees and they're supposed to
> have a big say in what Oxfam does. In reality, there's a wall be-
> tween the overseas programmes and what happens in Canada.
> And, a lot of the people who are Oxfam members in Canada are
> students and they're political activists and they're really interest-
> ed in social justice in the Canadian context; but they do not have
> much connection to what we do overseas. And this is, in func-
> tional terms, a real problem within Oxfam: you have a big piece
> of the organization that doesn't know what the other big piece of
> the organization does. (Interview, Ottawa, Canada, 2007)

These kinds of challenges form part of the polemical nature of Oxfam's community programs and governing practices.

In what follows, we show how Oxfam International's approach to alleviation of poverty in the South, or developing world, focuses on practices of government that aim to liberate groups from their struggles through advanced liberal programs of empowerment that focus on community. We maintain that its promotion of international trade – which it advocates to reduce poverty – results in an untenable dilemma. This explicit emphasis leads to a precarious relationship with the instruments of advanced liberalism, one that is complicitous, not challenging. In addition to our analysis of Oxfam's programs, we look at its ongoing Make Trade Fair campaign. Release of the *Rigged Rules and Double Standards* report – which met immediately with controversy – spurred this endeavour. The campaign's polemical nature and its implications serve as a basis for us to analyse Oxfam's governing practices and how its programmatic statements and policy documents reflect these. We suggest that its governing efforts attempt to demarcate and direct relations among certain individuals, organizations, communities, and regions; yet its self-management and empowerment initiatives, and its global trade campaigns, obscure its means of governing the poor. We conclude that grassroots networks consisting of groups of the poor and marginal can better voice their own needs and direct development.

'DEMANDING JUSTICE'

Because *we* recognize them, we give them that kind of empowerment.
          Interview with Oxfam staff member, Windhoek, Namibia, 2007

We approach our case study of Oxfam International's poverty-reduction initiatives from a governmentality perspective that considers how specific programs of social reform emerge and how a rationality of governance works within and through the organization. As we showed above, this perspective does not conceive government simply in terms of the formal apparatus of the state or state activities that laws or policies legitimate; rather it views government as also including programs and practices that direct and shape peoples' actions. This approach requires an analysis of a particular regime or practice of government – Dean's (1999; 2007) "analytics of government." It seeks to identify the emergence of such a regime and to study the multiple sources of its elements and the processes that assemble them and establish them as forms of organization and institutional practice. Furthermore, such a perspective examines how such a regime gives rise to and depends on particular forms of knowledge and how, as a result, programs of social reform commence (Dean 2007: 91).

Among a potential field of international aid and development organizations of similar size, we choose Oxfam International[12] because of the scope of its operations, its high profile, and its international poverty-reduction initiatives. Notably, its Strategic Plan, *Demanding Justice (2007–2012)* (2007d), outlines its collaborative work with its partners and with NGOs and governments. The document emphasizes the need "to address growing inequality and to empower people living in poverty, particularly women, as a prerequisite to achieving Oxfam's five rights-based aims." Oxfam has committed itself "to supporting women, men and children, living in poverty, to claim their rights to sustainable livelihoods, to basic social services, to life and security, to be heard, and to an identity" (Oxfam International 2007d).

With its aim "to find lasting solutions to poverty, suffering and injustice" (Oxfam International 2007b), it has become synonymous, particularly in the English-speaking North, with secular, transnational development aid. It is highly visible among international and nongovernmental organizations, and celebrities have joined its current Make Trade Fair campaign (2007e). Furthermore, Oxfam International, like CARE International and World Vision International, uses publicly available web-based documents to render its operations transparent. These web pages advance its public relations, informing the public about its programs, mission statements, financial needs, and accounts, all within an attractive, user-friendly visual environment that employs minimal text and extensive graphics.

An interview with an NGO staffer working in Namibia for more than a decade, and grappling with the region's pervasive and rising rates of hunger, HIV/AIDS, and malaria, reveals the complexities of Oxfam's public interface: "Oxfam is very poor at record keeping. When you try to find out about what Oxfam Canada is doing, you discover that the information just isn't there. And, yet, Oxfam is endlessly self-congratulatory about its website and saying, you know, 'everything anybody ever wanted to know is right there at their little … fingertips'" (interview, Windhoek, Namibia, 2007).

Despite its seemingly open, public set of discourses, there is room for critical assessment similar to those for other international aid groups (see, for example, Brauman 2004; Essex 2008; Hilhorst 2003). Indeed, as we demonstrate throughout this book, such bodies' increasing role under advanced liberalism warrants thorough examination (see also Duffield 2001a: 34), as do their practices of empowerment. Oxfam International, including its affiliates, constitutes a worthwhile case study because of its practices that direct the conduct of groups and populations and that, more specifically, engage in empowerment. Its nebulous use of trade goals that focus on human values, justice, and community is in fact advanced liberal in character.

COMMUNITY-TARGETED EMPOWERMENT

Oxfam inculcates particular ways of thinking about problems such as poverty and forms of intervention that depend on its use of governmental technologies. These technologies range from the complexity of routine programs, calculations, and apparatuses to plans to empower communities, through which it seeks to embody and give effect to "governmental ambitions" (Rose and Miller 1992).[13] One instance is its planning of and commitment to advanced liberal programs, which, Dean reminds us, emerge alongside the many new languages of community and new vocabularies of administration, from community care to community consultation (2007: 89). Its overwhelming emphasis on community-targeted empowerment involves enhancing the well-being of select individuals and groups as a task of government. This form of intervention by Oxfam approaches communities as zones for it to investigate, document, interpret, and ultimately transform, while making its members aware of their allegiance to the community through the work of anti-poverty campaigns, educators, and narratives.

In such a process of social reform, the underlying assumption is that once intervention heightens awareness of the community – through, for example, anti-poverty campaigns – and restores it for particular purposes and ends, the community can then govern itself. Oxfam International's mobile-education program in Darfur, western Sudan, provides a good example. In Darfur, Oxfam supported eleven mobile schools by supplying school materials and sheep to supplement teachers' salaries (Aikman 2003). Oxfam acknowledges that a vital part of this work in Darfur is its intervention in the community in order to foster greater self-management and self-empowerment: "Direct support to schools is complemented by capacity-building at the community level" (Aikman 2003: n.p.). Aikman claims that "the strength of the program is that schools are embedded in a community management structure, which means that parents and communities are actively searching for ways to solve the shortcomings of the mobile school model and to address the government's lack of interest" (2003: n.p.). It is through this program that the people of Darfur are made responsible for their own management. Like government more generally, self-management can, as Cruikshank contends, "swing between the poles of tyranny and absolute liberty. One can govern one's own or others' lives well or badly" (1999: 2).

The humanitarian crisis in Darfur has worsened over the past five years, and the mobile education programs have closed,[14] and Oxfam increasingly works on emergency aid and health and sanitation for the many settlements of internally displaced persons (IDPs) (Oxfam International 2007c). More than 2.5 million people have had to leave their homes and live in immense, crowded camps in both Darfur and neighbouring Chad[15] (Oxfam Canada 2008). According to Khadeja Mohamed Ibrahim, who lives with her family in one of the camps: "Life is very different; it's not like the life we were used to before." She adds: "There are no job opportunities, no income. There is not enough food. I hope peace will come soon so we can go back to the villages. I hope we can return to our lives soon" (Oxfam Canada 2007b: 14). However, and as Agamben (1998) would caution, the architecture of these and other such camps fosters the zone of exception where anything becomes possible and the politics of place and space emerges. This zone reminds us of how international aid organizations such as Oxfam International can enter the spaces and politics of poverty.

Oxfam's ability to co-ordinate and shape empowering projects concerning poverty and the poor is a focus of critical work on this organization. Akin to the way numerous transnational knowledge networks and communities have emerged, including "regional nodes in global networks" (Amin and Thrift 1992), "transnational innovation networks" (Coe and Bunnell 2003), and participatory development networks (Ilcan and Phillips 2008), Oxfam emphasizes regional networking communities to help empower communities. A prime example of this governmentalization of Oxfam's relations with the poor comes via its well-recognized Women's Linking Project. Oxfam brought together this vast group of women, soliciting and consolidating them from among NGOs in the South, where no such previous ties existed (Oxfam's Gender Team 1994). Oxfam intends the project to "create solidarity, and set up information-sharing exchanges and informal networks for Southern NGOs, Oxfam staff, and like-minded NGOs, in order for them to learn cross-regionally, and break through the isolation that many feel"

(Oxfam's Gender Team 1994: 29; see also Oxfam Australia and New Zealand 2006).

The Oxfam Gender Team identifies community empowerment in its post-project analysis of the early 1990s, even though the project sought rather to expand public *perception* of women's empowerment: "The rationale behind the visit [of eight women from the South to Britain and Ireland in March 1992] was ... to increase people's awareness of the women's existing and potential roles as agents for change" (Oxfam's Gender Team 1994: 29). Here, the language is that of agency, which Oxfam bestows on them. Women from the South who participated in Oxfam's Women's Linking Project conference in Bangkok, Thailand, 20–23 February 1994, called for Oxfam itself to be more aware of women's ability to empower themselves by choosing for themselves the development networks in which they wanted to co-operate. Further, they argued that women could empower themselves only if global aid organizations such as Oxfam International chose to work with partner organizations in the South that have this as an explicit goal. They also demanded "that Oxfam should cease funding gender-blind organizations" (Oxfam's Gender Team 1994: 31; see also "Gender Justice" in Oxfam 2007g).

In the decade since the project and analysis, gender mainstreaming – which involves strategies for making the concerns and experiences of women and men an integral part of the design and evaluation of policies and programs in all political, economic, and societal spheres – has continued to inform Oxfam's activities in its 100 countries. In fact, the practice, which aims to achieve gender justice, is an organizational mandate to which all affiliate members subscribe and which the Strategic Plan for 2007–12 cites as one of four key goals, along with economic justice, essential services, and rights in crisis (Oxfam International 2007d). Yet criticism continues of Oxfam's attempts to empower poor women without working towards gender equality within the organization itself. One anonymous Oxfam worker stridently echoes the earlier participants: "Could we realistically expect to achieve at the programme-level what we could not achieve in our own workplace?" (quoted in Mehra and Gupta 2006: 6).

Oxfam International, as we demonstrate, continues to mediate relations of power and resistance and acts as the radical organizer, exhibiting 'the will to empower.' Empowerment in this context leads to promotion of the idea of self-management, with the radical organizer acting as a conduit and relaying the concept that the people themselves, in this case the community of women from the South, can make change; yet Oxfam continues to construct the circumstances and conditions of that change. In this way, the subjects of community empowerment seemingly take over the organizer's function, and expert reformers such as Oxfam – which cast off their role as organizers – therefore participate in the "nongovernmental means of government" (Cruikshank 1994: 50–1; see also Ferguson 2006).

Oxfam members' programmatic rationality of community-targeted empowerment views the world as consisting of powerful people and powerless people. It emphasizes a bottom–up approach that stresses advanced liberal participation and self-management. In the illustration above, for example, women from the South are said to be able to empower themselves by meeting and organizing for change. However, this form of empowerment ignores Oxfam's mediating role, which women participants themselves recognize and demand that it not use to control, influence, or divide their autonomy (Ranjo-Libang 1994: 44). The organization plays an enabling role, bringing together this group, facilitating temporary working communities, and therefore deploying the notion of community-targeted empowerment as a technology of governance.

Dean argues that programs of empowerment are clear examples of "liberal rationalities of government that endeavour to operationalize the self-governing capacities of the governed in pursuit of governmental objectives" (1999: 67). Even Oxfam itself recognizes that the twin goals of participation and empowerment are difficult to achieve and often remain rhetorical devices to govern the most disadvantaged people. More than a decade ago, Eade and Williams made this clear in *The Oxfam Handbook of Relief and Development*: "Empowerment is demonstrated by the quality of people's participation in the decisions and processes affecting their lives. In theory, empowerment and participation should be different sides of the same coin. In practice, much of what passes for popular participation in development and relief work is not in any way empowering to the poorest and most disadvantaged people in society" (Eade and Williams 1995: 14). While "the poorest and most disadvantaged" can perhaps achieve power through working with Oxfam on community projects, this form of empowerment occurs in a political context and is a relationship that experts of the poor establish and foster. Marginal groups, such as the poor, cannot therefore easily empower themselves while working under the advanced liberal organization's guidance and management.

The account of a researcher with an NGO in Namibia demonstrates how capricious the process of empowerment can be. She highlights the changeability in the direction of funding for NGOs and hence the target of empowerment programs. Here the language of empowerment serves to emphasize the partnership between communities, NGOs, Oxfam Canada as a funding agency, and the market: "Basically, the key is to address poverty and ... the people who are involved day to day, especially in rural areas, ... are the poorest of the poor. They don't have other sources of income generally ... There is less food security because they have livestock but no crops; so it becomes a little bit more challenging. So [what is needed] is capacity building, empowerment, training, but through ... commercializing [local products] as a way of trying to address poverty basically. And, basically, our role is a facilitative one between primary producers and commercial entities. And we try [to] link these two entities together in a partnership" (interview, Windhoek, 2007). Here partnership is a conduit to empowerment. And increasingly Oxfam's thirteen affiliates fund other NGOs operating locally to implement empowerment programs.

An example from the South Pacific highlights the many ways of employing ideas of empowerment. This example, unlike that above, does not feature market solutions to poverty; partnerships, however, are common. Oxfam Australia funds the Social Empowerment and Education Program (SEEP) in Fiji, which the Ecumenical Centre for Research, Education and Advocacy runs and the Australian federal government's development-aid agency, AusAid, supports. This program seeks to create spaces for exchange of ideas for local villagers in the wake of a 2000 coup in Fiji, in order to resolve issues of land ownership and governance that perhaps led to the coup. Oxfam Australia thus facilitates partnerships between local organizations and international funding bodies, but also sets up spaces of communication and participation for local people to direct their own development. This participatory program has attracted interest from government personnel in neighbouring Solomon Islands (see McErvale and Maclellan 2007) and shows the value of unearthing diverse genealogical relationships, even among Oxfam partnerships.

Empowerment ought ideally to enable people in diverse territories to be "active agents in, rather than passive recipients of, development strategies" (Oxaal 1997: 24). However, the emergence of an agency to do so would require a radical move away from the current practice of community-targeted empowerment, which serves as a measure of certain individuals' subjection. It would require recognition that poverty is a product of power relations and not a condition that advanced liberal empowerment initiatives or the global capitalist market can cure. For example, programs to ameliorate poverty and governmental interventions vis-à-vis the poor often reproduce political and international power dynamics that define relations of authority[16] and give only prescribed individuals and groups access to particular types of knowledge and information.

Agencies of empowerment may well call for progressive grassroots networks advocating social change and social justice. Local, national, regional, and global groups, co-operatives, and alliances may thereby challenge the inequitable programs and practices of advanced liberalism and the geographical mobility of global capital. This "movement of movements" (Mertes 2004) – heterogeneous, rather than singular and cohesive – global networks for social justice have called for sweeping changes to the primacy of global capital. These diverse calls have links through Fraser's "three major families of justice claims: claims for socioeconomic redistribution, claims for legal or cultural recognition, and claims for political representation" (2008: 396). Demands for social justice from diverse local and transnational networks have increased in the last decade in the face of strident, complex, yet interlinked challenges, as Brodie writes:

> Echoing [Karl] Polanyi's indictment of laissez-faire, Ronald Wright observes that 'the idea that the world must be run by the stock market is as mad as any other fundamentalist delusion' (2006, p. 22). It is a fundamentalism that has not displaced the residuals of over two centuries of struggles for citizenship equality and social justice. It is also a fundamentalism that is unable to comprehend and actively fuels the emergent crises of the early 21st century, among them, global warming, rampant insecurity, the polarization of the North and South, and pervasive antagonism to neoliberalism's imperial designs. And it is a fundamentalism which, having failed to deliver on its core promises of wealth, wellbeing, and freedom, increasingly governs as if we live in a 'state of exception' (Agamben, 2005) ... In the face of all of this, the necessary task of reforming social justice may very well

hinge upon our collective insistence on putting the social back into our way of seeing and contesting neoliberal times. (Brodie 2007: 105)

Social-justice networks may help initiate and support actions that strengthen the ability of marginal groups and citizens to challenge injustices, to influence the social, economic, and political processes that govern their lives, and to create new kinds of insurgent participation and new kinds of rights.[17] The building of these networks, however, is not easy, and these networks may not necessarily or directly improve the lives of the poor. International and transnational social-justice networks today seem unable to oppose unjust relations and to counter capital in its global dimensions. While these networks often lack the resources, planning schemes, and vigour of capital to globalize through the capture of trade and markets (Appadurai 2001b: 18), they may indeed help the poor. Nevertheless the dilemmas facing marginal groups such as the poor are not technological or managerial matters that they can leave to poverty experts and international organizations, including NGOs that espouse advanced liberal solutions to poverty or for 'making trade fair.'

MAKING TRADE FAIR?

One of Oxfam International's empowerment initiatives is its promotion of sweeping changes to international trade and to the practices of communities in the South. It views trade as an instrument of poverty alleviation for developing communities (see Oxfam International 2005j, 2007f). In what follows, we address its advanced liberal practices in terms of its view of trade as a broad social reform and method of development. We build on existing responses to its report on trade policy – *Rigged Rules and Double Standards* (2002d) – and analyse the ramifications of this document for its relationship with its community partners.

The 272-page report proposes management of international trade in a way that will allow it to act as an instrument of poverty alleviation and ultimately of social reform through economic growth. It concedes that trade itself may not reduce poverty – an assumption in keeping with the document's positivist stance that international trading under advanced liberalism is a given that people must accommodate and manage. However, trade under wise management can, it is assumed, help to lift millions of people out of poverty, creating new opportunities for broad economic growth (2002d: 27).

We focus here on the notion of managing trade. For Oxfam International (2002d), international trade operates under faulty rules, which need change. *Rigged Rules and Double Standards* sets out eight policy goals: improve market access for developing (or poor) countries and end agricultural subsidies and dumping practices of trade blocs such as the European Union and the United States; end detrimental market liberalization as a condition of IMF–World Bank programs in developing countries; create a new international commodities institution; establish new laws on intellectual property; prohibit conditions that require governments to liberalize or privatize basic services; enhance private-sector investment and employment standards; give developing countries a stronger voice in a democratized World Trade Organization (WTO); and change national health, education, and governance policies "so that poor people can develop their capabilities, realise their potential, and participate in markets on more equitable terms" (Oxfam International 2002d: 6).

The list of reforms does not make clear who or what will initiate and instigate these directives. Moreover, these policy goals understate the influential role of the Bretton Woods institutions – the IMF, the World Bank, and the WTO – in the new global-aid regime. The new regime operates within and beyond nation states. It is one of many global flows, comprising waves of aid organizations, information, knowledge, networks, objects, people, and risks that move across regions in varied, uneven, and unpredictable forms (see Urry 2007). Not only does it frame development goals in terms of creating conditions for successful participation in global activities and markets (Mosse 2005b: 4–5), but it also supports self-responsibility efforts to serve the interests of government. In this process, it sanctions various governing practices to influence international and nongovernmental organizations, such as Oxfam International, to engage in policy dialogues.

Similar to the administration of the U.S. War on Poverty in the 1960s, Oxfam International attempts to manage poverty and the poor by assuming that the "powerlessness of the poor" is the cause of their poverty rather than interrogating the actions of the powerful and the complex dimensions that produce poverty and famine (see Chandler 2001; Edkins 2000). It argues that trade reform is a possible remedy to poverty (Oxfam International 2002d: 7). This initial approach, however, quickly gives way to more theories about the global-trade regime and empowering the "economically excluded" through it (2002d).

Rigged Rules and Double Standards proposes making trade work for the poor by managing it properly. Even many of the aims above may seem radical, but they actually mix Oxfam International's public desire for radical change with a push for reform within the existing economic and trade relations and arrangements. The detailed discussion in the report reinforces the latter position. For example, the publicity slogan "Make Trade Fair," which appears on popstars and activists' T-shirts alike at WTO, G8, and G20 summits, has strong reformist connotations and may be a call not to overhaul economic and trade relations but rather to make them work better for developing countries. Even as an interim measure, it does not, for example, call for South–South trade, economic, or political blocs, which a number of economists and activists in the South espouse as a means of subverting Northern dominance and dictation of trade terms (see, for example, Bond 2006b). Instead, the reformist, liberal approach is in line with Oxfam International's more general and long-standing trade and market policy.

The *Oxfam International Strategic Plan for 2007–2012* (2007d), available to the public via Oxfam's website and in print, seeks progress towards broad, open outcomes such as reform of global trade: "Together with partners and allies Oxfam will ... achieve fairer trade rules for poor countries. People living in poverty must get a fair share of the wealth and opportunities generated by world trade" (Oxfam International 2007d: 6). The emphasis on empowerment of "economically excluded people" relates to the market and to the international-trade paradigm premised on advanced liberal agendas. For example, in October 2006 Oxfam initiated an international campaign to encourage Starbucks – the world's largest chain of coffee shops – and other coffee roasters to engage directly with Ethiopia on initiatives of trademarking. In 2007, Ethiopia continued to challenge the unfairness of the international coffee market by seeking to trademark the names of its high-value specialty coffee beans.

Oxfam wanted the Ethiopians to use trademarks – part of the modern arrangement for intellectual property – to benefit and empower poor farmers (Oxfam International 2007h). On 21 June 2007, Starbucks honoured its commitment to Ethiopian coffee farmers by becoming one of the first members of the industry to join the trademark initiative. Raymond C. Offenheiser, president of Oxfam America, praises the campaign:

> Congratulations to our Ethiopian coffee farming partners and to Starbucks on an agreement that recognizes Ethiopians' right to control the use of their specialty coffee brands. This agreement represents a business approach in step with 21st-century standards in its concern for rights rather than charity and for greater equity in supply chains rather than short term profits ...
> Harnessing market forces and allowing poor countries to benefit from intellectual property rights are keys to creating fairer and more equitable trade. In a modern economy, companies must bring their business models in line with the demands of good corporate citizenship, which goes beyond traditional philanthropic approaches to dealing with poverty. (2007c: n.p.)

In this case, Oxfam supported development of market-based strategies to gain more benefits from trade. Such an initiative is advanced liberal in character, attempting to make vulnerable or excluded groups increasingly responsible for their actions through self-management initiatives (see, for example, Larner and Walters 2000; Mosse 2005a).

Oxfam International's current fund-raising practice provides a further example, albeit seemingly benign, of its entanglement in the existing international trade paradigm. Many people, particularly in Britain and Australia, identify Oxfam with the Oxfam charity stores (see Figure 3.1). These stores sell either donated used goods or, in Australia, for example, goods made by Oxfam International's target communities. This part of Oxfam's fund-raising mimics the trade policies that the organization advocates at the macro level. The shops serve as a highly visible sign of twin foci: attracting funds and support from Northern publics *and* providing a sales venue for vulnerable groups in select Southern communities whom its programs seem to have empowered.

In September 2007, Oxfam launched Britain's first online charity shop – www.oxfam.org.uk/shop – with which it hoped to raise some £2 million a year to help fund its 'fight against poverty.' Oxfam aimed to have, at the time of its launch, over 120,000 items on sale, including more than 100 types of new fair-trade goods, ranging from jewellery to chocolate and coffee. Volunteers select and upload new

Figure 3.1 Oxfam fair trade. Authors' photo.

donated items each day onto the site, which promotes such lines as "Ethical Collections," "Fair Trade Fashions," and "Oxfam Unwrapped Wedding and Engagement Wish Lists." Tricia O'Rourke, a spokesperson, said that the online store would operate alongside existing Oxfam outlets and not mark the end of bricks-and-mortar charity shops. "It's complementary to them," she said. "The items that come into individual shops will continue selling as before – this is an additional market for them. We see this with other retail business – the move online has actually meant more business overall" (Third Sector 2007).

In line with having more business, the organization hopes to tap into the growing trend for British consumers to shop online, with that activity making up at least 17 per cent of the country's overall retail market. Oxfam director Barbara Stocking comments: "At a time when how we buy is at the forefront of people's minds, Oxfam's online shop gives people a real way to buy more ethically." She added: "This is the one website where customers will know that all their purchases will directly support Oxfam working with people in poverty across the world."[18]

On the Oxfam GB web-based shopping site, one can find a local store at which to donate goods or buy used donated goods or link up to Fair Trade online in an effort to further development of fair trading relationships (Oxfam GB 2007b). Oxfam shops differ in their activities, with some operating as shops and others as retail outlets for handcrafts from the South. These retail practices echo the broader policy of trade reform – the stores mimic standard liberal processes of capital exchange, while also attempting to create a forum for a more equitable exchange for goods from developing countries. The organization's platform on trade reform similarly advocates operation within the existing trade paradigm while attempting to improve the situation of peoples in developing communities. This is a position unpopular with many social-justice activists, who also call for fair and ethical trade[19] but oppose the existing trade paradigm and the governing rationalities, politics, and institutions that uphold it (see, for example, Lacey 2005b).

In what Oxfam Great Britain (GB) terms a "market access parable," Bangladeshi woman Barna Ahmad tells of her work for Oxfam GB and the Irish relief and development agency Concern that involves marketing a local producer association's incense to lucrative Northern markets, such as the Body Shop chain. The association represents a community of over 150 poor migrant women (Oxfam GB 2007a). In its advertising of the relationship between Fair Trade and poverty alleviation, Oxfam presents empowerment of the poor as achievable through the liberal trade market. Similar programs organize producers into networks to facilitate "development of cooperatives; ... entry into markets, including Fairtrade and organic markets; and advocacy and campaigning skills to strengthen their voice" (Oxfam GB 2005).

It is the strength of the producers' skills that emerges repeatedly in interviews and program documents with Oxfam staffers and affiliates

as synonymous with empowerment. For example, a program director in Namibia identifies empowerment of the poor as involving recognition: "Because we recognize them, we give them that kind of
empowerment." As with other like attempts, governmental authorities promote empowerment to produce rational economic and
entrepreneurial participants and to effect the actions of others in the
future. In the words of Oxfam GB: "But while changing trade patterns and ways of trading can be a cause of poverty, they also offer
a possible solution. Through trading, campaigning and working
with producers, Oxfam aims to enable poor producers to take part
in trade and overcome the significant hurdles they face" (2007c).
While good intentions may underlie the will to empower or, as we
see above, work "to enable," it is a strategy for constituting and governing a wide range of the subjectivities of the recipients.

REACTIONS TO *RIGGED RULES* AND *DOUBLE STANDARDS*

Immediately after Oxfam International (2002d) launched its report
on trade, globalization, and poverty – *Rigged Rules and Double
Standards* – two prominent academics who study development released individual critiques. Bello (2002b) and Shiva (2002) point out
factors that jeopardize Oxfam's claim to represent the needs of poor
people in developing communities. Shiva describes its report as a
"schizophrenic analysis," attempting to reconcile two incompatible
paradigms: "one which gives precedence to people's democracy, another which gives precedence to trade, commerce, markets" (Shiva
2002: 10).

The first paradigm is prominent throughout the document, particularly in its rhetoric. The report uses a colourful analogy to describe the inequity of international trade: "Rising tides are supposed
to lift all boats. Over the past decades, international trade has created a rising tide of wealth, but some boats have risen more rapidly
than others, and some are sinking fast. It shows how unequal trade
is limiting the rate of poverty reduction, reinforcing global inequalities, and marginalizing poor countries and poor people" (Oxfam
International 2002d: 64). In contrast, chapter 4 emphasizes the
growth of export markets in developing countries. Shiva finds the
confusion of Oxfam's stance most apparent here, as its stress on
market access is simply a linguistic disguise of the World Bank's

traditional policies of export first, trade liberalization, and economic reforms. This focus "hides and renders invisible the economic, social and ecological costs generated by export obsessed and export dominated policies of agriculture in poor Third World countries" (Shiva 2002: 10).[20] It also ignores how trade liberalization can facilitate competitive pressures on global markets by IMF and World Bank initiatives and by partnership arrangements that private- and public-sector organizations set up with international trade and financial organizations.

Bello's critique appeared in *Focus on Trade*, a publication by Focus on the Global South. Like Shiva, Bello concentrates his critique on two issues: Oxfam's promotion of WTO-style market access (see also Oxfam International 2003d) and the incongruity of this stance with its own broad goal of poverty alleviation that centres on people (Bello 2002b). The report's concentration on reforming trade by increasing developing countries' access to markets leads Bello to argue that Oxfam has "emerged as a civil society advocate for the Cairns Group position (a position that involves a group of agricultural exporting nations, formed in 1986 in Cairns, Australia, just before the beginning of the Uruguay Round, to lobby for agricultural trade liberalization)" (2002b: n.p.). However, Bello tempers this claim, refuting the *Washington Post*'s assertion that Oxfam has joined the free-market camp. He attacks Oxfam's advocacy of market access while recognizing its role in the "movement against corporate-driven globalization" (2002a: n.p.).

The strident public criticisms of Oxfam International's market-access campaign prompted it to respond publicly. It challenged each of Bello's charges systematically, for example, claiming that he exaggerates its support for market access to ease poverty (Oxfam International 2002c). Yet the report clearly emphasizes market-access solutions, even though it often presents them in an ambiguous and somewhat contradictory light. General statements in effect nullify each other: "Participation in world trade has figured prominently in many of the most successful cases of poverty reduction – and, compared with aid, it has far more potential to benefit the poor. If developing countries increased their share of world exports by just five per cent, this would generate $350bn – seven times as much as they receive in aid. The $70bn that Africa would generate through a one per cent increase in its share of world exports is approximately five times the amount provided to the region through aid and debt relief" (2002d: 8). In addition, the report asks: "What impact would an increased share in world export markets have on poverty levels in developing countries? There is no simple answer to this question. The gains to be derived from exports are dynamic, and cannot readily be captured in static snapshots" (49). These statements reveal Oxfam's stance as indecisive, and the report is replete with "obfuscation rather than clarification" (Bello 2002a: 13).

For Food First co-director Anuradha Mittal and *Z-Magazine* contributor Patrick Bond, the report is only somewhat clear (see Mittal in Bond 2002). While neither explaining clearly how developing countries can increase their access to markets nor providing a clear statement of the effects of such a change, the report undermines social-justice activists' criticism of economic growth policies that focus on exports. Oxfam's policy strategy, which Bond calls "insiderist" (2002: n.p.), can be viewed as a response to what Dean describes as the reduplication or reflexivity of neoliberalism that occurs when the market becomes a global entity that challenges national governments (1999: 161). Oxfam responds to the weaknesses of the global-trade regime by employing its language and remedies. Export-led growth is simultaneously problematic and a solution. The outcome of further stress on market access will depend on how national governments respond to existing economic and trade relations while also awaiting change from international trade organizations. Oxfam International thus participates in a broad, ongoing process of advanced liberal reform that validates and enforces itself.

Under advanced liberal agendas, Oxfam International is circumscribing and co-ordinating relations among diverse individuals, communities, neighbourhoods, regions, and other organizations. Through its key campaigns for reform and trade that detail rules for making trade work at local, national, and international levels, Oxfam governs poverty relations and the conduct of the poor. Notions of community-targeted empowerment interweave themselves in the organization's practices of government. Its programmatic campaigns operate through advanced liberal rationalities that emphasize the need for particular groups, such as the poor, to improve themselves and to take responsibility for their own life conditions. Like other international aid organizations, Oxfam has high hopes for empowerment to transform trade and reduce global poverty without adequately recognizing the critical problems inherent in export-led growth and market access as solutions to poverty.

CONCLUSION

In the name of empowerment, advanced liberal programs concerning the poor, the homeless, and the unemployed continue to receive support from NGOs, Western liberal states, and international development and aid organizations. Several organizations at the global level embark on governmental initiatives to assemble territories in the name of community and as sites of empowerment.

Through our case study of Oxfam International, this chapter has revealed that advanced liberal programs of empowerment target marginal populations on the assumption that they lack the skills of self-management to steer themselves as active members of communities. In the light of Cruikshank's analysis of the will to empower and Dean's critical work on the practices of government, we argue that such initiatives ultimately turn empowerment and participation into an object of governmentalization and intervention. A case in point is the increasing emphasis that Oxfam places on individuals and their immediate communities of allegiance as sites of social reform. In this way, it becomes an agent of government among a multiplicity of agents possessing governmental authority in fields ranging from social reform to promotion of trade.

Oxfam International's promotion of trade and the expansion of market relations bring into question its relationship with such bodies as the IMF and the World Trade Organization, which other aid agencies excoriate for not living up to their promised goal of reducing poverty on a global scale. The organization's trade campaigns, and the self-management and empowerment initiatives it advances as solutions to poverty, have obscured its means of government. Some researchers might well claim that it is difficult for Oxfam and similar international aid organizations to do things differently for the poor, as they routinely establish partnerships with international financial organizations, such as the World Bank. These organizations support advanced liberal solutions to poverty.

However, it is precisely for these and other reasons that international aid organizations advocating solutions to global poverty should convey a clear message and policy directive with grounding in solid research and support from grassroots groups. These policy directives need to bring about a more socially just environment while upholding aid recipients' rights and to promote knowledge that can shape new forces as well as new futures. Although knowledge is highly mobile and can bring about demands for social justice, Tsing cautions that universal forms of knowledge can motivate "*both* imperial schemes to control the world and liberatory mobilizations for justice and empowerment" (2005: 9). On the issue of liberatory mobilization, such as that involving advocacy networks, there are other cautions.

Appadurai (2001b) asserts that international and transnational advocacy networks are unable to counter capital precisely in its global dimensions. These networks often lack the resources and the planning ability to transform understanding and treatment of the poor and how development experts, policy-makers, and governing bodies deal with poverty. Nevertheless, participation in grassroots networks can make a difference, no matter how small, to the lives of the poor in ways that benefit the poor. Advanced liberal solutions cannot ease poverty; but ongoing dialogue on and commitment to social transformation by the poor themselves and by participants in local, national, regional, and global networks can do exactly that. These are participants who are willing to bring the organizations of power to task for not fulfilling their promises or not developing thoughtful and robust ways to reduce poverty; challenge social hierarchies in culturally and politically perceptive ways; and provide other progressive and social-justice solidarity groups with ideas and allies for political strategizing.

While political strategies and tactics may often face challenges within and beyond progressive networks, these alternative networks may nevertheless disrupt the prevailing mechanisms and technologies for governing bodies, populations, and poverty issues; they may also advocate and practise a social-justice life-politics that involves, but moves beyond, the poor themselves to promote multiple levels of analysis, dialogue, and political intervention. It is fitting to return to the idea of empowerment at the close of this chapter. Self-empowerment is a concept that can serve as a tool of responsiblization and of government, whereby, for example, communities in the South, because of their participation in Oxfam's advanced liberal projects and practices of empowerment, seek to manage their poverty themselves. Community empowerment can, however, be an emancipatory concept and practice. Iris Marion Young, in her early work on participatory democracy and justice, asserts that group empowerment is essential to achieving social justice for self-organized marginal groups (1990: 184), in this case poor communities in the South. In the light of our analysis of Oxfam International's programs of empowering the poor and its global reform and trade campaigns, we see a stronger need to create spaces to establish progressive, grassroots networks that aim to deal with powerful organizations and institutions that govern marginal populations such as the poor.

In order to create viable political initiatives and debate, these grass-roots networks would involve the active participation of marginal groups to deal with poverty as an issue of social justice on multiple levels. These progressive aid and anti-poverty networks would need to consist of and engage a range of participants – including poor people, alternative co-operative and community groups, urban, regional, and national coalitions, and members of international and nongovernmental organizations – and generate forums, among themselves, to voice their concerns for social change. Such issues may range from wages and health and living conditions to the dislocation that often marks the lives of the poor. The poor would discuss these matters on their own terms and in their own language, rather than in that of individualization and trade liberalization that organizations may have imposed on them. Grassroots networks may call for forums for negotiating long-term remedies to poverty with national and regional governments; they may also ask for culturally particular forms of social reform, empowerment, and self-determination that neither depend on global capital markets nor make the marginal responsible for their impoverishment. While such alternative networks prevail and may invoke the kinds of social justice that can alter the everyday lives of the poor in various parts of the globe, they are not easy or rigid solutions to the global governance of poverty.

The complex arrangement of relationships between aid agents and authorities of poverty reform is the focus of the next chapter. Authorities of development aid aim to shape the poor as a social and political grouping in a variety of contexts, and in the next chapter we reveal convergence in the increasing role of aid in developing economies. We suggest that the proliferation of practices of global aid in post-apartheid Namibia reflects the role of advanced liberal governance in current efforts of poverty reduction and its ties to development initiatives. Our analysis points to the continuing and often-reconfigured place of national territory within contemporary forms of power and rule. Yet, and as we argue, that theme is also part of a language of regions and communities that exist above and below conventional notions of the nation state and of practices that govern the poor from afar.

4 Global Aid in Post-Apartheid Namibia

In Namibia, inequalities, social inequalities, economic justice, social economic justice ... are, for me, some issues that are within the current
Millennium Development Goals that can still be highlighted; but by no
means should the MDGS be seen as a complete package. There are other
issues for Namibia that need attention.

> Interview with member of nongovernmental organization, Windhoek,
> Namibia, 2008

Attention must be paid to the formidable institutions that are 'governing'
Africa from afar: the transnational financial institutions (World Bank,
IMF, foreign banks) and development agencies (USAID, UNDP, UNHCR,
etc.), as well as the churches, missions, and so-called nongovernmental
organizations.

> James Ferguson, *Global Shadows: Africa in the Neoliberal World Order*
> (2006: 87)

INTRODUCTION

Despite a large volume of research on international development
and NGOs, and the increasing role of network relations in international development efforts,[1] we know little about the ability of
such groups to shape issues relating to the poor and to work on
poverty with other businesses, organizations, and national governments. We need to figure out how those partners connect to the new
regime of global aid. As we saw above, advanced liberal agendas
frame development goals to align with an emergent and contingent
global market, support self-responsibility in the interests of governance, and encourage nongovernmental and international organizations to engage in policy dialogue, consultation, and participation

on reducing poverty and helping the poor. As such, these agendas are transforming the character of development and various government-al plans and initiatives.

Rather than analysing government only in terms of state activities that laws or policies legitimate, we understand government more broadly. In this chapter, we demonstrate how it increasingly involves a collection of agents and organizations within and beyond the state apparatus. One form of government, advanced liberalism, consists of initiatives whereby various authorities act on particular populations to ensure effective governance. Poverty-reduction initiatives, for ex-ample, often assume decentralization and a locus in community that shift responsibility for some economic problems onto local actors. These actors participate in global markets (for example, Porter and Craig 2004: 415; Rojas 2004), in hybrid zones of government and citizenship (for example, Brodie 2008; Ilcan and Basok 2006; Isin 2008; Latour 1993; S. Phillips 2006), and in new entrepreneurial ar-rangements. Such forms of governance are emerging within Western liberal states (see, for example, Blaser, Feit, and McRae 2004; Carroll 2003: 43), in international organizations such as Oxfam International, the UN, USAID, and the World Bank, and in a range of developing countries such as Namibia[2] and Solomon Islands.

In comparison to recent analyses of international aid organiza-tions,[3] we focus on post-apartheid Namibia – a site of increasing development aid that has links to the new global-aid regime. This regime is altering the character of development and its political rela-tions in the country. The case study attempts a unique scholarly con-tribution to the overlapping areas of research on advanced liberal governance and international development aid to challenge poverty. In this regard, this chapter examines how and through what means the private sector, NGOs, the national government, and international organizations aid development in Namibia. We hope to demonstrate their consistent ways of thinking about aid or its rationality; we also seek to show their ability to shape ideas about the poor, to foster solutions to poverty, and to develop relations with other aid organ-izations on these and similar efforts.

The first section outlines colonial and apartheid forms of power in Namibia, namely German and South African, respectively. This dis-cussion sets the context for contemporary development aid and its links to poverty reduction and the poor. The second section describes the regime of global aid to reveal how it operates in post-apartheid

Namibia. Rather than presenting poverty reduction as an empirical condition to measure, we view it as a mobilizing and integrating concept that has emerged recently in Namibia. We suggest that plans to that end, as a rationality of aid, reflect demanding and complex forms of global co-ordination. This co-ordination involves private companies, NGOs, government departments, and international organizations, excluding equitable and democratic considerations of marginal groups. It reveals what Dean (2007: 108–29) describes as 'authoritarian liberalism,' whereby an advanced liberal government of civil society is intrinsic to authoritarian measures by the state and increasingly by international organizations.

We base our analysis on policy and program documents, reports, media items, official correspondence, and interviews with policy and research staff in international aid and NGOs in Windhoek. We collected these and other research data during two lengthy trips to the capital in 2006 and 2008.

THE BACKGROUND: COLONIAL NAMIBIA

Namibia – formerly German South West Africa and then (British) South West Africa – was the continent's last colony and, until independence in 1990, virtually South Africa's 'fifth province.' It borders Angola and Zambia to the north, Botswana and South Africa to the east, South Africa to the south, and the Atlantic Ocean to the west. It consists of various ethnic groups, of which the majority live in rural areas. These ethnic groups include Afrikaner, Baster, Caprivian, Coloured, Damara, English, German, Herero, Kavango, Nama, Ovahimba, Ovambo, San, and Tswana. About half of the population belongs to the Ovambo people and one-tenth to the Kavango; the other ethnic groups are much smaller. The San peoples are viewed as the original inhabitants.

Segregation under apartheid aimed to keep 'black,' 'coloured,' and 'white' Namibians separate from each other. It also separated other ethnic groups and kept them to their sections by municipal administrative designations (see, for example, Becker 2005; Melber 2005; Tvedten and Nangulah 1999). Today, Namibia retains social and economic inequalities and gender, ethnic, and social class divisions that it inherited from over half a century of apartheid rule, and many people told us that these inequalities are among the most intense in the world today.

Colonial power has a long history in Namibia; it aimed to immobilize old forms of conduct by methodically breaking down their conditions and to mobilize new forms to replace them. These new ways involved new classifications of people, resource extraction and demand for new types of labour, and new meanings for differential rights and irreconcilable categories – Mbembe's "manufacturing of a large reservoir of cultural imaginaries" (2003: 26). As an activity to produce effects of rule, one form of colonial power – Scott's "colonial governmentality" (Scott 2005) – became visible under German rule from 1884 until 1915. The colonial power renamed the land German South West Africa (GSWA) and made German law applicable.[4] This territory sustained one of the first genocides of the twentieth century.[5] The war of the colonial administration and the settlers against Namibians ended with the German victory at Ohamakari (14 August 1902) and pushed the Ovaherero people into the arid Omaheke (Kalahari) region on the east, where most died of thirst.

The next stage of the war involved annihilation of the Nama (Khoi) people, including those under Hendrik Witbooi, a Nama chief who tried to join the Herero and Nama against the Germans. The Witbooi rebelled against German rule on 4 October 1904. Those Witbooi who did not die in battle became prisoners and died later because of conditions in German prisoner-of-war camps in South West Africa, German Togo, and Cameroon (Steinmetz and Hell 2006: 156–7).

Thus German colonial power was not merely about domination by one group but also about its mobility, particularly its ability to circulate in and through the lives of individuals and groups that identified and constituted them as an effect of colonial relations of power (see Foucault 2003b: 29). Moreover German colonization was not simply about governing the territory through economic and political rationalities of control. It also involved governing groups and populations through new forms of knowledge, cultural imaginaries, institutions, and technologies that aimed to reconstitute the territory as a new colony and its subjects as new colonial subjects.[6] However, like other forms of colonial governmentality that failed because of defeat in war and similar phenomena (Redfield 2005), the German authorities lost control of the colony in 1915 as a result of defeat in the First World War; this war nevertheless was as much a means of achieving sovereignty as a way of exercising the colonial 'right' to kill – a critical point that Mbembe (2003: 12) raises in his analysis of colonialism.

The second colonial power in Namibia was South Africa. South Africa appropriated the territory from Germany in 1915, initially in the name of Britain. While formal German occupation ended in 1915, German influence was by this time firm and would last.[7] From 1915 on, the territory was British South West Africa (later South West Africa) (Hartmann, Silvester, and Hayes 2001: 14). In 1921 the new League of Nations mandated the Union of South Africa to administer the territory in its own right. South Africa made its own laws applicable there; in 1926, it established a settler parliament, the Legislative Assembly (UN 1990: 949). During the 1920s, Namibia lent its territory for settlement by poorer whites in the land-hungry 'new South Africa' during its early nation building (Hartmann, Silvester, and Hayes 2001: 3). This settlement practice later become part of South African apartheid relations of rule – the violent social and political policy of racial segregation and discrimination that white-minority governments set up in South Africa beginning in 1948. We discuss these territorializing practices, and their racial-biopolitical dimensions, in the context of a former Namibian township in chapter 5.

Like other forms of colonial and authoritarian rule, South Africa employed race to mobilize populations to support colonial schemes and technologies of government. Through its strategies, it organized native societies on the basis of tribal groupings, a practice affecting most black Namibians today, as they still live in 'homelands' – now 'communal lands' (Legal Assistance Centre [LAC] 2006). Under South Africa, for example, the Damara, Herero, Kavango, and Ovambo peoples received large 'homelands' where they could continue their livelihood practices, and the regime dispersed the San widely in other people's homelands (2006: 2). Furthermore, and as part of the colonial administration's labour system, in 1925 it created two recruiting bodies: the Northern Labour Organization (NLO) provided labour for the northern mines and commercial farms, with labour in the Police Zone[8] going to farms; the Southern Labour Organization (SLO) supplied the diamond mines with workers largely from Owamboland and the Okavango (Frayne 2004: 491).

In an effort to foster greater claims to the territory, South Africa encouraged a new wave of non-German white immigration and investment during the 1920s. It publicized the territory and solicited 'white' settlers through its leading travel journal, *South African Railways and Harbours Magazine*, and sought as well to create an attractive tourist site. According to Hartmann, Silvester, and Hayes, "The administration made its support for visiting expeditions conditional on their advertisement of the territory to their constituencies abroad. This formed part of the contract, for example, with the Denver Africa Exhibition in the 1920s ... Photography was central to these efforts to project South Africa's image of Namibia as a desirable destination for new white settlers" (2001: 15).

Although German cultural organizations, ranging from choirs to gymnastic associations, continued to advance German interests there, by the late 1920s the National Socialists controlled all German-speaking organizations in the territory (Gewald 2001: 123). The colonial state responded to the famine of 1929–31 in eastern Ovamboland by hiring people to dig dams in exchange for food relief.[9] This project involved "the mass entry of women and children into the public space. Most 'able-bodied' men were encouraged to work on public projects in the south." It shifted the gender division of labour but formed part of an effort to colonize the region (Hartmann, Silvester, and Hayes 2001: 87).

Shortly following the National Party's establishment of apartheid in South West Africa in 1948, urban centres began growing, and town planning aimed to control urban areas and black Namibian social relations. South Africa extended most of its apartheid legislation to the territory, including pass and vagrancy laws, population-registration permits, entry restrictions for public places, exclusion of land ownership for black people, and prohibition of mixed marriages, creating social and political environments very similar to those in South Africa. For example, the Vagrancy Law (Proclamation 25 of 1920) prohibited anyone from being in the Police Zone (most of central and southern Namibia was appropriated for white settlement, an area formerly known as the Police Zone) without employment or other obvious means of support. The Native Administrations Proclamation (Proclamation 11 of 1922) required permits for travel within and outside the territory and also forbade squatting on private property (Frayne 2004). The pass laws prevented most blacks from moving into the towns or the southern parts of the territory. Also, homeland policies forced these people into small settlement areas on designated communal land with inadequate and poor social infrastructure, while the rest of the land became large commercial farms. Thus, alongside urbanization came apartheid policies that circumscribed social relations and urban environments.

Colonial and apartheid rule employed the concept of race to assemble populations to support the government's agendas and inscribed an authoritarian understanding of the use of space, including colonized and apartheid areas, and the conditions of life and death there. Carefully planned urban apartheid settlements divided the territory into settler areas and ethnically designated homelands and facilitated strict surveillance of and restrictions on the conduct of 'nonwhites.' According to Müller-Friedman (2008):

> The colonial/apartheid regime in Namibia initiated a vast spatial reorganization enterprise not only to create room for and to meet the needs of the white settler society, but also to contain and control local populations ... Namibian urban practitioners, like their South African counterparts, were concerned with different issues, depending on the types of spaces they designed. The Namibian urban landscape at large was perceived by these white practitioners as white spaces. The Windhoek-based architect Lentin, for example, revealed that his interest for urban development in Windhoek was a concern for the development of white space. He considered the black and coloured townships as 'physical barriers', similar to mountains and industrial zones, and as obstacles for future development. (2008: 33)

An immense array of architects and urban planners set up residential suburbs that depended on the modernist neighbourhood model, including "monofunctional land-use zoning, hierarchical road systems and pro-rata amenities within residential areas. For its black and coloured residents, urban practitioners implemented the 'native' housing schemes developed in South Africa and they did so on a large-scale" (2008: 33).

The large-scale planning and building of townships occurred during the late 1950s and early 1960s and included construction of the well-known township of Katutura, a site of the new global-aid regime, which we explore further in chapter 5. These townships were several kilometres beyond the 'white towns' and often replaced former 'blacks-only' locations. Additionally, not only did highways, 'green belts,' and industrial zones separate the townships from each other, but other design features, such as single-access roads to townships, facilitated police control (Müller-Friedman 2008: 33).[10] Policing reflected dispersal of colonial and apartheid relations of

Namibia's Independence

THE UNITED NATIONS General Assembly sneaked in another political atrocity the other day. Though negotiations for independence are under way in Namibia, the African name of the land South Africa rules as the colony of South West Africa, the Assembly shouted through a resolution endorsing "armed struggle" to end Pretoria's control. It is true that the resolution, approved by the kind of margin (107-6) that has come to signal Assembly hysteria, adds no guns to the guerrillas on the ground. The idea behind it, however, is appalling: The United Nations is ostensibly devoted to the peaceful resolution of international disputes. Others, not the United Nations, are in fact trying to resolve this dispute peacefully. Yet here comes the Assembly to endorse a solution by violence. The vote tramples on the U.N. Charter and on good sense alike. Anyone wishing to understand why the General Assembly has fallen into such low repute can end his inquiry here.

Behind the vote, of course, lies a shabby political exercise. Some time ago, the Namibian group called the South West African People's Organization (SWAPO) got the Assembly to anoint it the "sole" representative of the Namibian people. SWAPO is the Ovambo tribal faction that is probably the best organized political/military operation in the country. But its claim to speak for all Namibians is absurd—at least in the eyes of a plain majority of Namibians, those whose leaders are engaged in negotiations now. By skillful diplomacy and by brandishing its Marxist cre-

dentials, however, SWAPO won the Assembly's uncritical sanction all the same.

This is the context in which the new Assembly endorsement of "armed struggle" should be viewed—as another diplomatic victory for SWAPO. Its great fear, you see, is that other blacks in Namibia will negotiate the sort of independence that leaves to SWAPO, at best, only that share of power that it could hope to command by its own political resources. SWAPO would prefer to use the leverage of its guerrilla activity and its diplomatic strength to win total power. The U.N. is its patsy.

SWAPO's greatest ally, however, is not the General Assembly. It is South Africa. It is mainly South African rigidity that has stalemated the negotiations on Namibian independence, discouraged the moderate black tribes and mixed-race communities participating in those negotiations, and given SWAPO the opening that its guerrillas and diplomats are trying to widen now. Many Africans expect Jimmy Carter somehow to breathe new life into the negotiations when he takes office in January. Far more important is whether Pretoria changes its strategy and takes an approach that will permit the prompt establishment of an interim government in Namibia, the immediate ending of apartheid there, and an orderly transition to full independence—as promised by South Africa. By that process, SWAPO would have an incentive to join with its fellow Namibians in the building of the land they share.

Figure 4.1 SWAPO and Namibia's independence; *Washington Post,* 29 December 1976. Courtesy of United Nations Archives, New York.

rule throughout everyday life and helped generate a plethora of social movements and resistance efforts against apartheid and for independence. Life histories of struggles highlight some of these contestations, including activists in the South West African People's Organization, or SWAPO (see, for example, Leys and Brown 2005).

In response to the devastating social and political conditions of apartheid, nationalist movements emerged, most notably SWAPO. Like other southern African liberation movements,[11] it used the language of human rights as a way to demand Western liberal civil rights from the white minority who enjoyed them for the black majority who did not (H. Becker 2007: 30). Beginning in the early 1960s, SWAPO increasingly operated in exile (see Figure 4.1) as various resistance groups coalesced over South Africa's effort to incorporate the territory, which began in 1946. After more than a decade of petitioning, mainly the UN, the nascent liberation groups had to go into exile and began taking up arms in 1966 (Kössler 2007: 369).[12] In the end, the struggle for independence resulted in many deaths and much suffering and hardship, population dislocation, and military rule (see UNICEF 1991).

The international community played a large role in bringing about independence. Petronella Coetzee, a SWAPO activist, reports:

I went to Switzerland, France and Germany to campaign [in 1988] for the implementation of [UN Security Council] Resolution 435 [that set out proposals for a cease-fire and UN-supervised elections in *South African*–controlled *South West Africa* with the aim of creating an independent Namibia]. I was invited by people from Switzerland who know me. They were also SWAPO supporters ... They worked with the SWAPO office in Germany. I was so optimistic. I campaigned for nearly two months in various countries. When I was returning to Namibia I even told the people in Europe, "See you next year." I thought that we would get our independence in 1989. I was so sure they would start implementing Resolution 435 that year. (Leys and Brown 2005: 53)

From the UN perspective, "1989 saw the beginning of the end of colonialism in Africa, as Namibia – the largest Territory with a colonial background anywhere in the world – began an irreversible march to independence" (UN 1989: 789).

In particular, the UN set up its Transition Assistance Group (UNTAG) in accordance with Resolution 632 to assist the special representative of the secretary general to advance independence through free and fair elections under UN supervision and control. Additionally, it aimed to help the special representative ensure the end of hostile acts, confinement of South African troops to bases, and their eventual removal from Namibia. During the transitional period, the South African administrator general continued to govern the territory but worked closely with the special representative to "ensure an orderly transition to independence" (Bauer 2001: 235). The aim was to repeal all discriminatory laws, release political prisoners, allow for return refugees, and maintain 'law and order' (UNTAG 2008).[13]

DEVELOPING AID FOR POST-APARTHEID NAMIBIA

Namibia has a specific approach towards non-state activities because, before Independence, non-state activities were [affiliated with] SWAPO, which was the ruling party. So it took us quite a while to be able to make

us see the possibility of support for non-state activities which would not
be seen by the government and the ruling party as supporting the political
opposition.

Interview, European Commission of the European Union,
Windhoek, 2008

After a long struggle by many people, groups, and organizations,
which SWAPO planned, the SWAPO Party came to power on 21
March 1990. It set out to reverse the effects and practices of apartheid, including segregated social spaces and institutions and the kind
of colonial subjectivities that they required. Its key objectives were
restructuring of the state, including redemarcating regions and local
authorities without regard to race and ethnicity (Ramutsindela
2001: 62–3),[14] national reconciliation, socioeconomic development,
and integration into the economy and 'community of nations'
(Gonzales 2000: 105). The de-apartheid process attempted to eradicate authoritarian rule that shaped institutions and social spaces and
fostered white superiority. It involved widespread activities by local,
national, and international organizations, as well as various social
and political groups (see Figure 4.2).

During the war of national independence, international organizations sought to propose ideas of development in an effort to transform
ways of thinking about change and shape future development. In the
struggle for independence, these ideas – ranging from growth of agriculture, cash cropping, and poverty reduction to expansion of rights,
security, and development aid – received support from international
organizations, including the UN agencies (UNDP, UNESCO, UNHCR,
and UNICEF) and their expert advice, conferences and meetings, and
development programs. These programs covered such matters as peace
and security, education, human rights, aid, and poverty reduction.

From our perspective, and in the light of the work of Escobar
(2005), Ferguson and Gupta (2005), Goldman (2005a), and Rojas
(2004), development operates as a rationality of global government. It
gives rise to technologies, experts, and apparatuses to administer and
transform peoples' lives and launch courses of action to develop countries. As a governing rationality, development orders relations between
people and things to generate a desired effect. At the time of independence in Namibia, this rationality came to represent forms of social and
economic change, which involved various organizations and agencies
fostering practices of development, as we see next.

U.N. Demands Namibian Independence

UNITED NATIONS, Dec. 17 —The Security Council voted unanimously today to demand that South Africa make a "solemn commitment" to give up the territory of Southwest Africa, or Namibia.

The United States backed the council action by declaring that "South Africa should act quickly and positively to end its illegal occupation of Namibia."

U.S. Ambassador John Scali called for a "specific, unequivocal statement" from South Africa, involving "self-determination in the near future," the abolition of discriminatory practices, and freer political expression in the territory.

The United States, he said, has informed Pretoria of these views, and of the need to "re-examine its basic policies" in light of the changing realities in Rhodesia and the neighboring Portuguese territories.

The resolution, significantly, was the product of negotiation and compromise between the Africans and the West. In recent months, the Third World nations have pressed the U.N. to adopt radical resolutions on colonial questions, eliciting a triple veto in the Security Council on a drive to expel South Africa from the U.N., and Western complaints in the General Assembly that a refusal to compromise was creating a "tyranny of the majority."

Yesterday, the Africans sat down privately with the U.S. and other Western delegations to hammer out a compromise text on Namibia. This text dropped an explicit threat to impose U.N. economic sanctions on South Africa, and pushed the deadline for a South African response to the council back to May 30 from March 14.

Thus the Africans answered the Western criticisms—they compromised. Scali was then able to answer the Third World complaints—he demonstrated U.S. support for change in the global status quo.

"We are pleased," Scali said at the end of his council speech, "that we were able to join together with members of the African group to adopt this important new resolution."

Specifically, the resolution demands that South Africa declare to the council its willingness to comply with U.N. resolutions and World Court decisions on Namibia and that Pretoria recognize "the territorial integrity and unity of Namibia as a nation."

Figure 4.2 UN demands independence in Namibia; *Washington Post*, 19 December 1974. Courtesy of United Nations Archives, New York.

Although many international organizations helped establish and disseminate development initiatives in Namibia, UNESCO was at the forefront. As an organization that promotes collaboration among nations through education, science, culture, and communication, it began its work there in the 1970s. It first provided instructive training for exiles through SWAPO Educational and Health Centres in neighbouring Angola. Additionally, UNESCO supplied fellowships for educational literacy and media training abroad and training in radio broadcasting, film, and video production to cadres through group training in Lusaka, Zambia. For example, a project to help 'women in development' emerged in 1978 at the first Namibia National Planning Workshop in Lusaka: "This intersectoral project provided upgrading in English, mathematics, agricultural skills and journalism, as well as institutional support to the Women's Council. It was jointly implemented by UNESCO, UNDP, the UN Council for Namibia and SWAPO and ended just prior to Independence in March 1990" (UNESCO 2008a).

In 1989, UNESCO[15] began to shape post-apartheid education through the International Conference on Teacher Education for Namibia in Lusaka, under SWAPO's sponsorship. The gathering formally adopted SWAPO's goal of transforming the apartheid educational system after independence. Teacher education was vital to the plan's success, and UNESCO focused on developing syllabi and designing and printing modules for training teachers at planned workshops. Within five years, by 1994, some 500 students had enrolled for first-year studies (see UNESCO 2008b).

While international organizations were channelling development aid to South West Africa in support of independence, many non-governmental organizations there were working on large-scale aid and related issues, such as community initiatives, youth education, health training, poverty reduction, regional development, and social empowerment. For example, a community development agency, the Rural People's Institute for Social Empowerment (RISE), began in 1987 to address poverty through saving-and-credit schemes for communal farmers and rural entrepreneurs. In 1993, it launched Savings and Credit Associations in affiliation with local farmers' co-operatives in the Hardap and Karas region in the south. In 1999, it started to encourage formation of such bodies in collaboration with farmers' co-operatives in the north (Ohangwena, Omusati, Oshana, and Oshikoto regions) (interview, Windhoek, 2008). In partnership with regional farmers' co-operatives, it currently implements savings-and-credit arrangements to assist rural farmers, women, youth, and other groups unable "to secure financial support from commercial banking institutions due to lack of collateral" (RISE 2008). While partnerships can represent co-operation and mutual understanding, they can also focus on making profits.

Another local NGO, the Namibia Development Trust (NDT), emerged in 1987 to funnel resources from the European Union to 'victims Apartheid.' NGOs founded it, including churches under the Council of Churches of Namibia, student movements in the Namibian National Students Organization, and trade unions within the National Union of Namibian Workers. During the late 1980s the NDT helped set up COSEDA (at that time the Namibian Job Creation Services), the Namibia Credit Union League (NACUL), the Namibia National Farmers Union (NNFU), and the Saamstam Housing Cooperative. After independence, the NDT became an intermediary organization to promote rural community development (NDT Report 2004–6).

Today, the NDT mobilizes marginal groups to work for social change, fostering self-sustaining and economically viable communities. It still continues to raise awareness about poverty and inequality (NDT 2004–6 Report: 21), support 'self-reliant communities' capable of 'self-management,' and assemble local and external resources and participants for such communities. It supports 25 projects for youth groups that foster self-reliance and seek to mitigate HIV/AIDS and poverty through self-employment. A long-standing member comments:

Certainly the need for rural communities to upgrade their skills is very important, fundamental; that's the success of capacity building ... The key idea of capacity building is, you know, the sort of skills that are needed, attitude change, changing the mind set, behaviour. For me that is the crux of the matter; because once that is unleashed, you help to unlock that ... inferiority complex, that feeling of needing to wait for government to come and do or NGOs to come and help. But, if you unlock that potential and know that self-reliance is the key to your own development, you start doing things for yourself. What are the gifts in you? What are the talents that you have? What are the skills that are available? What are the resources around me? Training and capacity building needs to encompass those skills. (Interview, Windhoek, 2008)

Capacity building here is an act of empowerment, of providing actors with skills and resources to improve themselves. However, these programs alter human conduct in other ways. They can, for example, exemplify a technology of government that shapes and controls vulnerable populations in their engagement with markets and enterprises (Gould and Ojanen 2005: 45; L. Phillips and Ilcan 2004) or a 'technology of citizenship' (Cruikshank 1999) that aims to constitute and direct certain groups such as the poor. Capacity-building initiatives can also embody a 'technology of subjectivity' that relies on forms of expert knowledge to encourage self-government so that citizens can optimize their choices in unstable markets (Ong 2006b: 6). Non-party political and development organizations emerged in Namibia with the aim to help poor people build such capacity.

Discussion of Namibia after apartheid raises complex questions about its peoples and its policies. Our interviews and discussions with anti-poverty activists, NGOs, and policy researchers and analysts from international organizations reveal many troubling issues. These include ongoing racial segregation, violation of human rights and land claims, a fractured opposition, weakening pro-democracy movements, ethnic and political conflict, armed conflicts in parts of the country, and numerous unsuccessful local, national, and international initiatives to further sustainable development and reduce poverty. The next section discusses the new global-aid regime and its international participants and sets the context for an analysis of Namibia's poverty-reduction initiatives. As we see below, these exercises bring together existing practices, organizations, and networks of development aid. They also highlight the diverse expectations of the poor vis-à-vis their 'problems,' relations between them, and authorities who attempt to rule them and make clear the social inequalities and divisions that affect everyday life in post-apartheid Namibia.

INTERNATIONAL AID ACTORS

Unlike the realist precept of state as the main actors promoting national interest and foreign aid ... philanthropists, international institutions and market actors all participate in different forms of government through aid practices.

Cristina Rojas, 'Governing through the Social' (2004: 99)

Around the globe, many nongovernmental and international organizations have worked to promote human welfare and emergency relief – 'humanitarian aid.' Such efforts expanded rapidly after 1945 in response to various crises. The International Committee of the Red Cross, for example, offered 'universal' humanitarian aid around the world. Similarly, the UN established organizations for the same purpose, such as the UN International Children's Emergency Fund (UNICEF) in 1946. Private charities providing famine relief during the war, such as the Oxfam Committee for Famine Relief (Oxfam) of 1943, have continued since 1945 (Chandler 2001).

Humanitarian aid boasts a history of contradictory actions, politics, and conflicts (Nyers 2006: 29; Yannis 2001: 45).[16] In the 1960s, the 'Decade of Development,' NGOs, national governments, and international organizations realized the inability of relief or charity to overcome crises and underdevelopment, including poverty and population increases. As Rojas (2004) argues, they 'developmentalized' aid, representing it as a condition of countries with specific economic, geographical, and social features (2004: 101). This global governmentality of aid gave rise to international organizations encouraging the poor to participate in development programs. For example, in 1960 the World Bank created the International Development Association to reduce poverty by providing interest-free loans and grants to stimulate economic growth (World Bank 2008e). Other banks had a similar focus: the Inter-American Development Bank (1959), the African Development Bank (1964), the Asian Development

Bank (1966), the Caribbean Development Bank (1969), and the Development Bank of American Samoa (1969). Likewise, international NGOs, such as Oxfam, switched from emergency relief to development and fighting poverty.

During the 1970s and 1980s, international aid actors, including NGOs, came to rely more on nation states, which urged them to administer government relief and development funds in regions around the world (Teichman 2004).[17] This kind of development aid was visible during the apartheid regime in South West Africa and South Africa, and many governments and international organizations demanded reform and called for development to that end. For example, as a humanitarian-aid partner of the International Committee of the Red Cross, the Namibia Red Cross Society – which parliament set up (act 16) in 1991– was to address the basic needs of the most vulnerable communities in health and care, and disaster management, such as orphans and vulnerable children. Today, it develops communities in Caprivi, Karas, Kavango, Khomas, Kunene, Ohangwena, and Otjozondjupa (five of these regions are in the north, where 70 per cent of the population lives). The Namibia Red Cross Society aims to "develop working partnerships with identified vulnerable communities" and to assist their residents in accordance with the principles of the International Red Cross and Red Crescent Movement (Namibia Red Cross n.d.).

Partnerships are a key rationality of the new global aid, and not all of them are antithetical to the self-directed or expressed needs of the poor, for they can promote social justice in pro-poor ways. An example involving the Namibia Red Cross Society shows how they can counter other dominant rationalities of the new regime of global aid including the market. This and similar instances further our search for an ontology of change (Gibson-Graham 2006). By unearthing accounts of efforts for social justice, we hope to help alter the subjectivities of the poor. It is in this way – through alternatives to advanced liberal, colonial, and authoritarian governmentalities – that the poor will be able to voice and enact their own demands and requests for change, their own life-politics.

The Namibia Red Cross Society's newsletter in 2009 describes a partnership to assist local community members' recovery from ongoing food insecurity. In this arrangement, the Namibia Red Cross distributes funds from the European Union's ECHO (European Commission's Humanitarian Aid Office) to local communities in the north, with emphasis on consulting residents. Community members received agricultural support to prepare for the next planting and harvest and to help them recover from floods (Namibia Red Cross Society 2009). Here, we would argue, one can see the shifting nature of rationalities of rule: despite a genuinely consultative, pro-poor approach to poverty reduction, the dissemination of agricultural support may also responsibilize the poor vis-à-vis their recovery or escape from food insecurity. Our genealogy-style excavation fades in the face of the rhyzomatic spread of the new global-aid regime itself.

During and since the 1990s, expansion of international development organizations, including NGOs, has not so much provided emergency relief or short-term development but addressed, as Edkins (2000: 75) stresses, longer-term development. Organizations active in development aid, particularly poverty reduction, are numerous and include ActionAid, Christian Aid, Oxfam, the Save the Children's Fund, UN agencies, USAID, the World Bank, and World Vision. Many such organizations fighting poverty operate in developing countries. In Namibia, such exercises have brought together existing practices, organizations, and networks of development aid to influence the efforts of Duffield's "ineffective states" (2007: 131). They have also drawn attention to those issues of health, conflict, and displacement that undermine the self-reliance of particular groups such as the poor.

UNICEF (1991) identified the relationship between poverty and child survival in Namibia. The World Summit on Children in New York in 1990 had endorsed this finding. In UNICEF's words: "A profound understanding of the underlying determinants of poverty is especially important if the major internationally accepted Goals for Child Survival, Protection and Development (CSPD) are to be met in Namibia in the 1990s. These Goals for the Year 2000 derive from the Plan of Action agreed upon by the 159 nations, including Namibia, represented at the first World Summit on Children " (1991: 7).

As an organization seeking to improve children's welfare, UNICEF called for Namibia to address social inequity and improve the welfare of its majority. It identified key problems: the absence of key socio-economic indicators of poverty and aggregate statistical information at the national level, including lack of adequate household statistical frames, a weak national information base, and improper information on statistical time series. If the national government could resolve these problems, it was understood that UNICEF could begin its work on child malnutrition and infant deaths, which would target communities and women in "problem assessment, planning, implementation and monitoring" (UNICEF 1991: 29). Here UNICEF recognized women as responsible actors in easing and eradicating child poverty and in delivering certain state functions. Overall, and in places such as Mozambique, Namibia, Tanzania, and Uganda in Africa, Solomon Islands in the Pacific, and Timor Leste in southeast Asia, donor governments and international financial and other organizations, such as UN agencies and some nongovernmental bodies, are shaping the design and delivery of states' economic and welfare functions.

As part of the new global-aid regime, many international organizations aim to provide continuing development assistance through relations with local NGOs, national governments, and international financial organizations, such as the World Bank. This form of aid emphasizes global markets as a way out of poverty, supports self-responsibility by groups such as the poor, and endorses such advanced liberal practices as good governance. In the process, international financial organizations shape these efforts by international groups offering development aid.[18] The World Bank, for example, pursues advanced liberal, pro-growth schemes of development that encourage participation via implementation and promotion of its Poverty Reduction Strategy Papers (PRSPs).[19]

The World Bank replaced its infamous Structural Adjustment Program in 1999 with its new Poverty Reduction Growth Facility (PRGP), while the PRSPs superseded its Structural Adjustment Policy Framework Papers. These policy initiatives have become preconditions for all of its concessional lending and debt relief (World Bank 2003). PRSPs – loan applications from governments – describe "a country's macroeconomic, structural and social policies and programs to promote growth and reduce poverty" (World Bank 2004). The World Bank requires recipients to meet advanced liberal standards (for example, privatization, deregulation, macro-economic stability) and work with stakeholders from civil society, such as nongovernmental organizations (Rathgeber 2005: 585). By thereby encouraging its relations with aid organizations such as Catholic Relief Services, Christian Aid, Oxfam International, Save the Children, and World Vision, the World Bank demonstrates its ability to 'govern at a distance' and hence shape many countries' efforts to reduce poverty.

In various parts of Africa and elsewhere, the PRSP process creates new ways of indicating, knowing about, and measuring the poor. It fosters, for example, new demands for calculations of poverty at international and national levels. UNDP economist Sebastian Levine, in Windhoek, states: "Demand is growing for estimates of poverty that are better and more systematically collected and analysed at the sub-national, national and global levels. A key driver of this increased demand has been the advent of Poverty Reduction Strategy Papers, or PRSPs. These are comprehensive and country-led strategies that set out a country's macroeconomic, structural and social policies and programs to promote growth and reduce poverty, and they are expected to include appropriate mechanisms for monitoring to ensure that progress can be measured" (Levine 2006: 90).[20] Estimates and indicators of poverty require identification, creation, collection, analysis, and dissemination of quantitative data. Like other measures such as human rights indicators (Rosga and Satterthwaite 2009: 255), they relate to the increasing number of global governing projects, such as the UN's Millennium Development Goals. They spread technocracies and expert forms of knowledge in the service of reducing poverty and generating growth.

The World Bank's PRSP process appears to foster people-centric, participatory attacks on poverty. Such plans are becoming increasingly integral to the new global-aid regime, wherein pro-growth development proliferates (McGrath and King 2004: 171) alongside participation and empowerment (World Bank 2005). These schemes have become ever-stronger since the late 1980s, when advanced liberal agendas influenced international and nongovernmental organizations with headquarters in Britain and the United States (Stubbs 2003: 328) and gradually shaped counterparts everywhere. The World Bank's activities in international development aid (Gould 2005b: 66) have disseminated this approach widely and deeply. Such endeavours assume that markets and private initiative are the best way to stimulate economic growth and provide maximum services to the most people. Diverse social, economic, and policy relations[21] prevail among various international, international financial, and nongovernmental organizations and people in the Third World receiving development aid. However, more specific research needs to focus on how and to what extent these relations shape international development aid as such bodies work against poverty among groups that they target, such as the poor in Namibia.

In the light of the above discussion of international actors in global aid, we now analyse this regime as it operates in Namibia. This regime not only depends on the concept of poverty reduction and of transforming the poor, but it also attempts to bridge divisions and bring together actors and sectors in development aid. We argue that the regime of global aid requires complex forms of global co-ordination that involve private enterprise, NGOs, governments, and international development aid organizations and fosters market relations, ties among participants, and ways of framing the poor.

GLOBAL CO-ORDINATION

From Tony Blair's Africa Commission, the G7 finance ministers' debt relief, the Live 8 concerts, the Make Poverty History campaign and the G8 Gleneagles promises, to the United Nations 2005 summit and the Hong Kong WTO meeting, Africa's gains have been mainly limited to public relations. The central problems remain exploitative debt and financial relationships with the North, phantom aid, unfair trade, distorted investment, capital flight and the continent's brain/skills drain.

Patrick Bond, *Looting Africa* (2006: back cover)

About the time of independence in 1990, the national government and aid agencies in Namibia acknowledged the need for development aid. The devastating situations facing many poor, vulnerable, and alienated people forced local NGOs to address critical issues, such as women's rights, community development, security, land claims, and poverty and development aid.[22] For example, some launched gender policies and programs that attempt to improve the lives of poor women.

One such group operating out of Windhoek is Sister Namibia. It aims to increase women's awareness of how political, cultural, and economic relations may act to control and oppress them. It works to eliminate gender discrimination, sexism, racism, homophobia, and xenophobia by raising awareness of the equality of all human beings through the use of media, education, and advocacy. Its activities include gender education in schools, advocacy with other NGOs, such as the Legal Assistance Centre, on social, political, and cultural issues affecting women, and a monthly magazine that it distributes widely (interview, Windhoek, 2008). The Legal Assistance Centre is a driving force behind improving the land rights and the lives of the San people, the country's poorest and most marginal minority, who have little access to political and economic institutions. It also initiates reform of gender law and engages in programs to improve women and children's rights, such as the Gender Research and Advocacy Project, which promotes gender equality and empowerment of women through legal research, law reform, and advocacy (interview, Windhoek, 2008; see also LeBeau and E. Iiping 2004: 9–10).

A forum for NGOs, NANGOF, started in April 1991. It is an umbrella network that promotes poverty eradication, democracy, and human rights. It operates through the combined resources of its membership and aims to create and sustain 'an enabling environment' for NGOs. It has three main goals. First, through advocacy, it encourages public participation and seeks to co-ordinate NGOs' efforts to address "the development needs of the poor and marginalized." Second, through networking and information, it aims to provide a platform for partnerships and experience sharing among member bodies, citizens, and international development agencies and to promote greater collaboration with regional and international networks of NGOs. Third, by building capacity, it aims to co-ordinate members' resources to strengthen NGOs so that their development services reach "their constituencies and thus contribute to the effectiveness of Namibian Civil Society" (NANGOF 2008).

NANGOF and its affiliates are increasingly delivering public services – a process that we demonstrate in chapters 2 and 3 is occurring around the world as part of the spread of advanced liberal agendas and the new global-aid regime. It relates closely to other advanced liberal practices, such as privatization, contractualization, responsiblization, and to decentralization of government itself.

In recent years, researchers have viewed NGOs' provision of services in terms of technologies of government. Here, they responsibilize marginal groups and create governable subjects, such as the poor, through technologies of self-management (Ilcan and Basok 2004; Larner and Walters 2000). This new role of theirs and their developing relationship with both the state and international organizations increasingly blur distinctions between the state and civil society (Dean 2007: 17, 100–30). For this reason, we concur with Dean: "Once we recognize that liberal political rationality might seek to create, work through or utilize freedom, then a set of complementary analytical openings emerges ... governing liberally does not necessarily entail governing through freedom or even governing in a manner that respects liberty. It might mean, in ways quite compatible with a liberal rationality of government, over-riding the exercise of specific freedoms in order to enforce obligations on members of the population" (2007: 109). In other words, it can be profoundly authoritarian.

A program officer working for Oxfam Canada in Windhoek describes the role and responsibility of NGOs in development programming. "Capacity building from Oxfam's point of view ... is when a local NGO or community-based organization is better able to carry out the activities and programs that it wishes to ... Certainly everywhere in Africa, one of the ongoing problems is with development programming. The expectation is that local NGOs will end up being able to implement and monitor and report and plan as well as, or in a very similar style to, a Canadian NGO" (interview, Windhoek, 2006). We see here both the entanglement of the new global-aid regime and the diverse ways in which advanced liberalism governs, including in authoritarian modes. This officer discusses how valuable it would be to have local NGOs implement development plans and take on responsibilities from larger aid donors. Such a sentiment reflects ideas of pro-poor development that Oxfam and other international organizations espouse.

Pro-poor development aims to link initiatives with poor people in ways that benefit them. Reducing poverty, for example, allows poor people to rectify their own impoverishment.[23] Pro-poor development occurs in many areas, ranging from housing and tourism to employment (see, for example, Chok et al. 2007). However, from our perspective, pro-poor initiatives tend to ignore such issues as racial segregation and authoritarian practices, advanced liberal programs, and the global governance of poverty and the poor. As we saw above, Oxfam increasingly undertakes pro-poor development and empowerment, which has proved ineffective in developing countries. Thus we must look at such efforts with scepticism, as Gould and Ojanen (2005: 60–1) contend, since they do not challenge advanced or neoliberal practices and often undermine political accountability and inhibit the democratization of public oversight. This study distinguishes clearly between, on the one hand, such globalized strategies, in local contexts, that reproduce social and political inequalities and the material conditions of the poor and, on the other hand, social-justice approaches that contest the power of, for example, international organizations.

Not only are NGOs becoming more responsible for development and poverty reduction, but so too are international financial organizations. For example, in the wake of growing concerns over Namibia's

economic and political stability and security at independence, the
World Bank launched a number of analytical and advisory activities. Some involved the national government and focused on a new
way forward for development. According to the World Bank,
Namibia "inherited a well functioning physical infrastructure and a
market economy, coupled with rich mineral resources and a relatively strong public administration. However, the social and economic imbalances of the apartheid system left Namibia with a
highly dualistic society. The structure of the economy has made job
creation and poverty reduction difficult, and inequality unaccept-
ably high, key challenges that are at the top of the Government's
development agenda" (2008c).

In 1990, Namibia, as one of the newest members of the World
Bank, also joined the International Bank for Reconstruction and
Development (IBRD), the International Finance Corporation (IFC),
and the Multilateral Investment Guarantee Agency (MIGA). In May
2007, the IBRD approved a Development Policy Loan – an advanced
liberal initiative – for Namibia, in the amount of U.S.$7.5 million.
The funding develops and implements specific policies and instruments for sector reforms and attempts to govern Namibia 'beyond
the state.' Likewise, the IFC has extended small investments, including a fisheries project (Pescanova), equity in the country's first indigenous life-insurance company (Namibia Life), and a loan to build
a Best Western hotel in the north. It has also worked with the
Namibian Agronomic Board to raise trust funds for a feasibility
study of a cotton-ginning industry (World Bank 2008c). Such advanced liberal instruments help implement the new global-aid regime, wherein Namibia is to engage in self-disciplinary or enforcing
standards to prepare for a new path of development that involves
investments, loans, and technical assistance.

In the early 1990s, USAID established bilateral relations with the
Namibian government in the area of development and technical assistance. A senior-level USAID policy analyst in Windhoek comments
on this early relationship:

The first [US government] relationships with the country really
began with the establishment of the Peace Corps here, but USAID
arrived within six months. A year after that, we entered into
what we traditionally acknowledge as bilateral relationships at
the development assistance or technical level with the signing of

a Bilateral Framework Agreement which I believe was September of 1991 ... That Framework Agreement is basically an understanding, between the government of Namibia and the government of the United States, that we would provide them with certain technical assistance. Traditionally, for USAID, that technical assistance runs the gambit from education and health, to the environment and democracy in governments. And pretty much what we established here in Namibia was a fairly traditional cluster of activities that's designed to help this fledgling democracy with some of its greater development challenges. (Interview, Windhoek, 2008)

The development challenges include HIV/AIDS, low life expectancy, widespread poverty, social inequalities, and a low-skilled workforce, which leave Namibia 'at risk': "Namibia is working to achieve transformational development but faces daunting challenges on a scale that leaves it vulnerable. A severe HIV/AIDS epidemic, as evidenced by an overall prevalence rate of 19.7 per cent, is already having profound impacts on Namibian society. Life expectancy has declined from 61 to 49 years and by 2021 up to a third of Namibia's population under age 15 could be orphaned" (interview, Windhoek, 2008). USAID stresses open markets as a way to reduce poverty: "Namibia benefits from a democratic government that follows open market policies and has met the Millennium Challenge Corporation's good governance indicators in the areas of ruling justly, investing in people, and promoting economic freedom" (USAID Namibia 2008a).[24] Thus USAID's message is that Namibia needs open markets to support the vision and agenda of the Americans' new Millennium Challenge Corporation (MCC).

As one of many international actors in the new regime of global aid, the MCC works with some of the world's poorest countries. Its key operating principle is that "aid is most effective when it reinforces good governance, economic freedom and investments in people."[25] In support of advanced liberal initiatives, its goal is to reduce global poverty through promotion of "sustainable economic growth," which includes investments in areas such as "transportation, water and industrial infrastructure, agriculture, education, private sector development, and capacity building" (MCC 2008). USAID's practices of aid form the subject of a broader account of partnerships as a rationality of the new global-aid regime below in chapter 6.

International development aid is increasingly building and regulating relations among the private sector, NGOs, and states in the
South. In Namibia, donors not only engage in political dialogue and
economic co-operation with the national government but also provide development aid.[26] In April 2008, the European Commission
(EC) of the European Union launched a development support package for Namibia of N$1.05 billion[27] – the largest of the EC's ten
packages to the country to date – over six years, with equal alloca-
tions to education and rural development (interview, Windhoek,
2008). With its mandate "to help to reduce and ultimately to eradicate poverty in the developing countries through the promotion of
sustainable development, democracy, peace and security," the EC ac-
counted for 72 per cent of official development assistance (ODA)
that Namibia received between independence and 2004 (European
Commission 2008).[28]

There are other businesses, organizations, and governments supporting new development projects and partnership relations, including management units known as conservancies and aid contracts
based on development.. The section that follows below looks at conservancies to bolster the private sector, the lives of local residents,
and the resources of participating communities.

PROMOTION OF CONSERVANCIES AND AID CONTRACTS

The Namibian government follows standard economic advice from
international financial organizations, such as the World Bank and
IMF, to expand the private sector, including stimulating public– private partnerships (PPPs) and free-market strategies and technologies.
The IMF recommends developing the private sector, making the
labour market more flexible, reducing labour costs, opening financial markets, tightening fiscal policies, and cutting wages (Kameeta
et al. 2007: 14).

Thus, and to stimulate the private sector and develop rural
communities, the Ministry of Environment and Tourism in 1996
introduced legislation that gave conditional use of wildlife to
communal areas that formed a 'conservancy,' or management
unit. A total of 31 conservancies had registered by the end of
2004 (Republic of Namibia, National Planning Commission,
2005: 15). By the end of 2006, there were fifty, housing more than
220,000 residents (NASCO 2007: 10). Such conservancies exist in

nearly all of the large country's regions and engage local communities in the tourist industry (NACSO 2007). They now form a very substantial source of income.

According to Deputy Director Menjengwa of the Division of Rural Development: "Over the past years, as part of its community-based natural resources management (CBNRM), the country has embarked on the promotion of conservancies, which are either managed by the local rural communities themselves or in conjunction with established tour operating companies. This initiative has culminated in the construction of joint venture lodges and resorts using local material and knowledge such as thatched roofs and verandas, thereby providing a local content and flavour, that is environmentally friendly and in harmony with nature" (National Planning Commission [Republic of Namibia] 2006: 12). Clearly the government sees CBNRM as a positive initiative. Diverse groups offering international development aid support enhancement of the conservancies.

One USAID policy analyst in Windhoek identifies the racialized dimension shaping communal land in Namibia: "You've got a relatively affluent white minority owning the best farmland and you have, north of this cordon line – which was ostensibly a veterinary cordon barrier for cattle – you have these communal areas which are occupied by many more people. And it's not just there; you've got other sections of the country that have sort of been divided off as communal areas. And a real part to how this system works, and the beauty behind this program, is that they have given an economic value to natural resources and turned that economic value, the management of it, over to the people who live on the land" (interview, Windhoek, 2008).

This analyst discusses USAID's early work in CBNRM and how it encouraged the government to set up conservancies:

What we began to see is that the conservancies took better care of those resources than anybody else because they had ownership of them. And Namibia is uniquely positioned because people value those resources ... and they're willing to pay a premium to access them and whether that is flying in for a five thousand dollar photo safari, or actually trophy hunting, which is an income generator (meat sales, live relocation of stock). So what we began to see, particularly in terms of bio-conservancy, is that these

conservancies and their structures actually began to safeguard
those resources and manage them. And what we've seen in the
last fifteen years is that things like wildlife populations have
more than quadrupled in Namibia because people are responsibly managing those resources. And they have options ..., as I
said, is it better to simply kill the kudu or does it make sense to
have somebody fly in to take photos of it, or even fly in and hunt
it, but hunt it on the condition that the meat goes to the conservancy members? (Interview, Windhoek, 2008)

While there may be some benefits to developing the conservancies
for people living and working there, one needs to be cautious.
Tourism in Namibia, which includes wild gaming and trophy hunting, small-enterprise campsites, and joint-venture lodges, may constitute a strategy for economic development, but what about the
authoritative ways in which access and rights are denied or limited?
Rights to land and natural resources in the communal conservancies
raise social, political, and legal questions. As the Legal Assistance
Centre notes, "The communal conservancies must have the legal authority to administer their own lands, with the support of their re-
spective Traditional Authorities and Communal Land Boards, to
meet the needs of the conservancy members" (2007: 58).

Proponents of CBNRM call for a new approach that reconciles the
truncated institutions of the post-apartheid state with pre-colonial
institutions of political governance, resource management, and conflict resolution.[29] Community development involves not just international development-aid organizations but also local NGOs in the
conservancies. According to the Namibian government, "The capacity of NGOs supporting conservancies should also be strengthened,
in order to enable them to support communities, in particular women
and young people, in natural resource management." As well, "It
would be helpful if more civil society organizations could provide
capacity building and training in project and/or community management, monitoring and evaluation, and leadership, financial and business management skills" (Republic of Namibia, National Planning
Commission, 2005: 16). As part of its engagement in CBNRM, the
NGO RISE, for example, has supported seven conservancies in the
Erongo and Kunene regions, covering about 3 million hectares of
communal land (interview, Windhoek, 2008).

International organizations such as the World Bank and the IMF are pressing for advanced liberal initiatives to expand the private sector via the conservancies and are involving NGOs in the process. Rather than reducing poverty in any significant way, their support creates, from our perspective, a ripe environment for controlling NGOs. They aim to manage the NGOs by encouraging members to think about the marketability of conservancies and about social transformation in particular ways and with particular objectives. This kind of development scheme is part of the new global-aid regime and is becoming a prominent trend among other international aid organizations.

Transnational private aid agencies operating in other countries, such as Tanzania, establish networks and partnerships with local non-state actors, such as NGOs. In a study on aid in Tanzania, Gould and Ojanen show that such agencies act as subcontractors for large-scale international aid donors, such as USAID and Britain's Department for International Development (DfID), and for UN agencies such as UNDP. "This subcontracting is no longer aimed only at transitional service delivery activities; it is increasingly shifting towards policy advocacy in the capital, and towards poverty monitoring, networking and capacity building at the district level" (Gould and Ojanen 2005: 49). The authors provide examples of how poverty-reduction partnerships among citizens, states, donor agencies, and transnational private aid agencies implement poverty initiatives. Particularly revealing, such alliances seem to be increasing in number.

Contractualization of development aid in Namibia, as elsewhere, engages businesses, NGOs, government, and international organizations. This process is part of the 'new public management' and generates accountability through such devices as performance indicators, contracts, competition, and budgets (see Rose 2000: 150). It involves regulatory plans that are apparent in the increasing contracting out of public services to private companies or community organizations and in performance agreements between national governments and providers of public services and between international organizations, such as UN agencies, and NGOs or private businesses (see O'Connor and Ilcan 2005; Trudeau 2008; Walters and Haar 2005). UNESCO provides a good example of contractualization in its development aid for Namibia.

UNESCO set up its Cluster Windhoek Office in 1991[30] and works closely with other UN agencies to implement joint programs in support of the government's Development Plan and other national initiatives (UNESCO 2008a). It relies on contractual arrangements, auditing techniques, partnership frameworks, and global compacts linking businesses, local agencies, NGOs, and governments. In particular, it relies on contracts with its numerous partners, including local NGOs, to deliver development. In delivering its services, UNESCO thus directs NGOs' activities through contracts, targets, and performance measures within the 'new public management.'

One senior UNESCO policy adviser explains how the organization elicits contracts from NGOs in Namibia in language that draws on the terminology of private business and risk management:

> We have two kinds of contracts. An NGO agreement is a kind of contract where they may come with a proposal for doing a program. That's the program side of it. And, based on working out what they can offer and what type of support they need, we have that NGO agreement; to do that NGO agreement we have to go through the same process as we go through with government. Do they have the financial capacities, risk control, risk management? ... We have to do these kinds of checks [first], and then we can enter into an NGO agreement. Whereas a product-oriented contract is like any other contract. We put out a tender in the newspaper saying we need this kind of product done. Come and pick up the terms of reference, put in a proposal, put in a bid, then we engage in a comparative selection process sometimes with government partners that we are working with, sometimes directly if they say just get the contract and manage it yourself, but it is a normal bid process. We look at the capacity to deliver ... what they've done before, samples, work samples, as well as the cost dimensions. (Interview, Windhoek, 2008)

UNESCO's strategy of contractualization seems to address a range of actors such as NGOs and to reduce uncertainty under UNESCO's environment of risk reduction. These contracts thus make NGOs active participants in common programs of development aid and privatizing responsibility by governing the NGO sector through private-sector measures of risk, accountability, and comparative advantage. UNESCO does this through its development programs and such thematic working groups as those for gender, HIV/AIDS, and poverty alleviation. Furthermore, its contracts govern the type of development aid, which becomes manifest in negotiation, in a logic of contractual-ization that rests on what Dean calls "negotiated intersubjectivity" (1999: 168).

UNESCO's educational work in the terribly poor region of Ohangwena has involved not only the national government but also local NGOs offering educational training under contract with UNESCO. Through a Joint UN Inter-Agency/Regional Council Pilot Poverty Reduction Program in the region, UNESCO has brought its know-ledge expertise and development experts to some key areas in the project in order to direct the conduct of the poor. Along with bring-ing in NGOs, it has set up a multimedia centre with a community radio station and library and provided material for an educational/information program within school curricula and an outreach pro-gram for rural youth and women (UNESCO 2008b).

During the national launch of Global Education for All (EFA) Week (24–30 April 2005) in Opuwo, Dr Claudia Harvey, director and representative of the UNESCO Windhoek Cluster Office, told lo-cal residents about the relationship between education and poverty and its importance for societal participation: "Ladies and Gentlemen, education can be the road out of poverty. It is a catalyst for human development, providing people with the necessary skills and know-ledge that enable them to fully participate in society. With relevant and quality education, one can also become efficient and productive, contributing to a higher income prospect at the individual level as well as at the national level" (UNESCO 2008b). Support for this kind of development aid was available, Harvey indicated, from a plethora of international organizations and their affiliated partners.

Through its Poverty Reduction Program in Ohangwena, UNESCO aims to reform the conduct of particular kinds of institutions, such as education, and individuals, such as the poor. It believes that they have 'problems' with economic performance, although it would not so consider similar situations in the North. In this regard, and in line with Hindess (1998), governmental activities under advanced liberal agendas involve assessments of economic efficiency and rationales for making social and political change and for transforming con-duct. UNESCO's aid to education in Namibia involves this kind of governmental activity.

International development aid from the European Union, UNESCO, USAID, the World Bank, and other organizations reflect an advanced liberal emphasis on international technical assistance, loans, and education and development initiatives to expand global markets and reform industries to 'secure' Namibia's economy and its poor people. As such, these initiatives and the underlying rationales form part of the new global-aid regime now operative in Namibia. This regime not only frames development goals in terms of establishing conditions for successful participation in global markets but also encourages international organizations to engage in policy dialogue, consultation, and participation with each other and with recipients of development aid.

The rationality of aid palpably indicates the ways in which the knowledge of markets and industries can authorize measures of reform and transformation under the aegis of international organizations and their development plans. This rationality of aid parallels other contemporary governing rationalities. For example, the rationality of globalization, such as economic globalization, expresses the way in which knowledge of the economic sphere (which is considered to lie outside political institutions) can authorize governmental reforms and transform institutional patterns of organization (Dean 2007: 128).

As we see below, the practices of global aid rearrange and direct populations and groups and categorize the poor and their 'needs' in new ways. These practices foster the ability to order people, things, and populations, a defining feature of global governmentality as a form of power, and frame the poor through a 'new epoch' of poverty-reduction initiatives.

FRAMING THE POOR THROUGH A 'NEW EPOCH' OF POVERTY REDUCTION

A small but growing field of research in governmentality is examining the government of the international – of international organizations, actors, policies, agreements, and networks and its domain of influence.[31] Further research becomes ever more crucial as states around the world continue to outsource their functions to private and not-for-profit sectors. As well, biopolitical and authoritarian dimensions can, under certain circumstances, shape the government of the international when, for example, certain populations may seem unable to exercise responsible market choices. Specifically, we need more research into how international organizations, working with national and local actors, frame the poor through poverty reduction and sometimes compel them to act in certain ways. The analysis in this section connects questions of government to formation of the new global-aid regime in Namibia.

As a component of global governmentality, the new regime of global aid in Namibia is shaping our knowledge of the poor and drawing together the autonomous aims of private enterprise, NGOs, national government, and international development-aid organizations. A range of NGOs, governments, and international organizations (including the European Union, Oxfam Canada, the UNDP, UNESCO, UNICEF, USAID, and the World Bank) have implemented on their own and with partners policy and programmatic efforts. These collaborative efforts, which operate in part from afar, are forming new ways of thinking about the poor and offering new solutions to poverty in Namibia. Since independence, for example, some international development agencies have provided technical assistance and funds to the National Institute for Educational Development (NIED) and the Ministry of Education to help transform education, particularly curriculum. In policy development and curriculum design for teacher education, the Swedish International Development Authority (SIDA) has, for example, provided substantial assistance packages. International development-aid agencies continue to shape education reform, just as other organizations work to reduce poverty and influence the poor. Namibia is a 'middle-income country' keen to lessen poverty, in line with its Vision 2030 initiative.

Reducing poverty through human and economic development is at the core of Namibia's national agenda: economic growth, job creation, poverty reduction, and income equalization appear in numerous policy documents, government speeches, and media reports and remain central objectives of the National Development Plan. Vision 2030 (2007) (launched 2 June 2004) connects directly to the UN's Millennium Development Goals (MDGs) and to demands from international development organizations. Its goal is to "improve the quality of life of the people of Namibia to the level of their counterparts in the developed world by 2030," transforming the country into "a healthy and food-secure nation, in which all preventable, infectious and parasitic disease (including HIV/AIDS) [is] under secure control; people enjoy high standards of living, a good quality life and have access to quality education, health and other vital services. All of these aspirations translate into a long life expectancy and sustainable population growth." Planners believe that fulfilment of Vision 2030 requires improvements in education, science and technology, and health and development and changes to produce sustainable agriculture, peace and social justice, and gender equality (Vision 2030 2007).[32] Further, this plan anticipates Namibia's move from a developing, lower middle–income country to a developed, high-income nation by 2030 (Van Rooy et al. 2006).

From our perspective, Vision 2030 has millenarian propensities. In order for it to receive support and achieve a public presence, it needs to demonstrate that the current situation calls for transformation. Millenarian tendencies, as Dean notes, stress 'a new epoch' or moment of rupture (2007: 55). Those of Vision 2030 emerge through its ties to the Millennium Declaration by the Millennium Summit in New York in 2000, whose co-chair was Namibian President Sam Nujoma. The conclave recognized that UN member states, including Namibia, would strive to meet the eight MDGs. The first MDG is to "eradicate extreme poverty and hunger with the specific target of cutting in half between 1990 and 2015, the proportion of people whose income is less than one US dollar a day" (Van Rooy et al. 2006). The MDG framework strongly influences current development thinking about the planet. It identifies what kinds of knowledge and practices are necessary to make a better world, without extreme poverty, and imagines a new regime of collaboration, responsibilities, and networks to reach that goal. For example, in their work on developmentalities, calculative practices, and the MDGs, Ilcan and L. Phillips (2010) focus on the governmental discourses that enable new ways of shaping social and economic affairs in development, or the "developmentalities" of the MDGs. As a resulting form of governmentality, these developmentalities recast certain development problems, such as poverty, and offer new solutions. They suggest that three neoliberal rationalities of government – information profiling, responsibilization, and knowledge networks – and their calculative practices shape new capacities for individuals and social groups. Similar to the way in which this approach recognizes the complex and uncertain relations between developmentalities and the new millennium, our research with local organizations and NGOs in Namibia reveals critical problems about the MDG framework.

The MDG framework advances ideas about change, with diverse businesses, governments, and international organizations providing development aid. Our interviews with local agencies and NGOs in Namibia raised concerns about the framework. Many worries centred on the global appropriateness of the MDG goals and their lack of integration with nation-level practices. An active member of the NGO Namibia Development Trust explains: "For me it's a question of each country taking the MDGs at a national level and saying: what are the issues for us? In Namibia what are the more burning issues? I mean, for example, in Namibia, inequalities, social inequalities, economic justice, social economic justice ... the number of children that die before they reach the age of five ... are, for me, some issues that are within the current Millennium Development Goals that can still be highlighted; but by no means should the MDGs be seen as a complete package. There are other issues for Namibia that need attention" (interview, Windhoek, 2008).

Here, the MDGs seem inadequate vis-à-vis the problems of the poor in Namibia and elsewhere, even taking into account both unique and common experiences of poverty. This account reminds us of the individualized solutions to poverty, a rationality of governance central to advanced liberal solutions to poverty, such as the MDGs. Janine Brodie, calling for reform of social justice in neoliberal times, argues that "responsibility for social crises, which find their genesis in such macro processes as the globalization of production, geopolitical and environmental displacement, racism or unequal gender orders to name a few, is shifted onto the shoulders of individuals" (2007: 103). In this regard, the experience of poverty, social inequality, and injustice in Namibia is reflected back onto the individual through the MDGs rather than contextualized at local, regional, and international levels.

Aside from criticisms of the MDG framework, it receives support from many international bodies – the World Bank, for one. In Namibia it provides technical assistance to sustain the government's efforts vis-à-vis poverty and HIV/AIDS, the private sector, local capacity, and management of natural resources. It has recently set up a Financial Sector Assessment Program (FSAP), an Investment Climate Assessment (ICA), and a country economic report on poverty, inequality, economic constraints, and statistical capacity building (World Bank 2008d).[33] In May 2007, it approved its first loan to the government for a project in education and training. Its own advanced liberal initiatives in development aid, together with efforts by other international bodies, form part of the new global-aid regime in Namibia.

Poverty-reduction initiatives work alongside international organizations' attempts to govern poverty and the poor. Many people feel that in southern Africa land ownership is the most common form of

land, household, and community development. Britain's Ruben and
Elisabeth Rausing Trust (now the Sigrid Rausing Trust) is funding
efforts to help poor households in Namibia secure land tenure for
housing construction. Taking its cues from the Universal Declaration
of Human Rights, it aims to generate effective advocates, organizations, and movements to defend human rights, equality, and environmental justice. It channels funds through the Shack/Slum Dwellers
International (SDI), an international network of grassroots organizations aiding "low-income communities" (Mitlin 2003: 184).

According to Mitlin, the SDI's grassroots approach seeks to ensure
that the poor shape decisions that affect them, control their own
development, and manage professional interventions (2003: 189–
90). She finds the housing grant unique: its "funds can be used flex-
ibly, blending with community finance, existing local funds, and
available government subsidies" (181–2) in order to maximize benefits to the poor. Yet, and less apparent, the SDI initiative gives the
poor a kind of flexibility that is based on participation. It depends on
individuals' abililty to participate in land tenure and constitutes the
poor as self-reflexive participants of their own life plans and as accepting the resulting responsibility.

As with other advanced liberal schemes to challenge poverty,
which Dean calls "ethical projects" (2007: 63), the SDI initiative
encourages individuals to adjust their conduct and transform themselves with the help of experts, training, and services. Numerous organizations and agencies support such endeavours, which involve
national and international actors and partner organizations and
shape individuals' capacities so they can alter their conduct. Donors
and managers manage the poor at a distance.

Other assaults on poverty, however, operate differently and may
facilitate articulation of demands on political authorities and contestations against them. These initiatives can range from poor peoples'
demanding assistance to feed their families to others' protesting lack
of work. Such efforts can establish a new and agonistic territory for
the organization of conflicts concerning the poor. One is a controver-
sial income-subsidy program to reduce poverty in Namibia.

BEYOND 'ETHICAL PROJECTS': SECURING THE POOR THROUGH 'BIG'?

The Namibian Tax Consortium (NAMTAX) proposed tax reforms in
2001 to boost economic growth but came to realize that it could

reach only five to ten per cent of unemployed people. Recognizing the potential of government grants to stimulate economic growth, the consortium is now considering paying each citizen N$100 a month until he or she reaches pensionable age. This basic income grant (BIG) has perhaps the potential to secure the poor by lowering the 'regressive informal tax' on the poor and stimulating the economy by allowing citizens to create viable businesses and spend more on local goods and services. Although politicians have greeted it cautiously, it has garnered much public support (Haarmann and Haarmann 2007: 3–5).

According to Kameeta et al.: "The Basic Income Grant is more than an income support programme. It provides security that reinforces human dignity and empowerment. It has the capacity to be the most significant poverty-reducing programme in Namibia, while supporting household development, economic growth and job creation" (2007: 23). This initiative lists security as a distinct goal. Security can refer to protection and fulfilment of a full range of needs and rights (Harvey 2005: 43), and this usage is in keeping with our own broad and critical understanding of the concept. In the account above, however, security acts to collectivize the poor and their needs; here, it becomes a rationality of governance. The insecurity of potential BIG recipients, their poverty, and their basic needs are risks that are part of the new global-aid regime in Namibia. Dean would find such governance in keeping with the proliferation of both sovereign-centred and global-oriented security concerns and their solutions: "The concern for security has not disappeared in a 'networked' world; it has increased and multiplied" (2007: 58). Security, as in the account above, serves to govern the poor, and we explore this theme further in the case study of Solomon Islands in chapter 7.

One official at a participating NGO, a strong supporter of BIG and very active in Windhoek and area, describes early support for the initiative:

We had an international conference on income security with other NGOs, with other churches, with government. And, out of that the basic income grant correlation developed, and so the desk for Social Development currently hosts the secretariat of the basic income grant correlation. So we are doing the administrative work and kind of correlation together with the secretariat, which is hosted here. And the basic income grant correlation has become, so far, the biggest civil society movement after

Independence. [It] has united lobbying for one purpose of poverty innovation that includes the federation of the unions, NUNW,
and then the federation of the NGOs – NARCOV, the Council of
Churches Namibia … , the federation of the umbrella organization of the AIDS Services Organizations, and then individual organizations like the Legal Assistance Centre. (Interview,
Windhoek, 2008)

We asked this participant to explain what the grant could mean.

The basic income grant is to give people an economic platform
from where they can start to work, where they move out of
the struggle for daily survival, into the economic … So how it
would work, everybody, every Namibian citizen, would receive
first of all the one hundred Namibian dollars; but that needs to
be financed and those people who are better off would adjust
the taxation so that they first of all would pay back the one
hundred Namibian dollars … One hundred dollars per month,
which is quite little but it's meaningful in that for the poorest of
the poor it would double their income and that is especially so
because the poorer the people are, the larger their household
usually is. So if you have five people, it's five hundred dollars, if
it's ten people, it's one thousand dollars per month. (Interview,
Windhoek, 2008)

He added, "Everybody would get it up until pensionable age. In
Namibia we have a universal pension, so once you turn 60 you qualify
for the Old Age Pension (N$370 [per month]); so then your basic in-
come grant would be converted into the pension, [and] then you would
get the higher amount, but it would not be paid out on top of the pension." Such activist views are common among other NGOs in the area,
such as the Council of Churches (CCN), the Labour Resource and
Research Institute (LaRRI), the Namibian Network of AIDS Service
Organisations (Nananso), the Namibian NGO Forum (NANGOF), the
National Union of Namibian Workers (NUNW), and the National
Youth Council (NYC).

The think tank and NGO LaRRI was formed in 1998 to provide
policy research and training to the labour movement in areas such as
legislation, collective bargaining, gender equality, and affirmative action. It aims to establish and maintain a database on the economy

and wages, design and undertake education programs for trade unions, help the labour movement to develop policy proposals, provide a resource centre on socio-economic and political issues for trade unions, NGOs, and students, and offer a platform for discussions on labour and socio-economic issues, such as BIG (LaRRI 2008; interview, Windhoek, 2008).

LaRRI views BIG as offering some interim security for the poor. One member observes that it "would have immediate impact on poverty levels because it goes to every person." As well, "because you give it to everybody across the board, you recover it fairly easily from the better offs through increased taxes at the higher end. So there is a redistributed component and, given the household incomes in Namibia, it would have an immediate impact on the poorest households." It would allow some people to "get at least some food," permit children "to stay in school longer," and enable other people to gain "a bit of mobility to even look for jobs, whereas currently they would be completely stuck. So, in terms of potential benefits, it seems logical to introduce that."

Yet government officials disagree about BIG. According to one policy analyst, some ultimately "decided it was too expensive, they didn't want to raise taxes for the middle class and upper classes to the level that they basically fund the basic income grant for the poor" (interview, Windhoek, 2008). In the light of the divided views (see Figure 4.3), many supportive groups wanted to prove to the government that BIG would work. One NGO participant from LaRRI explained:

We went and looked for a place in Namibia that's relatively small, that has the poverty characteristics of Namibia and where we could implement it [BIG] for two years with an accompanying study to show exactly how people's lives changed, how they're living now, and how they will live. That starts in fact on Wednesday [in January 2008], we pay out for the first time. It's only Tara, east of the airport, where a lot of former farm workers, who were evicted or retrenched from farms, are living with family members, who have nowhere else to go, squatter areas essentially. So that's as poor as you can get. And we did, in October/November [2007], the assessment of how people are living now, spending a week there and documenting exactly that, the survival. And we go to the same fifty households again in half a year, and then in a year, in eighteen months, and twenty-four months to see over time how their life changed. If it does change, and we can conclusively prove that it was due to the basic income grant that they received, then I think we will publish it in such a way that the government will be very hard pressed. And strategically we want to do it just ahead of the next election. (Interview, Windhoek, 2008)

A researcher for another local NGO explains how exercises of poverty reduction such as BIG make sense in the broader context of poverty and racial segregation. "One has to realize that Namibia has one of the highest inequalities in the world. The UNDP even says it has the highest inequality in the world. And so you get extreme poverty alongside quite wealthy people, like you see in Windhoek. And this is very hard for people, and there's a very strong racial connotation [in that] the formerly disadvantaged are still making up the majority of the poor; there have been a few people who have moved up from there to the rich side, but there is still mass poverty. About 60 per cent of the people are below the poverty line, of one U.S. dollar per day; so that is quite substantial" (interview, Windhoek, 2008).

From our perspective, BIG, while involving so many participants, will do little to reduce poverty. The problem of poverty cannot be solved by short-term solutions that do not facilitate more general actions and practices. These solutions do not achieve much. As with other exercises of poverty reduction in Namibia and that derive from the new global-aid regime, it does not reduce general poverty in any major way. From our perspective, the regime of global aid creates new phases and tensions of development aid via poverty-reduction plans that govern the poor, enmesh them in new entrepreneurial obligations, and entangle them in local, national, and international market relations and partnerships. These tensions remind us of Gould's (2005b) "aid game," "caught up in a persistent tension between the virtuous rhetoric through which aid relations are legitimized, and the consistently disappointing quality of its outcomes for recipient economies"(140). In many ways, unfortunately, BIG creates these kinds of tensions and qualities.

For BIG to reduce poverty and improve the conditions of the poor, it would need to go hand in hand with dynamic plans and programs to demolish racial segregation and to stimulate equitable employment,

Figure 4.3 Basic income grant for Namibians now! Dudley, *Namibian*.

adequate access to safe water, housing, education, day care, and many other social amenities. Such endeavours should not be part of the new global-aid regime and should rather redistribute wealth and undermine a capitalist economy that breeds ineffaceable social and political divisions. Such changes would involve a social-justice life-politics that generates modes of action and practices that engender transformation and link to other forces above and below the level of everyday actors' control. Such a life-politics is much more about producing new frames of reference, new kinds of questions, and new ways of becoming.

CONCLUSION

In this chapter, the case study of Namibian development relations has emphasized the overlapping areas of advanced liberal forms of governance and international development aid in the form of poverty reduction. Through original interviews and field research, we have demonstrated how post-apartheid Namibia links to the new regime of global aid at local, national, and international levels. In examining how and under what conditions local, national, and international participants engage in development aid, the chapter first looks at colonial and apartheid relations of rule prior to independence. We argued that these ruling relations infused social and political relations, produced colonial and apartheid subjectivities, and gave rise to struggles for national independence. During the Namibian war of independence (1966–88), for example, international organizations and their development programs sought to introduce new ideas of social change and to transform conduct in particular ways in relation to certain objectives and on a global scale. Shortly after independence, international humanitarian interventions and development aid emerged in conjunction with the new global-aid regime.

With its links to an advanced liberal agenda, the new regime of global aid encourages a wide range of local, national, and international bodies to engage in policy dialogue and participation concerning the poor and poverty reduction. These bodies and their activities, we show, frame development goals in terms of engagement in markets, market initiatives and obligations, and self-responsibility schemes, or 'ethical projects.' Our analysis emphasizes how this regime fosters new relations and contractual arrangements among participants in North and South and shapes new ideas about the poor, lessening of poverty, and solutions to poverty on a global scale.

Despite the grandeur of its aims, the breadth of the international players – ranging from NGOs and governments to the World Bank and UN agencies – and the numerable spaces of poverty that the new regime targets, poverty has not significantly decreased in and beyond Namibia. Instead, it has merged into new kinds of relations and new understandings of poverty that are more about governing the poor in the manner of advanced liberalism than about providing for more equitable and socially just solutions to deal with their impoverishment. Consequently, we have argued that poverty-reduction plans, as a rationality of aid, demand complex forms of global co-ordination involving businesses, NGOs, governments, and international organizations to the further exclusion of marginal groups. We have advanced, as a counter-orientation, a view of transformation that involves a social-justice life-politics and that fosters other actions and practices and moves beyond individuals, groups, and organizations.

Drawing on some of the ideas that we developed in this chapter, chapter 5 reveals how colonial and apartheid practices shape the territory of Katutura in Windhoek. Through resettlement processes, including their racial biopolitical features, Katutura is increasingly the target of anti-poverty speeches and of national and international aid that forms part of the new global-aid regime. It is to this analysis that we now turn.

5 Mobilizing Katutura: 'A Place Where We Will Never Settle'

> The apartheid state apparatus operated as a machine that was both territorial and deterritorializing.
>
> Achille Mbembe, "Aesthetics of Superfluity" (2008: 49)

INTRODUCTION

Social and political segregation continues to shape Namibia's local environments. Governmental domains carve out predominantly white, wealthy urbanite groups and black and 'coloured' (mixed African and European ancestry) urban poor populations. Such ethnic divisions and identities are palpably evident in urban and rural landscapes, wherein three to four thousand whites occupy almost half of the country's farmland, and over one million blacks the other half. Local legal actors and activists consider blacks "impoverished and with little hope of making a living from that mostly degraded land" and are very much aware of colonial and apartheid relations of ruling that forced thousands of them "from the communal lands to expansive squatter and informal settlements on the edges of every city in the country" (Legal Action Centre 2006: 2).[1] It is Katutura, a former apartheid settlement in Windhoek, that is of concern in this chapter. It serves as the object and target of governmental action, biopolitics, and sovereign decisions and as a site where a diverse range of actors participate in the new global-aid regime.

In the light of Katutura's colonial and apartheid relations of ruling, and their biopolitical dimensions, this chapter first offers a brief genealogy of Katutura's spaces of government and the mobilization of its population to demonstrate how resettling practices overlie these relations. Rather than viewing Katutura as self-enclosed, we reveal some of the differences, continuities, and transformations that mobilize Katutura as a governable and governed terrritory. Such an orientation opens up detail, complexity, and specific arrangements, statements, and visibilities and thus exposes Katutura as a site for the exercise of power, which is always discursively mediated.

As we reveal, the domain of Katutura is an 'intelligible field' (Rose 2007), amenable to discussion, assessment, analysis, and deliberation. It is increasingly characterized by problems that link to and identify its poor populations. It is also the target of anti-poverty and pro-poor government speeches and of local, national, and international development assistance from the new global-aid regime. In this analysis, we draw on reports from NGOs, government policy initiatives, information from local media, scholarly documents, and our research interviews and visits to schools, organizations, and NGOs in Katutura during one of our field research trips in 2008. We hope that the analysis will offer insights into the distinct lines of governmental change and global aid that form and travel through the territory of Katutura.

LARGE-SCALE MOVEMENTS AND RACIALIZED BIOPOLITICS

Each kind of uncertainty gains increasing force whenever there are large-scale movements of persons (for whatever reason), when new rewards or risks attach to large-scale ethnic identities, or when existing networks of social knowledge are eroded by rumor, terror, or social movement.

                                     Arjun Appadurai, *Fear of Small Numbers* (2006)

Like other apartheid-era townships such as Soweto in Johannesburg and Khayelitsha in Cape Town, Katutura emerged initially through intersecting colonial and apartheid relations of ruling. These relations shaped conduct in terms of a racialized biopolitics, which made many distinctions among races and invoked a hierarchy of races (Foucault 2003b: 255). This shaping controlled certain bodies of populations and ruled their movements, the ways of caring for them, and their experiences of life and death. It relates not only to what it means to be a particular kind of living species in a living world, but also to the promotion and directing of these living species. Biopolitical relations render a concern with "powers of the fostering of life and letting die" (Dean 2007: 92–3), a politics of life and death that Foucault identified as underscoring diverse political processes, such as those of state racism, war, genocide, and the Holocaust – "the right to take life or let live," he called it (2003b: 240–1). The analysis below examines these kinds of relations of ruling, or assemblages of rule. It focuses on the processes of racialized biopolitics that led to the making of Katutura during early-twentieth-century colonial rule and then later under the South African apartheid state.[2]

Windhoek's black township emerged in 1912 as the Main Location, later the Old Location, when the city moved its black populations from site to site and dominated them in exercises of racial discrimination. Its formation and development were in part the result of segregationist policies, which the German colonialists promoted and which demanded separate residential areas for blacks (Frayne and Pendleton 2001). These policies and practices formed part of the lethal amplification of the racialized biopolitics that came to characterize many life processes in the country and specifically in Old Location, which exemplified, as Dillon and Reid (2009: 49) might assert, a well-developed discursive, cultural, and political practice in many parts of the world. By the end of German colonial rule in 1915, Old Location was well established. From this time until independence, South Africa administered it as part of Windhoek. The relationship between apartheid rule and Location is of particular interest here, enfolding critical dynamics of racialized biopolitics.

Racial segregation began to intensify in Namibia with the National Party's victory in South Africa in 1948. A much more extensive politics of life and death emerged through apartheid rule, which assembled political and economic forms of power in the hands of the white minority. The ties between Namibia and South Africa tightened through social and economic relations of apartheid. Many white South Africans started moving to Namibia, and commercial farming came to constitute about 40 per cent of the land there.[3] All major paved roads, railway lines, and airline routes in Namibia led to South Africa (Frayne and Pendleton 2001: 207).

By the early 1950s relentless racial classification was clearly implicating the human sciences in the operation of an authoritarian governing regime. In 1950, South Africa passed the Population Registration Act and the Group Areas Act, which required strict classification of people by racial group to determine where they could live and work. Also, the Land Acts in 1954 and 1955 led to forcible and often violent removal of blacks from 'black spots,' or black residential areas, which the apartheid state considered too close to white settlements.

Racial classifications came to characterize political and cultural domains. Bowker and Star identify the four main groups: "Europeans,
Asiatics, persons of mixed race or coloureds, and 'natives' or 'pure-
blooded individuals of the Bantu race'" (2000: 197), which classification enabled "the bureaucratic underpinnings for a vicious racism"
(195). They mention other realms that became part of apartheid
laws – "political rights, voting, freedom of movement and settlement, property rights, right to choose the nature of one's work, education, criminal law, social rights including the right to drink alcohol,
use of public services including transportation, social security, taxation, and immigration ... The brutal cruelty, of which these laws
were the scaffolding, continued for more than four decades. Millions
of people were dislocated, jailed, murdered, and exiled" (197).

With Namibia under apartheid rule, racial classifications and
apartheid laws controlled populations through brutal application,
which involved a power capable of delegation, or what Dean (2007:
92) calls a "delegation of sovereignty."[4] The targeting of 'nonwhiteness' permeated Windhoek; as the city began to grow, the government established districts within it primarily for whites. Like South
Africa, Namibia came to have industrialized white areas and rural
black areas, and the poorest and most marginal city residents had to
live separate from white residents in areas of which the latter thought
poorly. Police rigidly enforced this spatial divide (Friedman 2000: 3).
Nadesan reminds us how various societies have targeted populations for their nonwhiteness and made them subject to sovereign
decisions regarding their exceptionality, such as the incarceration of
Japanese Americans during the Second World War and the more recent practice of incarcerating huge numbers of African-American
juvenile offenders (2008: 187).

One of the governing strategies of apartheid was forced homogenization of ethnically and culturally distinct groups, which the
Nationalists called 'separate development' (see Bowker and Star
2000: 197). Their rationalizations promoted a racialized biopolitics.
According to F. Friedman:

Separate development was justified on the grounds that indigenous traditions had to be preserved. The ideology was fostered by
the view that African peoples had 'traditionally' lived in isolated
and bounded communities. The colonialists argued that black
people would feel most comfortable, and be most able to develop

according to their 'nature', among their own ethnic group. Under the policy, all Namibian black and coloured people, classified into ten subdivisions based on race and ethnicity, were forced into 'homelands.' These homelands were marginal with regard to size and any natural resources base, and hence unable to sustain [their] populations ... They did, however, ensure a steady supply of cheap labour to the cities as a way to meet the economic needs of the white minority. (2000: 3)

'Homelands' were remote rural areas that the state created as part of separate development; however, they included both rural and urban areas and were the official places of belonging for blacks. According to F. Friedman (2000), Namibian cities were a "white domain," and "black people were tolerated in the city in order to sell their cheap labour" (3). Here, the racialized biopolitics shaping homelands controls a population and its individuals in order, as Ong might say, to "harness and extract life forces" (2006b: 12).

During the years of racial segregation, the government stripped vulnerable and poor people of their potential citizenship rights in South Africa or South West Africa: it treated them as temporary urban residents, denied them the right to own city property, and forced them to surrender aspects of their mobility. These are states and sites of 'inexistence' that Isin and Rygiel (2007) refer to as "abject spaces," where displaced and distressed people are outsiders and lack citizenship (the rights of becoming political) (181). Even the allocation of housing, which the state owned and operated, depended on possession of employment permits, which allowed blacks legal residence in the city (F. Friedman 2000: 13). Windhoek's city administration continued to use a language of whiteness and nonwhiteness and new strategies of racialized biopolitics that would assemble a black township further from the city centre. These strategies resemble the ways in which Nazi Germany regularly mobilized and reawakened anti-semitism, as Appadurai (2006: 54) asserts, through powerful campaigns of racial and political propaganda that portrayed Jews as non- and anti-German.

Racialized biopolitics took many forms and ranged from management of towns, cities, and particular human bodies to attempts to administer the life-worlds of certain populations. Apartheid rule subjected 'nonwhites' in Windhoek and elsewhere to removal at any time by the state. With expansion of the city, white developments moved westward until they were close to Location – a 'dangerous' situation for the colonialists and apartheid supporters. While seeming to threaten "one's place in the world," as Bauman (2006: 3) might claim, such 'danger' can link to colonial rationalities of power (including the targets, sources, fields of operation) that involve governing people without any concern for their well-being (see Scott 2005: 5). But the discourse on dangerousness narrated a relationship between life and politics wherein the state controlled the biological existence of specific human beings, or a racialized biopolitics. Crucial to our analysis are the social and historical dimensions surrounding Katutura as a governmental site and border zone. We consider this zone as one that exemplifies the 'friction' of mobile bodies and ethnic violence.

THE FRICTION OF MOBILE BODIES

The apartheid transcription of race took various discursive forms, most insidiously the medicobiological.

Achille Mbembe, "Aesthetics of Superfluity" (2008: 46)

The apartheid state used various colonial and apartheid governing rationalities to instigate Windhoek to resettle Location residents and accommodate and enlarge white neighbourhoods. By the early 1950s, the city centre had expanded to be close to Location. According to the official explanation, Location was a health hazard, and a new residential area northwest of the city, Katutura, would offer more "hygienic" living conditions (Pendleton 1996). Such racialized biopolitical ideas stimulated concerns about the care of healthy bodies and invigorated the relationship between the health of certain populations and apartheid practices, as in South Africa.

In his compelling analysis, Mbembe argues that the apartheid transcription of race invoked the "medicobiological." It borrowed its discourse, he argues, from a materialist anatamophysiology that ascribed to blacks a racial disposition to disease. Consequently, and under apartheid, concerns about the health of whites led to health acts that forced thousands of blacks out of Johannesburg (Mbembe 2008: 46). It is this kind of politics that links biopolitics and sovereign decisions. Dean (2007: 94), for example, notes that the biopolitical powers of the medical care of life can also involve sovereign decisions about its termination or continuation.[5] After all, biopolitics, especially its forms of reasoning, techniques, and power, involves the administrative imperative to "optimize" the health and life of populations (Dean 2010: 30; Weir 2006: 5).

While apartheid discourses on health sought to invent mechanisms for governing certain territories and their black residents, they did generate challenges. The residents of Location would feel and respond to the effects of injustice on their bodies, on their spaces, and on their lives, a kind of 'friction' (Tsing 2005) that enfolds authoritarian ruling relations and their practices of injustice and can inhibit universal colonial and apartheid reasoning. For example, residents questioned their living conditions and demanded to know why they could not expect improvement if concerns for their wellbeing drove large-scale plans to move them. Location was a site for shared memories, biographies, and histories, and residents knew that Katutura meant unjust enforcement of apartheid legislation and compulsory relocation. There would soon be a five-kilometre border zone between Katutura and the city centre, leading to more expensive commuting to work and, as Pendleton (1996: 29) stresses, vastly higher housing rents in Katutura. The move meant higher living costs and violent appropriation of their former homes.

By the mid-1950s, Windhoek, under direction from the South West African administration and apartheid state, decided on relocation (Pendleton 1996). Friction between the city and Location residents was escalating by the late 1950s. One contentious issue involved 'tombo,' a beer that residents traditionally brewed and that generated income for women. Until 1967, beer was the only alcoholic beverage that blacks could legally consume (Pendleton 1996: 73). However, the city restricted sale of beer in municipal beer houses, and women contested. In September 1959, women staged a protest march, but the police responded with tear gas. In December, when officials were evaluating houses for compensation, women continued their resistance, and over a thousand of them particpated in another march. Finally, they decided to boycott municipal services, including buses and beer houses (Vantaa City Museum 2008). The Herero word 'Katutura' means "a place where we will never settle."

On the world stage, in 1959 the Committee on South West Africa reporting to the United Nations General Assembly condemned apartheid rule and compulsory relocation. Its report highlighted highly disturbing developments in the territory: the regime's emphasis on reinvigorating "White" supremacy, its planning mass removals of "Native" inhabitants, and its preparing to "secure the eventual annexation of the Territory." The same document cited new defence and security measures, infringements of freedom of the press, and intrusions on freedom of religion (UN 1959: 320).

By late 1959, resistance to relocation had gained support from the Ovamboland People's Organization (OPO),[6] the South West Africa People's Union (SWANU), women's groups, and the Herero Chiefs' Council (Vigne 1987). While many resistance efforts ensued and met with much official brutality, one particular event of 'ethnicized violence' – Appadurai's (2006) phrase – erupted and spread into other events and practices. This distinctive and unrepeatable configuration of things and processes would exercise extensive, uncontainable effects on existing relations and arrangements, à la Grosz (2005: 159) – "always specific, historically particular emergencies" that do not form systems or cohere to patterns but induce intensities.[7]

On 10 December 1959,[8] residents were challenging relocation when the police opened fire on demonstrators. According to Foucault, violence acts "immediately and directly on others," while a relationship of power "acts upon their actions" (1978: 93). According to historical accounts by the National Archives of Namibia:

Local residents could see police near the local beer house and, curious, people began to gather. Pushing and shoving ensued when one of the women wanted to buy beer, under boycott at the time. When the police intervened, some people began throwing stones. According to witness statements, police responded by firing randomly. The unarmed residents were taken completely by surprise. It is now known that ammunition had been stockpiled some days earlier and that police were prepared for the assault.

Thirteen people were killed in the shooting, with a further 43 wounded. It led to a mass exodus from Location. Some left Windhoek altogether, while others sought shelter in churches or with friends and relatives. Most of those who died were buried in a mass grave. (National Archives of Namibia, in Vantaa City Museum, 9 July 2008)

The Committee on South West Africa reported in a similar fashion to the United Nations General Assembly and "deplored the police action in the Windhoek Location and urged the Mandatory Power to desist from the further use of force and not to proceed further with the enforced removal of Location residents to the new site." On 21 December 1959, the committee approved a resolution for the General Assembly expressing profound concern over these events (UN 1959: 325–6). In another report, it disclosed that blacks were being "deported from Windhoek," "dismissed from employment," and "intimidated by other means" as a way to enforce relocation (UN 1960: 488).

Authoritarian and biopolitical forms of power characterized the colonial territory of Location and fostered decisions on appropriate behaviour. These 'sovereign decisions' involve, according to Dean, "not merely a matter of letting die but a form of killing without the commission of homicide" (2007: 93). Their effects ranged from violence to death to resistance, and the event itself served as a catalyst for the OPO's transformation into SWAPO and its leaders' flight into exile in Tanzania in 1960 (McConnell 2000: 32).[9]

These authoritarian acts and decisions reverberated and led to transformations that interpenetrated new orderings and the intermingling of acts, bodies, and statements. By the end of 1959, the apartheid state forced many Location residents to move to Katutura, and its racialized biopolitics would continue to fragment and subdivide these populations under its control for years to come. The inhabitants, including Damara, Herero, Nama, and Owambo people, not only experienced the often-violent seizure of their land and property but also became separated from each other and had to live in ethnic quarters. The state operated as a "deterritorializing machine" – Mbembe's (2008: 50) label – appropriating land, disassembling territorial lineages, and forming new replicated enclaves, such as Katutura.[10]

Petitioners from Namibia, including those from SWAPO, who appeared before the United Nations' Fourth Committee in 1968 noted that "in defiance of United Nations resolutions, the Government of South Africa had continued to govern Namibia, by force, for the benefit of the European settlers and certain foreign economic interests in the territory. It had taken steps towards the creation of so-called 'homelands' in Namibia and the integration of the territory into South Africa, and had carried out the scheme for the forcible removal of the Africans from the Old Location in Windhoek to the newly built Katutura location" (UN 1968: 788). Furthermore, at about the same time, South Africa set up military bases in Namibia and took other actions involving various themes on racism (UN 1965: 595). The United Nations Council for Namibia[11] submitted one of several reports to the General Assembly demanding immediate change. One document declared that South Africa "had continued to refuse to comply with the demand that it withdraw from Namibia, unconditionally and without delay, all its military and police forces and its administration" and observed that it had sought "to consolidate its illegal control over the territory. The most serious step in this direction had been the implementation of the decision to create separate 'homelands' designed to destroy the territorial integrity of the territory and to facilitate its illegal annexation" (UN 1968: 781–2).

The United Nations Council for Namibia recommended that the General Assembly request the Security Council to act against South Africa and aid Namibia. It called for the occupiers to withdraw from the territory, for "all States to pursue all diplomatic, consular, commercial or other relations" vis-à-vis Namibia exclusively with the council, and for all transactions with South Africa in regard to Namibia since termination of the mandate in 1966 to be illegal. It also appealed for a provision in the UN budget for the council to assist Namibia via "establishment of a separate education and training programme for Namibians; an emergency aid programme in co-operation with the specialized agencies; the issuance of travel documents; and meetings with representatives of the Namibian people" (UN 1968: 781–2). While the General Assembly responded seriously, the apartheid state was persisting with its acts of violence and transformation.

Just prior to closure of Location in 1968, appeals from the General Assembly, the council for Namibia, and other organizations and groups continued. For example, on 20 December 1966 the General Assembly considered a statement from Reverend Michael Scott: "On 30 November 1966 the South African Minister of Bantu Administration and Development had announced the Government's decision to close the old Native location at Windhoek and, from a date to be fixed, to make it illegal to live in the old location or to hire anyone living there. Residents were to move to a new Windhoek location, Katutura" (UN 1966: 603). As far back as 1959, Scott recalled, opposition to establishment of Katutura had led to conflicts that killed

11 blacks and injured many others, and he noted that the first arrests in South West Africa of black political leaders (under the Suppression of Communism Act) had just occurred. He considered the current situation "explosive" (603).[12]

At the close of Location, the apartheid state assembled the Windhoek Urban Area into three townships: Windhoek for whites, Khomasdal for coloureds, and Katutura for blacks. Colonial and apartheid rule not only created the outer city, Katutura, but also governed the conduct of its residents by circumscribing how they would live and die and under what conditions. It produced Katutura, which contained about four thousand rental houses by 1968 (Pendleton 1996: 40), to govern urban blacks more effectively and relentlessly. In other words, it made them into abject citizens as they became invisible and were transferred to the outer city.

The poverty and brutality that frequently accompanied development of apartheid townships derived not merely from the inhabitants' 'minority' status but from difference itself (see Appadurai 2006: 11). The state used their difference as a reason for their governance and for colonial and apartheid technologies of 'security' to shape both their lives and Katutura. Katutura became a security zone through governing efforts that involved "enforced isolation, avoidance of ordinary foreseen inspections and controls, and politics of non-transparency," efforts that Basaran (2008: 350) analyses in his study of the embedding of illiberal practices of border zones in the everyday practices of liberal states. The state controlled residents according to authoritarian rule, and its practices echo the modes of authoritarian liberal governance that other states employ vis-à-vis indigenous communities in Guatemala and Mexico, Sierra Leone, Solomon Islands, and Australia and Canada. We recognize too that the rationalities and technologies of such authoritarian liberal governance in Katutura are not as distant from liberalism as liberals might claim.

Pendleton (1996) analyses the township's administration by the most rigid machinery of the apartheid era in South Africa or South West Africa and how it later displayed new forms of ethnic division and conflict. As we show below, Katutura is a site not just of state intervention but also of development aid from businesses, NGOs, and international organizations. These efforts are reshaping the elements and relations of Katutura and thus resettling the field of Katutura.[13]

RESETTLING KATUTURA FOR GLOBAL AID

Once in Katutura, our guide drives through the oldest suburb in the old location. We also take a short drive to the single quarters, one of the poorest areas of Windhoek. Along the way the local people sell traditional food called kapana and a traditional drink which is called Tombo. At the Soweto market you will be able to see traditional hairdressers and tailors, and the impressive open air butchery. Then to Babylon which is a low to zero income area offering an overview of a typical shanty town.

Finally we visit Penduka Woman's project where there is the opportunity to purchase some local arts and crafts and a nice relaxing view of the Goreangab Dam.

Namibia Travel (2008)[14]

Windhoek is an assemblage – à la Deleuze and Guatarri (1987: 504–5) – of intermingling built environments, memories, historical struggles, and practices. The putting together of certain ideas, forms of knowledge, and types of practices forged its territory. And like every place, it is not preset for all time but is rather being constantly made (reterritorialized) and unmade (deterritorialized).

As Namibia's largest city (population 250,000), Windhoek houses close to one-half of the country's city dwellers, and the majority of blacks there still live in spatially segregated areas. The best educational facilities (including the University of Namibia) and the finest health-care, recreational, and social facilities (health clubs, hotels and guest houses, the movie theatre, the municipal swimming pool, the national library, the national theatre, parks, private hospitals and clinics, pubs, and restaurants and cafes) are either in the city centre or near the former white residential areas.[15] Also, most large-scale commercial facilities (department stores, malls, and supermarkets) and the international organizations so prominent in the new global-aid regime (symbolized by the new United Nations House, which offers a plethora of development-aid programs) are in the city centre. In the central business district, most shopkeepers speak German, which is still common in Namibia, even though English is the official language. In fact, Windhoek is home to Africa's only German-language radio station and daily newspaper and to other facilities and services (churches, clubs, and schools) that support the 'German' cityscape (Owens 2008: 235). However, these fine central facilities and services remain beyond the economic reach of most Katutura residents.

Katutura lies four kilometres northwest of the centre of Windhoek, home to more than half of the city's people (more than 150,000). This former apartheid township exposes colonial and apartheid forms of power and their intermingling with contemporary apparatuses of governmentality. Among other features, it is spatially separate from all other city neighbourhoods. There is only one road to enter and leave Katutura, and in times of political unrest police and military forces can block it with tanks and control it (F. Friedman 2000: 6). A Katutura resident, Eixab, comments: "The road layout within Katutura is linear and there are main roads located around the perimeter of the settlement. For this reason, the military is able to encircle the settlement. Now they have installed these huge lights in every part of Katutura, like flood lights in a football stadium. These lights are so strong that there is no night in Katutura" (in F. Friedman 2000: 6). Katutura has over fifty communities, and most residents are black or 'coloured.' Even some of its streets are named after former German foreign minister Hans-Dietrich Genscher or Ewa Schumacher, wife of a former German ambassador to Namibia.

A coalition of development-aid and educational NGOs, community programs, 'ethical projects,' and churches has attempted to transform this township. Parts of the terrain convey the historical influence of colonial missionaries. For example, the Finnish Evangelical Lutheran Mission (FELM) worked there to shape the religious conduct of the poor. As an international partner of the Evangelical Lutheran Church in Namibia (ELCIN),[16] FELM has had a noteworthy presence in the north since the late nineteenth century. Since massive migration to urban centres after independence in 1990, the church has since expanded into new areas, such as Katutura, where it teaches church music, family guidance, financial management, and moral education, which often involves techniques of self-government and self-responsibility.

Currently, ELCIN, through support from the FELM, trains nursery school teachers, sponsors children's education, and operates three nursery schools in Katutura, which accommodate 100 to 150 children (FELM 2008). In Namibia and elsewhere in Africa, international and transnational Christian organizations, such as Campus Crusade, the Church of Jesus Christ of Latterday Saints (Mormons), FELM, Promise Keepers, the Salvation Army, and World Vision

Figure 5.1 A Katutura shantytown. Authors' photo.

International help shape and organize local events and services and build and operate schools where states have failed to provide or maintain them (see Ferguson 2006: 102; see also Bornstein 2003). For example, 240 FELM missionaries carry out and advance a conventional governmentality that aims to shape the conduct of the poor by emphasizing the proclamation of the Gospel and Christian service, and related practices, in more than twenty countries in Africa, Asia, Europe, and Latin America (FELM 2008).

In Katutura, thousands of people live in informal settlements in the north of Namibia, such as Babylon, Kilimanjaro, and Okahandje Park. This immense area receives a continually increasing number of migrants from the rural north looking for a better life. On arrival in Katutura, however, they face very few job options and have little access to education, housing, medical care, and transportation. In these and other areas of Katutura (see Figure 5.1), poverty is widespread, as are high rates of HIV/AIDS and unemployment,[17] and many people, groups, and advocacy organizations in and outside of Katutura work to overcome the alarming social injustice.

Overwhelmingly, Katutura has deplorable living conditions, with shortages of clean and safe drinking water, safe and adequate facilities for human waste, electricity, and health and education. The many shebeens (informal taverns joined to a house) bear big Coca-Cola signs (see Figure 5.2), and small tin-roof homes (see Figure 5.3) accommodate several family members.

Figure 5.2 A shebeen in Katutura. Authors' photo.

Figure 5.3 A home in Katutura. Authors' photo.

The life-worlds of Katuturans permeate the numerous small-scale commercial activities on the streets, including trading, sex work, and liquor and drug exchanges. These activities coexist alongside repair, construction, taxi, and restaurant businesses, United Nations Plaza, and the markets, including the Soweto Market, with its stalls for food, spices, clothing, and tailor and hair-styling services and its open-air meat butchery. Less visible are memories of historical resistance to apartheid, such as the roughly 5,000 schoolchildren who marched on 4 May 1988 to commemorate the massacre by South Africa at Kassinga, the largest Namibian refugee camp in Angola, on the same day ten years earlier. "Apartheid police using tear-gas, rubber bullets and truncheons" attacked the youngsters, killing and injuring many (UN 1988: 764). Furthermore, there are numerous small buildings throughout Katutura that accommodate local kindergartens and primary and secondary schools, as well as half-built church structures, the dilapidated hospital (a historic site of the struggle for national liberation), the Katutura Community Arts Centre (KCAC), the Katutura Community Hall, and SWAPO headquarters.

On 30 May 2008, at the Katutura Community Hall, a highly charged and emotional event reflected what Grosz (2005: 159) would view as the "affective impingements of an outside, of forces on living subjects." It marked the centennial of the release of Namibians from German concentration camps, such as those set up in 1904–5 in Windhoek, in Karibib, Lüderitz, and Okahandja, and in the coastal town of Swakopmund. Hundreds of people congregated with traditional, political, and church leaders to commemorate the genocide that took place between 1904 and 1908. The event also recalled the emergence of other massive problems, including poverty, unemployment, and landlessness.[18] The struggle to survive in the 'camp' of Katutura – to survive displacement, poverty, underemployment, and much more – is an endemic problem of this ambiguous zone. As an NGO member from Sister Namibia told us,[19] the shared communication of such struggles occurs through social and political channels, including Katutura Community Radio (KCR), which Sister Namibia and other NGOs currently support.

Local NGOs, using funds from international organizations such as UNESCO, opened the radio station in 1995 in response to the appalling living conditions, white control, and social and political inequalities.[20] This station provided a platform for participatory communication, education, and advocacy, allowed residents of Katutura and nearby

Khomasdal to speak on their own terms, and became a vehicle for
socio-economic justice. The NGOs, however, gradually disengaged
themselves, and the station closed in 2006, but it reopened in 2008.
Four NGOs – the Desert Research Foundation of Namibia, the Legal
Assistance Centre, the Namibian Planned Parenthood Association
(NAPPA), and Sister Namibia – along with students from the College
of the Arts, now produce programs on local social and economic
life.

AN INTELLIGIBLE FIELD, A GOVERNABLE TERRITORY

Discursive and programmatic initiatives foster other kinds of meaning to the territory of Katutura, and they become, as Edkins argues,
"socially embedded and institutionalized in their interactions with
other social practices" (2000: 68). They work across and through its
multiple relations and infuse its government as an economy that harbours relations of bodies, of community and partnership, of participation, and of self-governance. The government of an 'economy,'
Rose contends, "becomes possible only through discursive mechanisms that represent the domain to be governed as an intelligible field
with its limits, characteristics whose component parts are linked
together in some more or less systematic manner" (2007: 33).

Katutura is a collection of heterogeneous elements (of bodies, acts,
and statements) that come together and move apart. It has become a
new intelligible field amenable to discussion, assessment, analysis, and
deliberation and to its always-emerging conditions of the present. It
is, among other things, a site of the new global-aid regime: its residents enter into relations with national and international aid programs that attempt to establish new ways of seeing and thinking
about the future, new ways of arranging and organizing lives and
ways of life, and new forms of interchange that involve contacts and
partnerships with local organizations, NGOs, and the private sector.
Katutura is increasingly the target of national and international programs that range from education and health plans to large-scale development aid that governs the poor. A diverse range of political
authorities targets the territory for its ensuing problems.

Projects that aim to govern relations in Katutura often involve associations between political authorities and the local poor. As a governable territory, Katutura receives much public attention on poverty
and how best to 'assist' the poor living in the area. State officials, for

example, implement relations of power through plans of national development that target the local poor and demand action from them. In these relations, governmental actors increasingly view residents in terms of their potential levels of enterprise, resourcefulness, skill, and flexibility. These diverse outlooks and plans tend to support a temporality that focuses on a future that is unachievable and unfamiliar – that, as Grosz (2005: 2) argues, overwrites and redirects the present in an indeterminacy that also inhabits and transforms an understanding of the privilege of the present.

During a recent visit to Katutura, Regional and Local Government, Housing and Rural Development Minister John Pandeni stated: "The time is long overdue for Namibians to stop sitting around and just wait for handouts from government, but they should actively become involved in development by helping themselves out of poverty and unemployment." This 'blaming the poor' statement emphasizes the state's poverty-reduction plans and its authority in advising the poor and in urging them to transform their impoverishment. It can remind us too of the increasing blurring between liberal and authoritarian modes of rule (Dean 2007), both of which govern populations 'at risk' – who cannot 'look after themselves' – as though they are incapable of autonomy. Furthermore, the minister was in Katutura's Goreangab informal settlement, opening the brick-making initiative of the Shack Dwellers Federation of Namibia (SDFN) (Africa News Update 2007) – its partnership with the Standard Bank of Namibia to construct low-cost houses in Katutura.[21]

It is through such efforts to influence the poor that a state represents itself as an entity that sits above and contains its localities, regions, and communities – Ferguson and Gupta's (2005: 106) "spatialization of the state." Such official statements present the poor not in social terms but as enterprising and economic actors who can cure their own dilemmas. The emphasis on their enterprise resembles findings in studies that reveal unemployment, as Walters (2000) stresses, as a site of government and the jobless as requiring skills and flexibility that will earn them work in a reimagined and competitive economy.

Through associations between authorities and the poor, governmental relations display optimism about the region's future. In highlighting the role of the poor in Vision 2030, Pandeni emphasized: "We would like to call upon all the people of our country, particularly the rural and urban poor, to participate in their own development because it is only through hard work that we will achieve our national Vision 2030. Don't sit back, work hard" (Africa News Update 2007). Such official pronouncements frame the poor as responsible for their own poverty and for finding remedies. They represent an advanced liberal responsibilizing ethos that encourages groups to pursue their own choices or goals. In Namibia and elsewhere, such processes often have links with decentralization, marketization, and development – for example, poverty-reduction strategies, 'good governance' programs,[22] and national development plans, such as Vision 2030.

International bodies providing development aid and their experts look for a niche in Katutura's economy from which to improve and adjust its residents. Katutura is the target of such initiatives as the numerous plans and programs of UN agencies, USAID, and other bodies. For example, USAID and the Namibian Institute of Democracy support a program that operates 'at a distance' through expert advice and 'optimizes' poor children through exercise. The new 'life skills through sport' biopolitical project started in 2003 through the Katutura Youth Enterprise Centre (KAYEC). A life-skills and sports officer may spend several mornings a week teaching cricket to children in grade seven (USAID Namibia 2008b).

Political and other authorities in Katutura are advising the poor to take responsibility for their own security and their families' in such matters as employment and health. Such discourses often promote investment in future behaviour and ways of life that emphasize individual rather than collective or state responsibility (Isin 2000: 155), and that order people's lives by rendering their reality in an assessable or calculable form (Nadesan 2008: 129; Rose 1999). There are many risk discourses infusing the territory of Katutura, perhaps most notably the International Day for Natural Disaster Reduction (8 October), which the UN launched in 1989 to focus on disaster prevention, mitigation, and preparedness.

A message from the UN secretary general on 8 October 2007 in effect presented Katutura as an intelligible field that comprised poor individuals in need of new kinds of knowledge and educational training. He announced "a disaster risk reduction learning session with a Grade 4 class and [plans to] initiate a painting competition for the students on natural disaster reduction." He also mentioned a commemoration ceremony and prize distribution for the same school (International Strategy for Disaster Reduction 2007). Such programs require particular knowledge to make risk thinkable, such as statistics, management, and accounting, which form part of the broader "audit culture" (Strathern 2000). The language of educational development therein embodies expert knowledge and stresses management of uncertainty, risk, and insecurity. Such new forms of training aim to govern the poor as active agents of decision and choice as they participate in risk-reduction programs, which create new subjects in 'high risk' environments. They can also turn territories such as Katutura into calculable space for new private–public partnerships, institutional demands, and campaigns for change, and they can, as Duffield (2001b: 314) suggests, guide policy.

The focus on risk reduction is part of a broader UN campaign that declares "Disaster Risk Reduction Begins at School." The campaign aims to mobilize individuals, communities, and governments to ensure that the subject "is fully integrated into school curricula in high risk countries" and that school buildings be able to withstand natural hazards (UNISDR 2008). The risk-reduction campaign has links to the UN Decade for Education and Sustainable Development (DESD) (2005–14) and to efforts by business, NGOs, and governments to achieve the Millennium Development Goals. Partners include ActionAid International, UNESCO, UNICEF, and the United Nations International Strategy for Disaster Reduction (UNISDR) (UNISDR 2008).

Training in risk reduction represents part of national and international attempts to assist people at risk and in need of aid and to institute surveillance, as Nadesan (2008) and Rose (2007) show in the context of risk management.[23] In Katutura, for example, control of ways of life forms part of an unyielding emphasis on risk management. One can recognize ways in which risk is managed in certain zones and forms of conduct, such as when security vehicles observe the road into Katutura, security guards or cameras scan certain buildings or districts, and some school classes learn about risk through, for example, the drinking habits of young girls or the dietary habits of poor children in school settings. These arrangements, which 're-responsiblize' the individual to manage personal risk, produce, according to Rose (1996), a field of uncertainty that opens the way to new problems and new solutions.

Initiatives in development aid look for a productive venue in Katutura for linking the poor to the market. The Zero Emissions

Research Initiative Regional Programme for Africa (ZERI) is one such endeavour, which gained its support through the UN University (UNU), which began in September 1975 and has grown into a decentralized, global network comprising UNU Centre in Tokyo, a world-wide network of institutes in 13 UN member nations, and liaison offices at UN Headquarters in New York and UNESCO Headquarters in Paris. ZERI emerged in 1994 and currently has its base at the University of Namibia in Windhoek. Its goal is to direct certain populations to think about the rich biodiversity in local ecosystems and to catalyse application of science and technology to create new jobs, especially for rural women and youth; to improve people's health and welfare; and to produce sustainable development and regenerate the environment in rural and urban communities. Its Khomas Women in Development (KWID) Project in Wanaheda, Katutura, produces mushrooms and has "the potential to provide mushrooms for the kindergarten children at the Centre and to serve as a training centre for more people in Katutura" (ZERI 2006). Approximately 25 rural farmers at Okaku and 25 jobless women have learned about mushroom cultivation there. This market-development project is a local, national, and international initiative: it is in Katutura and receives support from the University of Namibia through partnership with and bridging funds from the UNDP and NEDBANK Namibia (ZERI 2006).

Like other such endeavours, the ZERI projects may reduce poverty with short-term jobs for particular groups, such as women and youth, who often face urban seclusion and lack sustainable work. However, these projects can also serve as justification for advanced liberal reforms that govern the poor. These projects frequently invoke private enterprise, free markets, and corporate autonomy, as do advanced liberal employment initiatives more generally, according to Nadesan (2008: 80–1).

In Katutura, the cultural politics of 'choice' is still part and parcel of long-standing practices of colonialism and apartheid, which continue to reinscribe relations of power and the politics of exclusion. And authorities call on people with little or no work to make themselves productive or to participate in aid projects with ties to the market and little effect on reducing poverty. Such transformations are reminiscent of the broader social effects of governing the poor through advanced liberal reforms, especially in the world's poorest cities, such as Cape Town, Caracas, Casablanca, and Khartoum, which provide a desolate outlook for slum-dwellers' futures, as urban theorist Mike Davis shows (2006).

In an effort to improve conditions for the poor in Katutura and elsewhere, many NGOs work in fields ranging from market trade and poverty reduction to children's rights, women's issues, HIV/AIDS, and education and religious training. Many of these NGOs work with other international organizations that aim to reduce poverty and form part of the new global-aid regime. For example, Penduka employs several hundred women in women's crafts in rural Namibia. These projects have national and international sponsors and produce handicrafts that sell at home and abroad. Penduka, at the Goreangab Dam in Katutura, boasts craft-making facilities, a craft centre, a shop, a restaurant, and accommodation for tourists. In the Oshiwambo and Herero languages, Penduka means 'wake up' (see Figure 5.4). It has become a rallying cry to rural women in Namibia to build on their own skills and resources as a way out of poverty. As in other countries, such pro-poor development shapes the lives of the poor by involving them in economic growth, new jobs, new commodities for national and international markets, and urban centres. For the poor women at Penduka, their work habits no longer derive from their own ideals or ways of life. As they enter into market relations, the virtues of industry, regularity, discretion, and independence, and more generally discourses of enterprise, shape their lives. Rather than viewing the market as a naturally existing social order, Dean (2007: 123) describes it "as a way of naming a set of discursive-technical means for the regulation of conduct located within the domain of civil society" and, we would add, for setting limits on the knowledge of the people it engages.

BRIDGING GLOBAL LIVES

Other NGOs in Katutura are non-profit, rely more and more on national and international partnerships, and orient their agendas increasingly towards national and international concerns.[24] The Italian NGO Terre des Hommes defends children's rights in developing countries such as Namibia. It was founded in Milan, Italy, in 1989 as a non-profit association affiliated to the International Terre des hommes Federation and sharing its vision and charter. Since 1998 it has managed over 50 projects in Africa (Algeria, Burkina Faso, Democratic Republic of Congo, Ivory Coast, Mozambique, Namibia, Uganda,

Figure 5.4 Penduka, "Wake up." Authors' photo.

and Zimbabwe), Asia (Bangladesh, India, Indonesia, Myanmar, and Thailand), Latin America (Brazil, Colombia, Ecuador, Nicaragua, and Peru), and the Middle East (Iraq, Jordan, and Palestine). Through these projects, it assists 100,000 children and 400,000 people living in poverty. It works in 67 nations and runs more than 1,000 projects involving over two million children.[25] It helps fund the Bridging School in Katutura, which receives no money from the Namibian government (see Figure 5.5).

From our research interviews and discussions with the school's staff members, we learned that it – unique among Namibia's NGOs – prepares children who have left school to re-enter the education system. Its students live in the poorest areas of Katutura: Babylon, Kilimanjaro, and Okahandja Park. In 2007, just over 2,000 people were attending this school, up from the previous year. Some are helping look after sick parents or younger siblings. One teacher was finding it "very difficult to just chase the children home at 4 p.m., and we are not an overnight shelter, but they feel much safer [here], and they can actually enjoy being a child."

Figure 5.5 The bridging school. Authors' photo.

The institution depends on its interns, including teachers and development workers, who design programs and implement short-term school projects. Most interns come from the Centre for Global Education, but some[26] are from Terre des Hommes, a major funding agency for the school: "That's why partnerships are important," observes one school-project organizer. This same person commented that education is very expensive for most people living in Katutura and generally in Namibia. Schoolchildren[27] pay an annual fee of N$200, in addition to costs for shoes, dresses, pants, and school bags. By comparison, the bridging program costs N$50 per term – too much for some families. When we asked about what additional resources the school needed, the organizer stated: "We would like to see more support from the government, because at the moment we receive [none]. I would love to see a few more classrooms and more sponsorship for teachers. There are always going to be children who drop out of school."

As organizations in Katutura take over some of the state's central tasks, such as education, NGOs are becoming much more 'governmental,' reterritorializing relations with the poor. Such situations entail, as Ferguson (2006) suggests, rethinking notions of 'grassroots,' the 'local,' and 'community' and their consequences for practices that depend on tropes of 'above' and 'below.' Ferguson emphasizes that international organizations can erode African states by working behind them and sponsoring activities via NGOs. "The role played by NGOs in helping Western 'development' agencies to 'get around' uncooperative national governments sheds a good deal of light on the current distain for the state and celebration of civil society that one finds in both the theoretical and policy-oriented literature right now" (2006: 102). He recounts the countless 'community organizations' in southern Africa that European church groups or USAID bankroll and tells of the World Bank's reference to 'BONGOs' (bank-) and 'GONGOs' (government-organized NGOs) (2006: 101).

CONCLUSION

This chapter focuses on the processes of racialized biopolitics that created Katutura during colonial and then apartheid rule. In the light of the resulting relations of ruling and their racialized biopolitics, our analysis stressed formation of Katutura as an assemblage of co-mingling memories, violence, struggles, and diverse practices. We began with racial segregation, which intensified with the National Party's victory in South Africa in 1948. As that country's ties with South West Africa tightened, there soon emerged new social, political, and economic relations, movements of people, and relentless classification that harnessed the racialized biopolitics of authoritarian relations of rule.

One of the central governing strategies in implementing apartheid politices was the forced homogenization of ethnically and culturally distinct groups, a strategy based on 'separate development,' the Nationalists' euphemism for apartheid. The racialized biopolitics took many forms and included management of towns, cities, and particular human bodies and administration of the life-worlds of certain populations. By the mid-1950s, the apartheid state was relocating people from Location to Katutura, which created much 'friction' (Tsing 2005) with residents. And like all territories, Katutura was persistently experiencing re- and deterritorialization.

As we demonstrate, Katutura is a site for the exercise of power and one amenable to discussion, assessment, analysis, and deliberation. Its 'problems' link to and identify its poor populations and it has been the target of anti-poverty and pro-poor government speeches and of local, national, and international development aid within the new regime of global aid. In the context of that regime, aid from NGOs not only embodies a significant local dynamic but is a creation of national and international forces, and these NGOs act as partners for larger organizations that offer aid and aim to reduce poverty. These organizations give funds, resources, specialized knowledge, or skills training to targeted and 'risky' groups. In return they expect individuals, groups, and institutions to change, and they shape the NGOs' actions and efforts through joint relations and networks.

A similar trend operates in other parts of the world. Chapter 6 examines partnerships in relation to the governing of the poor. It provides in-depth analysis of the discourses and practices of partnership within development-aid agencies in general and in USAID in particular. It is to this analysis that we now turn.

6 Partnering the Poor: USAID's Poverty-Reduction Partnerships

The new aid paradigm is not designed to solve problems of areas such as Africa so much as to contain them. What is at stake is whether the inequalities and polarization between regions of the world (which are growing, not becoming smaller) and the instabilities to which they give rise can be managed effectively.

Jenny Edkins, *Whose Hunger? Concepts of Famine, Practices of Aid* (2000: 138)

INTRODUCTION

Partnerships have become ubiquitous in many aspects of social life. The terms 'partnerships,' 'partnering,' and 'partners' have become synonymous with more participatory and transformative modes of social reform. They often imply joint action and mutual understanding and support. The discourse of much policy in education, welfare, and social housing, for example, employs the notion of partnership to cover arrangements between individuals, business, community, and national governments. Partnerships are increasingly central to a vast range of ventures in and among an equally far-reaching spectrum of organizations and physical locales. The complexity of arrangements is typical of globalizing patterns of social reform, which since the 1980s have largely involved advanced liberal governance at local, mezzo, state, trans-state, regional, and international levels.

This chapter examines how notions of partnering target particular populations, such as the poor, as a distinct social group needing transformation. Increasingly, development aid and efforts to lessen poverty reach the poor via partnerships within the new global-aid regime. These arrangements collectively constitute and actively guide poor individuals and communities of the poor. We analyse partnerships as an advanced liberal technology of governance that shapes poverty reduction and in turn targets the lives of the poor. The underlying rationale is collective reform of the poor.

The chapter begins with a brief genealogy of partnerships both of the poor and of other targets of reform. It contextualizes today's partnering mentality as part of a continuum of governmentalities. The chapter next explores a number of partnerships to reduce poverty, including global corporate partnerships, offers case studies from actors in the new global-aid regime such as UN agencies and the World Bank, and looks at how these organizations commonly employ advanced liberal rationalities of governance that emphasize responsibilization within partnerships as a way out of poverty. An investigation follows into the partnership arrangements of USAID, focusing on the many ways in which partnerships can simultaneously group partners and the poor; engage the poor as aid recipients in responsibilization and market enterprises; and govern them by a rationality of security within reflexive partnerships and networks.

PARTNERSHIPS FOR SOCIAL REFORM

The history of poverty reduction, as we showed in the Introduction, is one of reform of the poor. Authorities have traditionally constituted the poor as a singular group, albeit within their own distinctive geographic settings, as in Britain via its old Poor Laws, colonial regimes in South Asia, Africa, Central and South America, and the Pacific, or in 'workhouses' in western Europe and North America (see, for example, Thomas 1807; Kidd 2002; Walker and Foster 2006). If one thinks it possible to fashion the poor into a population, one can understand that people may imagine them as possessing certain qualities and that they are amenable to shaping and directing. Looking at social reform in eighteenth- and nineteenth-century England, M.J.D. Roberts, for example, notes the shift in efforts by moral reformers from social control to self-control (2004). Writing about the United States, Joel Schwartz argues that nineteenth-century reformers believed that the "poor could conquer or at least alleviate their poverty by exercising virtues like diligence, sobriety and thrift" (2000: xiv). Both accounts identify a temporal shift towards self-responsibilization – one that we argue has continuously outlined how the poor can escape poverty, though with different emphases. One method of responsibilization is via partnerships. As we demonstrate throughout this chapter, partnerships can deliver policy and further constitute and govern the poor.

Over the past decade, partnership has appeared a cost-effective route to responsible market governance (L. Phillips and Ilcan 2004: 399). Many international organizations, such as the World Bank and the United Nations, have embraced a 'partnering mentality' to deal with social issues ranging from poverty to underdevelopment. Partnering can imply equality – each participant equal in negotiating and carrying out the terms of the partnership. Further to this normative notion is an assumption of likeness between partners. The scope of the relationship inherent in partnering can bring together the most unlikely actors. The terms may be negotiable, or one party (or several parties) may prescribe them. Again, the normative assumption – of distributing and assigning responsibilities – is one of negotiation. This chapter explores that assumption, proposing instead that partnership is a process of governmentality and thus a process of equilibrium, encompassing "complementarity and conflicts between techniques which assure coercion and processes through which the self is constructed or modified [by the subject]" (Foucault 1993: 203–4). Furthermore, it considers how partnerships shape poor people's experiences of poverty, specifically of its reduction. This deliberation of partnerships and their governmentality takes into account individuals' institutionally formed self-governing capacities and how these capacities govern individuals and groups (Dean 2007: 68), including the poor.

Poverty itself has seemed to observers variously a social ill or the fault of the poor themselves, but, despite these important differences, authorities and poverty experts have agreed on the need to reform them. This reform has entailed leading the poor from impoverishment. The two intersecting, variably interdependent methods employed to do this both relate to the governmentality of partnerships: mentoring and adaptation. Mentoring the poor takes place not in 'one-on-one' relationship building, as in Big Brother and Big Sister programs, but indirectly, as through sponsorship by one individual from the developed North of a child in the developing world. Here, monthly donations can apparently transform a child's life, and the donor's – a financial mentoring with clear transformative aspirations. This goal appears in the discourse promoting, for example, the non-sectarian CARE Canada's child-sponsorship program: "Point. Click. Be the Solution. Change a Child's Life. www.careconnects.ca"

(CARE Canada 2008) or UNICEF New Zealand's Global Parent campaign (UNICEF New Zealand 2008).[1] The program's immediacy contrasts starkly with other aspects of CARE Canada's work with youngsters in, for example, drought-stricken northeast Kenya, where it attacks poverty in partnership with local NGOs and individuals (Coates 2006). Such development aid reaches recipients nevertheless via dense, complex, sometimes-opaque partnerships, which, we argue, are typical of the new regime of global aid.

Various experts and organizations present partnership as a means to guide the poor and adapt their behaviour as a way out of poverty. Guiding is central to partnerships, especially in mentoring, which can be described as the act of leading by example. Like partnership, mentoring conveys normatively positive ideas of sharing skills and information, of support and care. However, at the heart of mentoring, as this chapter reveals, and of partnerships more generally, lies reinforcement of hierarchical relationships, which emphasize power and its receipt. For example, Manathunga finds academic mentoring a form of academic discipline and self-reproduction (2007). Such ideas transcend the academic environment and are common to partnerships, of which mentoring is a form. Mentoring, for example, can silently structure leadership and thus coercively reinforce relative power. Partnership, be it explicit and formal or implicit, acts as a means of governing; it is but one of the arts of governing (Foucault 2003b: 264).

Under advanced liberalism, social reform revolves around partnerships, which become the medium not only of delivery, but of change and reform – a mode of advanced liberal governance that, we argue, constitutes a partnering mentality. Advanced liberal states present partnerships as active engagement, yet they actually signal a retreat by the state. The language of partnership, of *being* a partner, implies an active relationship. But the advanced liberal state's partnering is often passive – the state is an initiating associate rather than an ongoing collaborator, initiating a partnership between itself, a program provider or deliverer, and citizens. Citizens, while acting as partners, are actually becoming less dependent on the state, and the partnership therefore distances them from the state. Partnerships thus act as one means of responsibilizing both individuals and citizens as a group. The state's withdrawal does not mean its absence. Instead, the state may not provide so many social programs and services, but it can actively shape their delivery.

The state's stress on responsibilizing individuals for their own welfare is common today. It reminds us that advanced liberal states work not in isolation but as part of an array of actors. Barry Hindess, after Cooke (2003), argues that "the governmental use of empowerment, responsibility and self-control as instruments of regulation" (2004: 35) is a particular focus of governmentality analysis that reveals the partnering mentality of NGOs, national governments, and international organizations. Partnerships regulate the partner; they offer control over partnership programs and, as we demonstrate in this chapter, over projects' objectives, design, and implementation.

In the recent genealogy of poverty reduction, local organizations, governments, and international organizations simultaneously assemble, control, and make populations accountable for fixing their own poverty. Partnerships and their use as a means of governing the poor, however, are not new; rather, their analysis is a phenomenon of recent decades. Responsibilization of the poor antedates advanced liberalism. William Thomas Thornton's work of the 1840s, for example, exalted social reform, through such means as philanthropy and education, in order to alleviate such tragedies as the Irish famine following failure of the 1840 potato harvest (Thornton in Donoghue 2007). Before this, the original (Elizabethan) Poor Laws regulated the poor in England. These laws required recipients of aid to enter parish workhouses ("indoor relief") or public works ("outdoor relief") (Donoghue 2007: 218). The income supplements were a form of partnership between parish authorities and the poor.

Poverty-reduction partnerships and advanced liberal schemes have governed the poor – for example, 'welfare to work' under the Clinton administration in the United States after 1996. Here, welfare itself is a partnership of sorts, directing individuals into a relationship with the state. Thornton believes that such arrangements should "avoid giving direct encouragement to improvidence" (Thornton in Donoghue 2007: 224). From the Poor Laws to advanced liberal states, welfare partnerships between individuals and the state have emerged. They do not comprehensively shield the poor[2] but force them out of immediate need into partnership at a distance; guidance, individually and collectively;[3] and responsibility for solving their own impoverishment. Thus the partnering mentality does not simply assemble the poor but also empowers them to act (Ilcan and Lacey 2006).

In her influential work on the will to empower, Cruikshank (1999) argues that Foucault's conception of governmentality explains how governmental authorities define the poor – in the words of Foucault, "recognize" them – as powerless and then empower them so they can participate in and be amenable to anti-poverty policy (1999: 81–2; see also Bourdieu 1992: 236–7n). The process of empowerment centres on participation and association (Procacci 1991: 166); and these twin ideas, we show, recur in the rhetoric and practice of partnership as a policy instrument for governing the poor and reducing poverty. We argue that just as governmental authorities actively constitute the poor at local and national levels as a site for policy action through programs of empowerment, they now construct partnerships as normatively just and responsible tools of social policy for governing the assembled poor on global scales.

Governmental authorities and organizations constitute partnerships as tools for empowering the poor and facilitating people's participation in poverty reduction, as well as broader development programs (Ilcan and Lacey 2006; Shamsul Haque 2004: 272). Empowering partnerships are, however, antithetical to ideas of social justice that characterized many grassroots nongovernmental organizations after 1945; instead, they often aim at "the liberal notion of empowerment wherein the poor are encouraged to be entrepreneurial and find solutions to their livelihood needs" (Kamat 2004: 169). The poor thus become "self-sufficient, active, productive, and participatory citizens," and programs of empowerment constitute them as a unified group or community (Cruikshank 1994: 35) and part of the responsibilizing ethos. In accordance with the aims of poverty-reduction policy and advanced liberal governance, the poor become responsible citizens – empowered, rational decision-makers. The sites of responsibilization in this global social-policy process become nebulous, as globalizing policies partner and thus govern the poor in multiple constellations – at the local, national government, and international levels.

THE PARTNERING MENTALITY

The partnering mentality is increasingly far-reaching, both within and beyond advanced liberal states, and typifies a partial shift to advanced liberal governance globally. Partnerships as a mode of social reform in advanced liberalism of course extend beyond poverty reduction. Outsourcing and political and administrative decentralization encourage individuals and groups to take on duties that were previously the responsibility of states (Dean 2007; Larner and Le Heron 2005), employing empowerment to regulate behaviour (Hindess 2004: 35). Here, individuals and groups begin to govern themselves or control aspects of their lives that states formerly regulated. Such empowerment, and hence responsibilization, becomes social policy through outsourcing and decentralization, which target diverse areas from waste management (Ilcan 2006), through homelessness (May, Cloke, and Johnsen 2005), to national Poverty Reduction Strategies (World Bank 2008b).

Outsourcing and decentralization accelerate the transition to market economies in developing countries, increasing competition and economic efficiency, reducing public debt, and improving public services (Ghosh Banerjee and Rondinelli 2003: 1527). These schemes nevertheless shift responsibilities to groups of citizens, private enterprise, and NGOs. An example is Britain's assemblage of local government authorities in Improvement Partnerships (Nunn 2007), which reformulate local authorities' powers to emphasize partnerships. This framework, according to the Department of Communities and Local Government (DCLG), encourages local authorities to determine their own programs and form suitable partnerships. Moreover, the department urges partnerships and empowerment not only for local authorities but also for their communities and individuals, who can thereby improve their own lives (DCLG 2006a). There is a corresponding emphasis on "greater responsibility for local authorities to secure improvement, themselves and with partners" (DCLG 2006b: 119). This link between freedom and responsibilization is the focus of an analysis of governance under advanced liberal agendas, including its global manifestations, as we see later in this chapter.

Partnerships are a key mode of advanced liberal reform. Vincent Lyon-Callo describes U.S. policies on sheltering the homeless as part of a continuum of "individualized, market-based views of the social" (2004: 12), and partnerships form a crucial element therein.[4] In their Canadian counterparts, partnership and partnering are a central "mentality," bringing together "communities, provinces and territories, partners in the private and not-for-profit sectors and Aboriginal partners," as well as an "alignment" of federal, provincial, and territorial agencies (HRSDC 2007). Partnership then is about the assemblage of actors and formulation of new relationships. Although Human Resources and Social Development Canada (HRSDC) does not speak directly of responsibilization, the technology is evident in the assemblage itself. Partnership can bring together competences or organize actors to share duties and accountability.

The proliferation of partnerships often brings together expected arrangements, particularly in advanced liberal states in the North. National governments are, for example, contracting service deliverers and bringing on board NGOs, often as consultants, which act as contractors and deliver services themselves. Philanthropic partnerships often draw together seemingly unlikely participants, however, and, as businesses, NGOs, national governments, UN agencies, and 'venture philanthropy' operations work together more and more, such relationships have increased rapidly. Corporate partnerships bring fund-raising and management expertise to the non-profit sector and produce what Larner and Butler call "unnatural groupings" (2005: 87). Certainly there are success stories, where additional funds from corporate–NGO partnerships have facilitated expansion.[5] Greater publicity and more donor activity may follow. Indeed, publicity for corporate–NGO partnerships has proliferated in the last decade, and they seem almost a new form of philanthropy. Many such groupings also incorporate inter-governmental and governmental bodies.

The years since 2000 have seen the growth of multi-partner, multi-sector philanthropic partnerships, joining rock stars with multi-national financial enterprises, for example, to address broad issues in development, poverty, and health. At the same time as the Live8 concert series to raise global awareness of poverty (Bond 2006a; Glennie 2006), Bono, of Irish rock band U2, for example, joined with fashion corporations Converse (Nike), Gap, and Giorgio Armani and financial-service provider American Express to channel one per cent of funds from the sale of special 'Red' goods to the Global Fund to Fight Aids, Tuberculosis, and Malaria. This branding and fund-raising partnership – Product Red – started in 2006 at the World Economic Forum in Davos, Switzerland:

At a news conference to launch Product Red, Irish singer Bono, of U2, commented: 'This is really sexy to me. It is sexy to want to change the world.' [He was holding aloft a new American Express Red Card, whose reverse side carries the statement:]

'This card is designed to eliminate HIV in Africa.' Designer
Giorgio Armani said: '... An ordinary person can simply walk
into a shop and feel that they can participate in helping the
needy by simply buying a perfume ... And cynically I would add,
without us changing the price of the product.' [According to
John Hayes, chief marketing officer at American Express,] 'It's
conscientious commerce, and it's our hope it will both reward
our shareholders and the global community.' (Reuters
Newsagency 27 Jan. 2006)

Here philanthropy has merged with the market. No longer does a
philanthropic partnership benefit the benefactor by enhancing his or
her morale or reputation; instead, the donor gives, either explicitly
or implicitly, through purchase and acquisition. John Hayes refers to
the demise of the traditional philanthropic model and heralds a new
era of charitable venture (Weber 2006), relying on enormous commercial marketing budgets to make the connections between purchase, consumption, and charitable donation (see Figure 6.1). This
approach ties the security of the poor – or in this case, the poor and
people living with HIV and/or HIV/AIDS – to that of the rich.

Product Red is just one of many examples of a new type of philanthropic enterprise; a high-profile case would be the Bill and
Melinda Gates Foundation and its increasing role in global development aid. Again, wealthy families have long participated in public
life via charitable trusts – for example, the Carnegie and Rockefeller
in the United States and the Joseph Rowntree, Leverhulme, and
Wellcome in Britain. Martin Bulmer, however, describes foundations
such as the Bill and Melinda Gates Foundation as novel and representative of "a new form of giving" (1995: 276), whereby donors
receive immediate public recognition for their contributions to the
public good through the branding of their initiatives generally and
the association between the foundations and particular types of philanthropic purpose. The Rockefeller is synonymous with support for
social science research, for example, and for funding agricultural
reform, joining with the more recent Gates Foundation to sponsor
increases in agricultural productivity in Africa at a cost of U.S.$150
million. The latter is now the largest charity in the world, with an
endowment of U.S.$28.8 billion in 2005 (*Lancet*: 911).

The Gates Foundation funds global health projects in partnership
with the Global Alliance for Vaccines and Immunization (the GAVI

Figure 6.1 Product Red Logo. Authors' photo.

Alliance), which it helped to found. The GAVI Alliance is itself a partnership and part of the Millennium Development Goals framework. It is "a unique, multi-dimensional partnership of public and private sector resources" and includes civil-society organizations (the International Pediatric Association), donor and implementing governments, financial institutions, the Gates Foundation, other private philanthropists, public health institutes (the Johns Hopkins Bloomberg School of Public Health), UN agencies and organizations (UNICEF, WHO, and the World Bank), and vaccine-industry representatives, whose collective efforts and expertise are enabling rapid progress in public health (GAVI Alliance 2008).

Partnership then is a means of assembling expertise and addressing global health through collective efforts and expertise and specifically immunization programs. It is the range and reach of these partners that are of particular interest. GAVI's shape is representative of the vast, far-reaching partnership "architecture"[6] characteristic of today's new global-aid regime. Partnership has emerged as a means of governing not only development aid, including in the form of health funding, but also the poor themselves. Partnership is thus a technology of governance and, we argue, one that is having widespread and novel effects on the lives of poor people within, across, between, and beyond nation states.

What is new and distinctive is that partnerships such as GAVI embrace businesses, charitable organizations, national governments, and international and non-state organizations.[7] The assemblage of these actors reflects the broader shift to advanced liberalism. Under advanced liberal agendas, there has been a profound rethinking of government, whereby partnership among local, national, and international actors has become a tool for promoting social, economic, and security objectives, including immunization for everyone and responsibilization of the poor for their own route out of poverty. Security is a crucial element of this approach. Mark Duffield links this change to liberal governance more generally, arguing that "a liberal problematic of security is concerned with people and all the multiform processes, conditions and contingencies that either promote or retard life and well-being" (2007: 4). Security then is another arena of control of the population and facilitates securing of spaces at local and global levels (Foucault 2007: 99).

Development aid and projects are flowing more and more from partnerships; indeed, in poverty reduction that route seems almost compulsory.[8] Partnerships themselves act as a mode of governance. We contend therefore that poverty reduction through that method shapes the lives of the poor. Partnerships have been a key component of local, bilateral, and global development aid since the 1990s. In 1992, for example, the United Nations Earth Summit in Rio de Janeiro called for a "global partnership" to address development and the environment (UN 1993: 43). This particular emphasis on partnership has continued. Paul Stubbs observed "a linguistic shift towards 'partnership'" when, for example, the OECD strategy paper of 1996 spoke of "development agencies" instead of "aid donors" and of "developing country civil societies" instead of "stakeholders"; "recipients" became "partner countries" or "partner governments" (2003: 336). Duffield argues that this internationalization of partnerships has facilitated social control of populations in the South that the North has constructed and grouped in regulatory techniques that transcend colonial experiences (2001b: 313). Partnerships – a new cornerstone of development policies (Crawford 2003a: 139) – offer a means to regulate and shape the conduct of the poor and to govern them at a distance.

World Bank President J.D. Wolfenshohn, in his annual address to the institution's board of governors in September 1998, lauded partnership as one "led by governments and parliaments of the countries, influenced by the civil society of those countries, and joined by the domestic and international private sector, and by bilateral and multilateral donors" (cited in Crawford 2003a: 141). Since this time, partnership has further entrenched itself in development-aid policy. Many national, regional, and international organizations now develop and deliver aid via partners, and, as we argue below, this assemblage of actors has transformed governance of poverty and the poor.

GLOBAL PARTNERSHIPS FOR POVERTY REDUCTION?

After the UN and the business community have successfully proved that they can partner for mutual benefit, the partnership era is now approaching its second chapter: opened by the possibility of estimating partnership's impact for development ex-ante.

Carlos Lopes, assistant secretary general of the United Nations and executive director of UNITAR, 2007

Since the 1990s, the concept of partnership has been operating within a development paradigm that supports responsible market governance. Development aid now reaches its targets via partnering relationships. Many development advocates within advanced liberal programs are employing the concept to promote accountability and transparency in government and a notion of governance fostering international trade. This approach draws the poor into partnerships with private businesses, NGOs, the public sector, and international financial organizations to plan development. The aim is to transform the conditions of the poor and make them, as choice-makers, more responsible for their circumstances. The World Bank, for example, views partnerships with NGOs as ideal vehicles for penetrating developing governments and economies. It advocates global public–private partnerships, for example, as a new form of global governance (2004). Various international organizations and programs are using this method to shape poverty through the World Bank's Poverty Reduction Strategies (PRSs).

Many countries now use PRSs to plan broad poverty-reduction initiatives. The World Bank and IMF require their inclusion in plans if a national government is to qualify for Bretton Woods development loans and/or other forms of assistance. Applying governments prepare PRSs through a "participatory process involving civil society and development partners, including the World Bank and the International Monetary Fund" (World Bank 2008). Since donors made commitments at the Gleneagles (Scotland) summit of 2005, emphasis has increased on participatory processes and national governments' responsibility for processes and outcomes of the PRSs, according to the World Bank (2008b). The PRSs, as part of the World Bank's Comprehensive Development Framework, represent the institution's effort to ensure people-centric and pro-participatory poverty reduction and self-help and -responsibility (see, for example, Craig and Porter 2006; Ilcan and Lacey 2005; Sumner 2006). By encouraging partnerships with NGOs, it demonstrates its ability to govern at a distance and shape poverty reduction on a global scale. This governing at a distance in turn affects how partnerships shape the lives of the poor.

World Bank descriptions of projects, aims, and objectives are replete with the language of partnerships. Its projects to reduce poverty in Orissa, India, are under the aegis of its International Development Association, which lends money to the world's poorest countries. They exemplify the diffusion of partnerships as a general guiding framework of poverty reduction at the local, government, and international levels and in NGOs. They also display the increasingly international nature of social policy aiming to lessen poverty (Duffield 2001a), facilitating a transnational and/or global policy network (Stone 2008: 35). Information about the Orissa: Rural Poverty Reduction Project and subsequent Targeted Rural Initiatives for Poverty Termination and Infrastructure reveals that acute financial crises in local government in Orissa and in India's national government are reducing spending on poverty (World Bank 2006: 1).

In response, a multi-faceted approach is emerging. The national government works with local and international NGOs to strengthen the Self Help Group (SHG) movement in Orissa, which NGOs initiated to facilitate microcredit and microfinance for the poor (World Bank 2007). This World Bank project seeks to further merge these SHGs and link them to banks and public financial institutions. It harnesses the language of empowerment and partnership, or "clustering" (World Bank 2006: 4): "The proposed project will contribute towards fulfilling the CAS [Country Assistance Strategy] goal of improving government effectiveness, investing in people and empowering communities and promoting private sector led growth through a community driven development approach" (World Bank 2006: 3).

Supporting this project in Orissa are the British and Danish development agencies, as well as consultancy firms such as Orissa's Sutra Consulting and international NGOs such as CARE-India, as well as other international organizations, including the International Fund for Agricultural Development (DFID 2007; World Bank 2006). This complex myriad of partner agencies is increasingly typical of delivery of development aid at the site and global levels. The Orissa initiative also demonstrates that these bodies see participation in private enterprise as the route to security for the poor. Development and poverty reduction have close links to microcredit enterprises and self-assistance, a common feature of the new global-aid regime.

A further demonstration of the prevalence of complex partnerships and self-responsibilization through microcredit and microfinance is the development-aid project Banking the Unbanked in Fiji and Solomon Islands. Here, the UNDP is partnering with the commercial ANZ (Australia New Zealand) Bank to establish rural banking services. First in a pilot project in Fiji in 2004 and later in an application of the model in Solomon Islands, these services have been mobile and offer savings, microcredit, and financial literacy services for "unbanked" populations (Liew 2006; interview with UNDP, Solomon Islands, 2007).

In promoting Banking the Unbanked, the UNDP shows how it governs target populations: "Instead of managing money effectively, instead of spending it on nutritious food, improved housing or better health care, money is often spent on junk food, betel nut, trips to Honiara and alcohol," said Linda McMillan, UNDP's financial literacy officer in Solomon Islands (Tabureguci 2007). These new partnerships thus act to govern and regulate the lives of the poor. They apply the language of financial empowerment, identifying financial literacy and services as a means to escape poverty and improve one's life. These routes also lead to market. Participation in the commercial financial sector facilitates participation in commercial market activities.

The new partnerships for poverty reduction represent a pattern of intervention in "governance states" (Duffield 2008) – 'fragile' sovereign post-colonial states.[9] International development organizations and donors operate with these states and their people through partnerships (Duffield 2008). Such partnerships aim ostensibly to reduce poverty, but we argue they regulate the poor and direct them to market participation, self-regulation outside a welfare system, and responsibilization for livelihood, education, and health, among other effects.

Development aid organizations, including NGOs, national governments, and international organizations, all like to assist development through partnerships – which form part of 'the new global-aid regime.' As an integral part of this regime, partnerships act as a framework for governing and assembling the poor. This aid regime facilitates their governance by responsibilizing them vis-à-vis both their impoverishment and their route out. Proponents often couch such processes of responsibilization in the language of participation, empowerment, and capacity-building; the route out of poverty is participatory – through partnerships – and empowering – responsibilization enables and liberates the poor and helps them build their own capacities. It is this language and these tools of governance that become operational in the example of the partnerships of the United States Agency for International Development (USAID).

USAID IN PARTNERSHIP WITH THE POOR

We consider USAID as one element of the new global-aid regime. It is the U.S. government's 'foreign assistance agency.' The Kennedy administration set it up in 1961 to run economic aid to foreign states separately from military aid (USAID 2008c; see also Essex 2008). As we explore in the next section, partnership is one of the nine principles that guide USAID's development and reconstruction assistance. As one of its policy analysts states: "We find it's very important to have that full range [of partnerships] because no country is purely represented by government and none purely represented by civil society. And so you have to have that partnership, or at least that's where it works best" (interview, Windhoek, Namibia, 2008). Moreover, partnership acts to assemble the poor as targets for USAID's other principles, which include capacity-building and ownership (USAID 2008a). This assemblage of the poor occurs when it sets up programs that regulate the poor to increase their security as part of that "massive smooth surface of the great global sea which envelops them" (Dean 2007: 27). The "smooth surface" resembles the new global-aid regime itself – the complex coming together of diverse actors and their many governmentalities vis-à-vis the poor. This surface highlights an advanced liberal global order and, in the case of USAID, the security of the donor state.

USAID terms its partnerships 'global.' We contend that they exhibit four key features: assemblages of the poor as subjects of partnerships; processes of responsibilization for the poor; market solutions to poverty; and securing the poor through global and reflexive partnerships. While USAID is not unique in these characteristics, it typifies one donor of global aid under advanced liberalism – and the world's largest state donor in gross volume,[10] influencing and under the influence of diverse states (Ong 2006b: 98–9) and their policy partners.

Through complex typologies of partnership relationships and networks, USAID assembles the poor. It shapes and fosters particular forms of partnerships that seem to vary yet have many similarities. In providing a range of partnership memberships and non-memberships, USAID assembles their subjects – the poor – for development aid. It also orders and regulates the poor, as well as its own partners. Foucault writes: "But discipline was never more important or more valued than when the attempt was made to manage the population: managing the population does not mean just managing the collective mass of phenomena or managing them simply at the level of their overall results; managing the population means managing it in depth, in all its fine points and details" (2007: 107). The "fine points and details" of USAID's policy discourse reveal its particular rationalities of governance vis-à-vis its partners and their effects ultimately on the poor themselves.

USAID presents its partnerships as a technique of governance throughout its discourses. Secretary of State Condoleeza Rice opens the joint Strategic Plan of the Department of State and USAID for 2007–12 by describing these agencies' joint mission as "a vision rooted in partnership, not paternalism – in doing things with other people, not for them" (USDS/USAID 2007: 4) and citing partnerships as a framing technique of governance. The strategic plan provides an overarching structure governing U.S. development aid; as well, the Policy Framework for Bilateral Foreign Aid: Implementing Transformational Diplomacy through Development (2006a) sets guidelines for bilateral aid, and a number of initiatives aimed at partnerships and their formation, such as USAID's Global Partnerships (USAID 2005a, b, 2006b) and the Global Development Alliance (USAID 2008a). These documents allow us to discern the extent of partnerships as a technique of USAID's governance of the poor.

"OUR PARTNERSHIPS ARE VITAL"

Partnerships are a method of assemblage, bringing disparate units into a cohesive series of connections and intersections. They perform

this act by organizing individual parts into a purposeful and transformative entity. In a broader context, USAID shapes its partnerships
according to a typology of membership – close collaboration with
"governments, communities, donors, NGOs, the private sector, international organizations and universities" (2005b). However, by
refining these classes of membership, it reveals a deliberative multiplicity of assemblages, à la Deleuze and Guattari's (1987) use of the
term as representing two types of assemblage – collective and machinistic (7–8).

The collective assemblage of enunciation comes in the typology,
and the machinistic in its acting out – bringing together units to
lessen poverty in a particular manner. The typology of these collaborative relationships with the various partners is formal and technocratic, although the agency's discourse suggests otherwise. There is a
binary tone to USAID's policy: the simplified public relations–type
descriptors (as above) of partnerships as a cornerstone of policy; and
the highly detailed and governing regulations of the conditions for
an international organization to register (USDS/USAID 2007).

There is a deep layering of types of organizations within the
Global Partnerships and the ways in which they can work with
USAID, including recognition of the different roles of faith-based
organizations (which comprise 25 per cent of USAID's partners) and
arrangements between companies, not-for-profits, and government
agencies under the Global Development Alliance. This complexity
thus marks USAID's partnership assemblage as reflexive, which we
discuss below. USAID engages in activities that include and move
beyond poverty reduction. For example, the Strategic Plan lists seven
strategic goals, with "Investing in People" and "Promoting Economic
Growth and Prosperity" the closest to poverty reduction–focused
aid plans. Yet this typology is an explicit conceptual apparatus
(Ferguson 1994: 296), a calculative rationality of governing the
poor, who are governed not only by USAID's partners, but also by
the partners' types, choice, and assemblage. Ultimately, these partnerships assemble the poor, as the following example demonstrates.

Food for Peace is part of a series of dense networks that encompasses a number of USAID programs, including the International
Food Relief Partnership, which allows U.S. NGOs and Faith-Based
Partners to help store, supply, and distribute international food aid, and
the Global Partnerships structure, which links in with the Faith-Based
and Community Initiative, again to bring on board private–public

linkages, now a central organizing node of USAID. Food for Peace shapes the poor and hungry recipients of emergency food aid into aware consumers of American philanthropy and into part of a supply chain. USAID administrator Andrew Natsios observes: "The secret of Food for Peace's success lies in the unique combination of American compassion together with the unmatched efficiency of our nation's farmers. It is less a triumph of government than of working Americans, for in its essence, Food for Peace is the work of farmers, businessmen [sic], grain elevator operators, truckers, bargemen [sic], freight forwarders, port operations, NGOs, PVOs [private-voluntary organizations], and government officials. Together they form an unbroken chain of humanity stretching from this country's fertile fields to hungry families half a world away" (USAID 2004 b). The efforts thus draw the global hungry physically towards the donor and render them consumers of U.S. aid – clearly a U.S. product.

PROCESSES OF RESPONSIBILIZATION: THE CAPABLE PARTNERS PROGRAM

The USAID promotes its poverty reduction as a partnership that facilitates "the ability of recipient nations to graduate from traditional development assistance to become full partners in international peace and prosperity" (USDS/USAID 2007: 6). These partnerships increasingly responsibilize the poor themselves for their own poverty reduction. Just as donor and recipient governments and international organizations, as we saw above, actively constitute the poor as sites for policy action through programs of empowerment, they now construct partnerships as normatively just and responsible policy tools for governing the poor whom they have assembled. Moreover, these tools, or rationalities of governance, promote responsibilization to challenge poverty. In this way, the poor will free themselves from poverty only if they become fully responsible and self-actualizing. Freedom is equal to participation and responsibility – notions, we argue, that derive directly from the market and hopes for security (see also Dean 2007: 108–29).

USAID states a clear objective in social services and protection: it will "help especially vulnerable populations manage risks and gain access to opportunities that support their full and productive participation in society" (USDS/USAID 2007: 24). It intends such aid to improve people's capacity to participate and eliminate their need for

Figure 6.2 Partnerships for the poor from Namibia. Authors'
photo.

assistance (see Figure 6.2). Efforts towards responsibilization include technical assistance from the Capable Partners Program. Here,
the discourse of partnerships is one of "increased capacity" and "improved enabling" (USAID 2005a). It is not, however, the poor themselves who are the immediate subjects, but rather local NGOs, which
will act as conduits, as they represent local people, the poor, and the
vulnerable.

The Capable Partners Program (CAP) offers technical assistance
within the private-voluntary co-operation program – a further demonstration of the complexity of USAID's partnerships. It aims "to
assist and collaborate with USAID missions in the field to strengthen
local NGOs and NGO networks ... It is expected that CAP will also
promote greater links between these local organizations and businesses, local governments, and international bodies" (USAID 2005a).
CAP provides an on-line resources database – NGO Connect – wherein local NGOs can gain access to resources for organizational "strengthening," "capacity," and "efficiency" (NGOConnect.Net 2008). The
information portal allows USAID partners to be active in networked
governance, evoking Foucault's assertion: "Power must ... be ana-
lyzed as something that circulates, or rather as something that

functions only when it is part of a chain ... Power functions. Power is exercised through networks, and individuals do not simply circulate in those networks; they are in a position to both submit to and exercise this power" (2003a: 29).

In this regard, local NGOs, working with USAID and its own myriad of partners, assume two positions in this network of power: their partnerships with USAID govern them, but they in turn govern their 'clients' – the local poor. The poor themselves are of course active in these networks of power, choosing to be active subjects rather than passive objects (see, for example, Butler 1997; Foucault 2003a; Gibson-Graham 2006). Donors assume that local NGOs are the most authentic representation of the poor (Nguyen 2005: 129) and that the poor are willing 'objects,' or recipients, of development aid and poverty reduction.

Programs such as the Capable Partners Program, in which U.S. private-voluntary organizations participate, govern by carving out new spaces of responsibilization. This governing by responsibilization affects both the local NGOs, which USAID trains to dispense development aid to the poor in certain ways, and also the poor themselves, who end up in the thrall of these very notions of efficiency, capacity, and enabling. The poor become responsible for their own futures at the behest of donors that render them capable and empower them, whether as recipients of short-term humanitarian relief or of longer-term development assistance. The governance of the poor then takes place in a network of power (Foucault 2003a; Rojas 2004) that operates through an assemblage of governing actors that shape their behaviour. By using ethopolitics, or the "self-techniques by which human beings should judge and act upon themselves to make themselves better than they are" (Rose 2007: 27; 1999), USAID recognizes its own rationalities of ethopolitical governance in the work of the private-voluntary organizations it registers and contracts – its agents "on the ground":

> USAID recognizes the significant and independent role that PVOs play in providing humanitarian and development assistance in rebuilding, transforming, and sustaining development in the countries where USAID operates. PVOs ... share a strong commitment to improving the quality of life of people in need. In their work overseas, registered PVOs demonstrate traditional American values of pluralism, voluntary action, and concern for others. In

addition, PVOs can foster sustainable selfhelp efforts at the community level by supporting programs that directly increase the
organizational and technical capability of local organizations
that empower and heighten the participation of the most marginalized citizens in the social and economic decisions that affect
their lives. (USAID 2007b)

USAID's partnership network governs the poor, and its partnering
mentality leads them to market. It clearly organizes these relations to
shape their connections to and conduct within particular kinds of
business environments.

LEADING THE POOR TO MARKET

The partnership framework not only assembles and responsibilizes
the poor, but also governs them by emphasizing market solutions to
poverty. This is a feature of the advanced liberal governance of the
poor. We now examine the role of the market in USAID's development solutions. This international aid organization promotes itself
as operating within an umbrella framework advancing freedom and
security. This discourse then links very clearly to participation in the
global market and market solutions to underdevelopment and more
specifically poverty.

USAID clearly articulates the links between development, poverty
reduction, and the market in its Strategic Goal 4: Promoting Economic
Growth and Prosperity. Here, it connects economic growth to economic development and explicitly associates both with reduction
and eventual elimination of extreme poverty (USDS/USAID 2007:
26). The Millennium Challenge Corporation (MCC), for example,
assembles the poor according to their own governments' behaviour
and performance. The U.S. government, via the Department of State
and USAID and their many partner governmental agencies, works
with states that they judge to be governing "justly," investing in
"their people" and fostering "economic freedom" (USDS/USAID
2007: 26). The MCC is another of the many umbrella partnership
structures shaping USAID programs and encompasses USAID's chief
mission – linking freedom and security with economic growth
(USDS/USAID 2007: i). It prioritizes the building of relationships between governments in developing countries with the private sector,
including U.S. businesses.

There is a clear synergy between the broad ambition of Strategic Goal 4 and a letter from the U.S. ambassador to Iraq, Randall Tobias, to "the American business community." "In the years ahead, we will build upon our diplomacy and development assistance successes in promoting economic growth and prosperity in opening markets, pursuing ambitious trade and investment agendas, assisting reform-minded governments to build the capacity to implement and sustain economic reforms effectively, multiplying development efforts through private sector participation and recipient country account-ability, supporting U.S. businesses through advocacy, and helping areas rebuild from war, terrorism, and natural disasters" (USDS/USAID 2007: 26).

Strategic Goal 4 offers a long list of prescriptions for transforming the lives of the poor. It requires the agency and its partners to lead the poor to market as a sure route to poverty reduction and ultim-ately to freedom and security. In Iraq's highly contentious environ-ment, USAID is seeking to transform the poor under its own business model – the Global Development Alliance. Again, USAID propagates a complex series of arrangements to introduce private–public part-nerships. In his message, Randall Tobias asks that American busi-nesses "join with the U.S. Government and Iraqi counterparts to build a public–private partnership" and notes that, "as Iraq address-es its challenges, it is essential to the country's future that American corporations become engaged in the country and facilitate private-sector development" (Tobias 2006). The relationship is, however, also clearly beneficial to the U.S. corporate sector, and examples in the letter demonstrate that U.S. corporations can gain access to hu-man and other physical resources and new markets by partnering with USAID.

The market's role in alleviating poverty is central to USAID's Global Development Alliance (GDA), which it launched in 2006 to attract more business money to fund overseas development and pov-erty reduction. President George W. Bush described the Alliance as representing "a collaborative effort"and claimed that "some of the best work in fighting poverty is accomplished in partnership in pri-vate institutions" (USAID 2006b). The centrality of the market orien-tation appears constantly in the agency's "stories" of development success. A policy document extrapolates from a successful partner-ship between Starbucks and Rwandan coffee producers: "By forging alliances with the private sector in which the different participants contribute money, human capital, in-kind contributions, or expertise, USAID leverages considerable, but always limited, public funds to attract a much wider and deeper pool of resources. Through the GDA, USAID combines resources and experts to transform the lives of poor people living around the world through a more flexible model ... The overall public policy objective is clear: to foster the growth and strengthening of societies that are free and well-governed while promoting economic development" (USAID 2008b). Certainly, the Global Development Alliance is one of USAID's flagship programs for incorporating private enterprise into the aid process and is representative of partnerships' effects on USAID governance of the poor more broadly. It also envisions eventual freedom – or the end of aid – through responsibilization of the poor via the global market.

SECURING THE POOR?

USAID governs the poor via a series of networked partnerships. In this section, we argue that these networked partnerships are reflexive and seek to secure the poor as a rationality of governance. They self-reference and shape regulation of the poor in terms of the *donor*'s security. USAID pushes individuals into reflexive partnerships that in fact ask them to self-manage and be responsible for their own futures (Seddon, Billett, and Clemans 2004: 132). These partnerships refer back to themselves in structure, content, and ability to govern by acting as a pro-poor, egalitarian rationality of governance. USAID comments: "U.S. foreign policy in Latin America and the Caribbean is designed to help governments respond to their citizens by strengthening democracy, creating widespread long-term economic growth, and promoting security. This policy has borne fruit in the emergence of democratic states, and improved social justice and economic competitiveness" (USAID 2008b).

First, USAID bases its view of social justice on enterprise; we, in contrast, value redistribution and recognition (see Fraser 1997, 2008; Fraser and Honneth 2003) but recognize that social justice can generate various outcomes. We stress dynamic measures that alter life worlds not through techniques of governance but through actions that move through and beyond individuals, groups, and organizations – a social-justice life-politics. Second, in terms of reflexivity, USAID and partners have achieved 'social justice' in collaboration with mining companies and broader MCC partnerships (USAID 2008b). At the beginning of this chapter, we posited equality between partners – a reflexive technique of governance; we return now to this idea in the context of USAID.

USAID sees partnerships as transformative. Its Policy Framework for Bilateral Foreign Aid of 2006 promotes them as guiding principles of development aid (USAID 2006a: 5). The agency aspires to "transformational development": "The ultimate goal is for countries to reach a level of development such that they can sustain further progress on their own, without relying on foreign aid" (2006a: 7). It sees development itself as a process of responsibilization. Its partnerships help allow it to transfer responsibility back to developing states and ultimately to the poor themselves. They intimate ownership and participation (2006a: 10, 24) and are therefore reflexive, drawing in participants – local NGOs, national governments, international organizations, and the poor – while telling them all how to act and formulate further ties in partnership networks.

The approach produces partnerships that may work to lessen poverty and deliver development, yet they are a technique of governance. One such partnership from Tanzania governs the poor, assembles them into a collective, makes them responsible for the route out of poverty, and forces them into the global market to bring about a more 'secure' future.

Tanzania set up reflexive 'smart partnerships' as part of its National Poverty Reduction Strategy of 2000 and National Strategy for Growth and Reduction of Poverty of 2004 (Mramba 2005). These smart partnerships assemble the poor in Tanzania, local and international NGOs, local governments, and Tanzanian ministries and a number of donors, including the European Union, the IMF, international businesses, UN agencies, USAID, and the World Bank. One links Tanzania's Ministry of Education and Vocational Training with South Carolina State University and USAID. Part of the President George W. Bush Education for Africa plan, it provides teaching and education materials by distributing local-specific textbooks but also establishes a reflexive social relationship of knowledge production (USAID 2006c). Yet while this framework spawns increasing numbers of partnerships, the subjects – the poor – seem less and less active participants, becoming instead objects of market-oriented programs that, in the words of USAID, "promote transformational development" (USAID 2006a: 7). This framework posits the poor abstractly and discursively as full partners for international peace and prosperity, along with their national governments and the U.S. government and people (USDS/USAID 2007).

USAID sets up Tanzania's smart partnerships to enhance economic performance through donor-driven and public–private local and non-local partnerships and to increase trade with the United States and other countries. Its policy recommendations and prescriptions centre on market activities that will "enhance sector market performance" through "public–private partnerships for export promotion and trade development." Partnerships are to also align with the agency's trans-formational aspirations (USAID 2004a: 4). Tanzanian producers and consumers, the poor and the non-poor, are led to the global market-place in export-oriented activities in such sectors as traditional agri-cultural production (for example, cashew nuts, coffee, cotton, tea), new potential agricultural markets (floricultural and horticultural production), the branding of agricultural and agro-processed products as "Tanzanian," and the mining and tourism sectors (USAID 2004a).

USAID's reflexive networks led more than 400 Tanzanian women basket weavers in the Iringa district, represented by the Kwanza market co-operative, to the U.S. retail giant Target, which purchased an order after the U.S. African Development Foundation gave the Kwanza co-operative a loan to increase its export capacity (Office of the United States Trade Representative 2007: 50). Here, one perhaps thinks of the complex Product Red networks that we mentioned above of market-oriented poverty-reduction and consumption rela-tionships. The Development Foundation – itself a partner of both the U.S. government and USAID – assists producers such as the Kwanza co-operative, rather than the weavers themselves, to facili-tate market access by "building their capacity" (Office of the United States Trade Representative 2007: 49). The partnerships that USAID and its own partners promote in Tanzania form part of the reflexive web. This network draws private actors, including the poor as produ-cers and consumers, and the national government into a wider frame-work of global partnerships, which reinforce and reproduce themselves. By penetrating simultaneously into the local and the global levels, part-nerships become seemingly legitimate, localized solutions to poverty.

The oft-beguiling complexity of USAID partnership relations in Tanzania is not unique, and this compelling case is illustrative of the reflexivity of the partnering mentality more generally. While the label 'smart partnerships' relays the market focus of the partnerships, this orientation links these examples to the global reflexive networks of partnerships and to USAID's countless other similar arrangements that appear in, for example, 'news stories' at <www.usaid.gov>. Operating simultaneously, however, is the often-more-overt discourse of security. The two propensities reinforce each other and confirm the reflexive nature of the partnerships.

Underpinning the mission and strategic goals of USAID is security – of the U.S. nation and its people and consequently of others. This relationship is causal – to advance U.S. security requires promotion of the world's security. Freedom serves as a synonym for security, just as empowerment and capacity have described regulation of the poor (Foucault 2007). In USAID's strategic plan, the secretary of state argues that "it is impossible to draw clear lines between our security interests, our development efforts, and our democratic ideals" (Rice in USDS/USAID 2007: 4). The coalescence of these interests operates throughout USAID partnerships; the security and market interests of the American state, as a donor, become operational modes in direct and indirect partnerships with businesses, national governments, other donors, and partnerships with the poor.

Security then clearly has many purposes and facets: securing the lives of the poor, within the framework of securing insecure nation states, in order to secure the donor. As we argue, the security of the poor in the new global-aid regime derives from their participation in certain types of poverty reduction that may render them less secure. Reflexive, ever-deepening partnerships that orient the poor towards the market occur within a broader restructuring and reorienting of developing countries and populations towards global markets. This transformation prevents realization of alternative forms of broader security. As a discursive and regulatory practice, security operates then as part of a wider disciplinary series (Foucault 2007: 8). Development, including partnerships for transformational development and diplomacy (USDS/USAID 2007), forms part of this disciplinary series of governing the poor. We develop this argument further in chapter 7.

CONCLUSION

This chapter has demonstrated that partnering the poor has long been a means of their governance. In efforts to make them more responsible and active, reformers have targeted them as a social group in need of dynamic and enduring partnerships. As we have argued,

partnerships now have novel primacy and qualities in the new regime of global aid. They operate as a technology of advanced liberal
governance that regulates them on a global scale. Partners – businesses, NGOs, national governments, and donors – are forming compacts for global change. Partnerships have far-reaching and profound
consequences for their constituents.

In our analysis of international efforts to reduce poverty, we have
argued that partnerships are a means of responsibilizing the poor
and embedding them in complex assemblages that govern their lives.
Our case study of USAID reveals how this international organization
regulates the lives of the poor through a variety of 'global partnerships' aiming at poverty reduction. These partnerships possess four
key features: assemblages of the poor as subjects, responsibilization
of them, market solutions to their poverty, and securing them
through global and reflexive partnerships. This global make-up of
partnerships alerts us to how partnerships for development and
against poverty are crucial to the investigation of contemporary
ways of governing the poor. The case study of USAID informs us of
the ways in which concepts such as partnership, as well as empowerment and responsibility, need examination as political and politi-
cized tools to constitute the poor as a governed entity within a
diverse global assemblage of companies, NGOs, national governments, and aid agencies.

Chapter 7 focuses on Solomon Islands in the context of its global-
aid regime. It examines poverty-reduction programs by international
NGOs and proposes that framing of these programs responds to discourses of security and that governance of the poor accords with
both advanced liberal and biopolitical rationalities of rule.

7 Spaces of Exclusion: Securing Solomon Islands

So when we're thinking about security here or when we're thinking about poverty elimination, we're thinking about human security in the sense that we're ensuring people are secure in all dimensions of their lives; and that's about security, about being secure, having safety, and what they are secure from, and provided for. And I guess when you look at some situations in the Solomons, I think you have to look at it through a human security lens, because the violent conflict size was actually in many ways a small blip; but security issues more broadly, people's general personal security, is an ongoing and fundamental issue.

Interview, Solomon Islands (2007)

INTRODUCTION

The relationship between poverty, the poor, and security may not be obvious; people usually associate security with the nation state, and poverty and the poor with social malaise and therefore social policy. It is a relationship, however, that is compelling and, we argue, more and more shaping governance of global poverty. This association between security and poverty is not new. Michel Foucault, for example, argues that governance of the state began to turn in the seventeenth century to the governing of its people. Security is a technique or technology of this governance. When U.S. President Lyndon Johnson declared a War on Poverty in 1964 and called for the American public to 'be troops' in this war, he explicitly linked security and governance of poverty. This connection, however, antedates Johnson's declaration and is more than rhetorical. It has crucial ramifications for governance of the poor.

This chapter presents an inquiry into the governance of the poor through security, showing this governing relationship to be more than purely discursive. It focuses on the ways in which notions of security are acting to govern the poor in Solomon Islands. This governance of poverty and consequently of the poor through security as a technology of governance makes use of space. International agencies, including UN bodies and NGOs, govern spaces of belonging and exclusion for the poor through their work in post-conflict Solomon Islands. This physical setting, as well as the policy spaces that operate there, act as post-colonial spaces of containment and liminality (Hamber 2002), or, as Duffield terms them, 'borderlands' (2001b). These spaces shape the experiences of the poor and, as we argue in this chapter, solutions to their poverty. By exploring Solomon Islands as a case study of the governance of the poor within the new global-aid regime, we argue that technologies of security are an everyday reality for many poor people. Whether in Solomon Islands or elsewhere, they face the exercise of governance in the form of national government and international organizations' policies and practices that shape their movements within, across, and beyond territorial borders.

Solomon Islands provides a pertinent case study of the complex dynamics of poverty reduction and discourses of security that shape it. For example, since the UNDP released its *Human Development Report* in 1994, human security has entered the lexicon of international security and development as a broad-ranging concept that incorporates protection both from poverty, disease, and hunger and from violence, abuse of human rights, and persecution (for example, Bellamy and McDonald 2002; Fouinat 2006; C. Thomas 2001). A range of international organizations, NGOs, and national governments are invoking it to inform policies on poverty reduction, such as those in Solomon Islands. The chapter considers its role in the biopolitical governance of poverty and the poor in Solomon Islands. The concurrent emphases on security and human security target populations and individuals and govern them via technologies that emphasize their capabilities and in turn responsibilize them vis-à-vis their poverty and insecurity. We base this analysis on policy and program documents, reports, official correspondence, and our interviews with members of policy and research staffs in international aid bodies and NGOs in Solomon Islands.

BIOPOLITICAL GOVERNANCE OF THE POOR

Authorities have assembled the poor as a population to regulate and control, as we demonstrate throughout this book. This assemblage of the poor is dynamic and multi-faceted, in a Deleuzian (1988) sense. It is simultaneously a territorial and a de- or non-territorial assemblage. It distinguishes the poor spatially from the non-poor in both developing and developed contexts. Many cities have, for example, neighbourhoods or zones of wealth and of poverty (Brenner and Theodore 2002; Leitner and Sheppard 1998). Markers and presumptions distinguish these areas physically and socially – for example, urban decay versus order, types of people on the street, levels of activity, and even individuals' appearances. While these distinguishing features differ – we are not suggesting uniformity of poverty or of affluence – their effects generate a hierarchy of space. The poor often inhabit socially separate spaces – in the North, one might think of urban areas such as the Lower East Side in Vancouver, British Columbia, the downtown of Detroit, Michigan, and south Auckland, New Zealand; in the South, shanty towns such as Soweto, South Africa, Katutura, Namibia, and Honiara, Solomon Islands. All these areas territorialize poverty and the poor therein (see Figures 7.1 and 7.2). Poverty, homelessness, drug use, crime, and sex work all gather in territorial associations of the poor with the necessity to control both the poor themselves and the spaces they occupy (Amstel 2003).

Simultaneously, the globalizing nature of the new aid regime deterritorializes poverty. Just as Duffield argues that the 'borderland' – a metaphor for chaos – animates aid policy (2005: 17), the poor and developmental solutions for their poverty belong to a physical space or territory that requires control – their poverty represents a form of chaos that is necessary to contain, monitor, and control. In this way, the governance of the poor operates via an assemblage that resembles Foucault's (1979) panoptical prison and means of discipline and power. Security is one of its technologies and operates through and beyond physical space, an idea that we explore throughout this chapter. The poor receive direction and governance in these spaces, but they also create their own spaces, both physically and as life worlds that promote their own solutions to poverty. These solutions are often antithetical to the governance of poverty that NGOs,

Figure 7.1 A Soweto shantytown with suburbs in the background. Authors' photo.

Figure 7.2 A street corner in Honiara, Solomon Islands. Authors' photo.

national governments, and international organizations enact (see also Lacey 2007) and may represent a social-justice life-politics by diverse peoples experiencing poverty.

In Solomon Islands, such social-justice practices do not usually take the form of large-scale collective actions; indeed, such practices are often evident at the micro, local level. In a country increasingly drawn into global trade and cash cropping (AusAID 2007), local barter and exchange of subsistence goods seem to enact a social-justice life-politics. Production in food gardens of bananas, cassavas, coconuts, panas, sweet potatoes (the nation's principal source of food energy), taros, and yams and their local exchange ensure food security and survival and challenge wholesale participation in global trade.

In this era of advanced liberalism, NGOs, national governments, and international organizations use security to govern populations. They invoke security to justify such governance. Security is a technology of governance that helps 'track' and 'manage' populations (Strange and Bashford 2003: 4), and it has become integral to biopolitical governmentalities. Biopolitics captures well the complexity, the almost-self-contradictory position of states' processes of control and retreat in advanced liberal governance. Nikolas Rose, for example, writes: "On the one hand, the state retains the responsibility that it acquired in the eighteenth or nineteenth century ... to secure the general conditions for health... On the other hand, within such a health-promoting habitat, the state tries to free itself of some of the responsibilities that it acquired throughout the twentieth century for securing individuals against the consequences of illness and accident ... Every citizen must now become an active partner in the drive for health, accepting their [sic] responsibility for securing their [sic] own well-being. Organizations and communities are also urged to take an active role in securing the health and well-being of their employees and members" (Rose 2007: 63–4). Advanced liberalism targets the poor as a global population, which it recognizes as perhaps territorially diverse but as sharing a common pathology. This is not a novel technology of governance – according to Foucault (2007), it typifies the very formation of the modern state.

In this age of advanced liberal global governance, this technology extends beyond states, however, and we argue that it is integral to the new global-aid regime. Technologizing people as a site for governmentalities fulfils the symbiotic relationship between security and populations. Populations, including the poor, become biopolitical subjects. "What does this new technology of power, this biopolitics, this biopower that is beginning to establish itself, involve? ... a set of processes such as the ratio to births and deaths, the rate of reproduction, the fertility of a population, and so on" (Foucault 2003b: 243). Building from this conception, Ong argues that biopolitical rule "centers on the capacity and potential of individuals and the population as living resources that may be harnessed and managed by governing regimes" (2006b: 6). Agamben (1998) sees the exercise of biopolitical power not only through the capacity of life, but also via the threat of death.

Death looms as readily as life is promised by development aid and poverty reduction in Solomon Islands. Particularly since 2003, inhabitants have lived under biopolitical governance as elements of the new global-aid regime impose development programs and policies to lessen poverty. Dillon and Reid (2001) write about "global biopolitics" and the role of threat and violence in liberal governance; we extend this understanding to the absence of social-justice solutions to poverty. Post-conflict security interventions have produced the biopolitical governmentalities – "the deliberations, strategies, tactics and devices employed by authorities for making up and acting upon a population and its constituents to ensure good and avert ill" (Miller and Rose 2008: 84) – that now shape the lives and deaths of the poor in Solomon Islands. We next analyse these governmentalities and their effects.

SECURING SOLOMON ISLANDS?

An examination of poverty reduction and development in Solomon Islands and their governmentalities shows security as a rationality of the governance of the poor, both there and abroad. Field work in Solomon Islands underlies our analysis of these policies and programs and grew from our desire to understand individuals' institutionally shaped ability to govern themselves – their responsibilization; it is these capacities that the aid regime shapes and implements to govern poor Solomon Islanders' lives and so-called solutions to their poverty. An examination of global governance in relation to these people and the governance of their poverty can reveal the governmentalities that aim to secure them both in the context of the state and beyond, as part of a global aid regime (see Burchell 1996, after Foucault: 140).

This chapter focuses on security as a governmental rationality of poverty reduction and development as international development-aid organizations implement them in Solomon Islands. This analysis draws on Foucauldian modes of analysis, which, according to Burchell (1996), connect Foucault's "'micro-physical' perspectives" with an "individualizing, disciplinary technology": "Liberal principles for rationalizing the exercise of political power outline a framework for a possible art of government which depends upon and facilitates a proliferation of techniques for the disciplinary integration of individuals at critical points in the social order. They delineate a space for the possible formation of a tactically polymorphous political technology for governing the lives of individuals which aims to fashion the forms of conduct and performance appropriate to their productive insertion into (or exclusion from) the varied circuits of social life" (Burchell 1996: 142).

Our choice of Solomon Islands as a case study may seem unusual, especially in the light of its seeming exotic quality. Yet this study can illuminate the global governance of both security and aid and its use of security to exclude or include the poor from/in, for example, poverty reduction. This case may seem distant and inconsequential – a 'failed state' or a unique small Pacific-island nation. Yet it offers critical insight into post-conflict governance by a combination of local, regional, and international actors. Solomon Islands, because of its recent conflict, can warn us of the possible danger of subverting the normative agenda of human security – as a development imperative responding to rights and needs – to reinforce a geo-strategic security agenda and advanced liberal rationalities of governance emphasizing market solutions.

The following excerpt from Kabutaulaka reminds us of the long-standing anthropological interest in Melanesia, and the writer argues that such interest continues (see, for example, Dureau 2001; Jolly 2007). In his review of a work about Tikopia, one of the Solomons' more-than-900 islands or islets,[1] Kabutaulaka also recognizes the flows between local particularities and global dimensions. The passage captures much of the nation's complexity, which Tikopia seems to mirror:

The island of Tikopia, for many people – even for many Solomon Islanders – is so far away that it seems like a mythical land; a place like Narnia, that magical land in C.S. Lewis' classic, 'The

Chronicles of Narnia.' Despite its remoteness – or maybe because
of it – Tikopia, its people, and their cultures have long fascinated
scholars, travelers, and casual observers. But, unlike Narnia
where you can get to by simply walking into a wardrobe, to get
to Tikopia you have to travel by boat for at least a week. Also,
unlike Narnia, there are no talking animals on Tikopia; only
people with interesting customs in the face of globalization. The
author of this book, Julian Treadaway, is one of those people
captured by the alluring attraction of Tikopia. As a result, Julian
has made a number of trips to the island in the past two decades.
This book is about his experiences, observations, and reflections
on Tikopia, its people, cultures, and the changes that have occurred. The book begins with a boat journey from Honiara. This
was no ordinary journey. Rather, it was one with symbolic significance; it took the author from modern civilization to a society
that seem to cling to another age – a place where the chiefs command respect, where you crawl into houses, where ritual crying
is an important part of ceremonies, where houses are built without nails, and where the spirits of the dead are forever present.
To a casual observer, Tikopia may seem to be an example of a
'pristine' Polynesian society. It was partly this that attracted
world renowned anthropologist, Raymond Firth, who went to
Tikopia in the 1920s and wrote eight volumes about the island,
its people, and cultures.

In many ways it is true that Tikopia has changed very little in
the past century. In this book, Julian comments on how many
things in Tikopia are the same today as they were described by
Firth and others who wrote about the island since the early
1800s. This book also stresses, however, that many things have
changed over the years. The agents of change include not only
'outsiders', but also Tikopians who left the island and then return
with new ideas and material goods: students, entrepreneurs,
church leaders, former public servants. Furthermore, Christianity,
money, and videos have had profound impacts on the society. This
book tells of the challenges of negotiating between the present and
the past and of how distant lands, peoples, and cultures deal with
the forces of globalization – a story that has resemblance elsewhere. (Kabutaulaka 2008, reprinted in *Solomon Star* 2008)

The focus of our case study is the period since 'the tensions,' which
started in 1998. A number of scholars have provided us with

insights, particularly Fraenkel (2004), Kabutaulaka (2001, 2002, 2005, 2007), Moore (2004), Pollard (2000), and Sofield (2006). We contend that the regional interventions since 2003 have incorporated Solomon Islands into the new global-aid regime as a site for development and poverty reduction. The peacekeeping Regional Assistance Mission to Solomon Islands (RAMSI) has made possible intense aid activity there by donors, despite the history of businesses, NGOs, and direct overseas aid since independence in 1978. The presence of both international and state-based aid organizations and of their personnel and programs and those of RAMSI has further inserted Solomon Islands into the new regime of global aid.

Solomon Islands received independence from Britain in a relatively peaceful process but has since experienced sporadic political tensions (Banks 2008; Dinnen 2007; Kabutaulaka 2001). This turmoil has arisen over access to resources, intense poverty and inequality, growing urban populations, and displacement from traditional lands and their matriarchal, tribal ownership (Bennett 2002). The period between 1998 and 2003 saw widespread conflict, which Solomon Islanders call 'the troubles' (see Moore 2004). Long-standing hostilities over land ownership had culminated in violent uprisings, as migration from the largest island, Malaita, to the most populous, Guadalcanal, increased rapidly. The five years saw violent insurgencies, counter-insurgencies, and a coup, resulting in deaths, internal displacement, and loss of livelihoods and property (Fraenkel 2004). The United Nations (UN 2002) reports "a perilous state ... The government is bankrupt, development has stalled, investment has ceased and the economy is at an all-time low. Lawlessness is rife on the streets of Honiara where 'order' is maintained through the barrel of a gun. The police force is incapable and unwilling to maintain law and order. Solomon Islands is a failed state. Its future is bleak" (2002: 1).

In the light of the crisis (see, for example, Fraenkel 2004; Moore 2007), the national government asked for outside assistance. In October 2000, parties signed a peace deal that Australia brokered. But lawlessness continued, and RAMSI arrived in July 2003. Australia and New Zealand set it up, with other Pacific states joining later (Moore 2004: 20–4, 2007). Its original mandate was to restore law and order. "On 17 July 2003, the Solomon Islands Parliament gave unanimous support for legislation to authorise and protect the presence of ... (RAMSI) under the auspices of the October 2000 Biketawa Declaration of the Pacific Islands Forum and loosely supported by the United Nations" (Moore 2007: 141; see also Alasia 2007; RAMSI 2008). Moore adds: "Because Solomon Islands recognises Taiwan, not mainland China, no attempt was made to get UN Security Council endorsement, which could have led to a Chinese veto. Both the Secretary-General and the Council President issued statements of support for RAMSI" (2007: 1).

The issues that underlay the 'tensions' are, however, still apparent, and violence remains a threat, as is evident in post-election rioting in April 2006 (Kabutaulaka 2007: 599). Authorities cite this rioting and instances of looting to help justify RAMSI's continuing presence. Australian Prime Minister John Howard invoked security, particularly in terms of territory, to explain his country's involvement in RAMSI:

> Even beyond the damage caused by the ethnic tensions that erupted in 1998, corruption has strangled many of the institutions vital to good governance, and violence has become endemic ... All the while a small group of criminals and militants have been looting the very future of the Solomons. They have terrorized the community – brought the nation to the very brink of collapse – and done a grave disservice to the reputation of the Solomon Islanders as a good and generous people ... In our interests to help ... it is vital that we do all that we can to arrest this downward spiral, which, if not addressed, could result in the total collapse of the Solomon Islands' governance and sovereignty ... A failed state would not only devastate the lives of the peoples of the Solomons but could also pose a significant security risk for the whole region ... If Australia wants security, we need to do all that we can to ensure that our region, our neighbourhood, is stable – that governance is strong and the rule of law is just. (Howard 2003)

We explore the links between security and good governance, and the security and governance of Solomon Islanders, in the next section.

'OPERATION HELPEM FREN'[2] AND RAMSI: A CONTESTED 'SECURITY' ACTOR

RAMSI's ongoing presence in Solomon Islands has generated controversy. Speaking at the 62nd Session of the UN General Assembly in

New York in 1997, Patteson Oti, the nation's foreign minister, spoke of a "continuing occupation." He told the gathering his government wanted more UN involvement and changes to the mission's rules (UN News 2007). None the less the World Bank and the Asian Development Bank soon reported that RAMSI was maintaining law and order and promised to continue lending and aid (Kabutaulaka 2005).

Between 1998 and 2003, Solomon Islands had experienced severe economic decline and fell into arrears with those two banks, its principal external creditors, both now playing a major role in reconstruction. In order to reach pre-tensions levels of economic activity, Solomon Islands would need ten consecutive years of 9 per cent growth – much more than its current rate of 2–3 per cent. Expansion is heavily reliant on unsustainable logging rates, with timber exports up by 30 per cent from 2003 levels. The economy revolves around logging, agriculture, and fishing, and more than 80 per cent of residents undertake subsistence activity (World Bank 2007).

RAMSI now calls its intervention "comprehensive state building" (interview with RAMSI, Solomon Islands, 2007) and uses a *pijin*-English phrase – *Operation Helpem Fren* – in its publicity to emphasize normative notions of helping, mentoring, and partnership. This label has gained wide currency, despite concerns that the mission does not address "Solomons' needs and reality" (Moore 2007: 147). Solomon Islands demonstrates how contingent security interventions can draw inhabitants further into governing relationships with regional and global organizations.

We find evidence of this new global-aid regime in relations between Solomon Islanders, local and foreign NGOs, the national government, RAMSI, major aid donors, and international organizations. Here, we see again that governance rarely operates in a vacuum and usually interacts with other arrangements in complex ways (Gould 2007). Among other researchers, Morison (2000: 100) and Mosse (2005b: 1–3) both argue that the range of governance has vastly expanded. Consequently, as we show above, it increasingly involves a collection of agents, agencies, and organizations that exist within and beyond the state. A link between 'good governance' and individual well-being is a central emphasis of an emerging new rationality of government, which shifts focus from society's well-being to that of the individual.

The promotion of such an active, responsible subject facilitates creation of certain kinds of expectations and specific types of human conduct (Borch 2005: 163). This rationality links these expectations and the governing of individuals' behaviour to the conduct of business, national government, and inter- and nongovernmental organizations. In fact, development of horizontal networks between these actors is central to advanced liberal 'good governance' (UNCDF 2003: 20; CDP 2004: 51). In Solomon Islands, as in many sites of poverty reduction, these networks take the form of complex partnerships.

Brinkerhoff connects good governance in failed states to re-establishing security and rebuilding effectiveness and legitimacy: "In fragile and failed states, weak governance is recognized as a contributor to conflict and civil war." Reform of governance is crucial in "establishing peace, pursuing state reconstruction, and avoiding descent into conflict in the first place" (D.W. Brinkerhoff 2007: 2). However, we would argue that 'good governance' is the standard term for this reformed governance and derives from the rebuilding of certain aspects of failed states. Good governance, according to J.M. Brinkerhoff and A.A. Goldsmith, assures security, restores law and order, and brings effective delivery of services and legitimate government (2005). This tripartite general understanding serves as a framework for development aid and delivery and is thus a technology, or rationality, of governance.

NGA HOE TUPUTUPU-MAI-TAWHITI[3] (THE PADDLES THAT BRING GROWTH FROM AFAR): GLOBAL AID AND HUMAN SECURITY?

The notion of human security is a powerful discursive tool for Solomon Islands, as aid donors and actors call for a more secure environment. Yet many particpants invoke a limited, if not false, notion of human security in order to emphasize a particular outcome – post-conflict security and stability and, more broadly, good governance. This attitude reflects the governmentality of policy at the discursive level (Ramazanoglu 1993 in Bäckstrand and Lövbrand 2006: 53) and in implementation (May, Cloke, and Johnsen 2005).

· Since the UNDP's 1994 release of its *Human Development Report*, human security has entered the jargon of international security and development as a broad-ranging interpretation of security. This interpretation incorporates protection from both poverty, disease, and hunger and the threat of violence, human-rights violations, and persecution (Fouinat 2006; C. Thomas 2001). D. Roberts argues that, in the absence of firm agreement on what the concept means, it is easier to define human *in*security (2006: 258) by focusing on causation in its processes. If insecurity is a consequence of human behaviour, then re-evaluate that behavour and influence it to enhance security. Bellamy and Macdonald (2002) and Bellamy and Williams (2005) think it crucial to include economic, food, health, environmental, personal, and community sources of insecurity; otherwise human security will simply mirror geo-strategic notions of state-centric security.

The linking of security and development – Duffield's "securitization of development" (2008, 2001a) – has placed citizens rather than the state as the site of security, so that social bodies are sites of intervention, monitoring, and securitization. Working with NGOs, national governments, and international agencies, the World Bank Group has developed a Country Assistance Strategy (CAS) for Solomon Islands. This action plan will help reduce poverty and promote economic development, while also promoting good governance. It emphasizes human security in securitizing the country, but to achieve good governance, not to address basic needs. Furthermore, it resembles the Poverty Reduction Strategy Papers (PRPSs), but for small nations or clusters of them it can act as precursor to them or a smaller-scale alternative. The CAS describes what type of support a country needs and how much it can receive during a three-year period. It set up a Pacific Regional Strategy for the Pacific countries (Fiji, Kiribati, Marshall Islands, Micronesia, Palau, Samoa, Solomon Islands, Tonga, and Vanuatu) to deal with the area's common problems.

The assistance program seeks to identify entry points for supporting reforms and constituencies for change, capacity-building, policy advice based on global experience, and communications/outreach. The Solomon Islands program consists of analytical/advisory services and small grants and work with governments and, where appropriate, communities. We believe it controls the policies and programs of other donor agencies and of local, national, and international organizations. The World Bank Group co-ordinates its efforts with other development partners, reinforcing the Asian Development Bank's idea of a co-operative effort for good governance and development (World Bank Group 2007).

Acute rural poverty is a continuing concern in Solomon Islands and generates social tension. The World Bank Group sees this type of poverty as posing a challenge to diversify and increase income-generating opportunities throughout the country so that local communities can begin to see more direct benefits from the restoration of law and order. The bank works with major donors, particularly AusAID, the European Union, and NZAID, to develop sector strategy and pilot projects for rural growth. It follows developments in forestry looking for opportunities to strengthen management and sustainability, despite worries of excessive logging. Solomon Islands is NZAID's single largest bilateral aid program – it received NZ$36 million in 2009/10. Aid priorities include education, restoration of law and order, sustainable livelihoods, and support to civil society (NZAID 2009). For example, NZ$12 million from NZAID went towards the Solomon Islands Education Strategic Plan in the period immediately after the arrival of RAMSI. This human-security development program aims to ensure basic education for all children by 2015 (NZAID 2009). NZAID also supports Honiara's Small Business Enterprise Centre, which has trained 3,800 potential and existing entrepreneurs (NZAID 2007). Leading responsible individuals to market seems a prime motive of NZAID's efforts, as with Oxfam International's market-access programs for poverty reduction and USAID's development assistance.

RAMSI has itself become a leader in development aid, facilitating reform and providing biopolitical governance via three pillars: economic governance, rebuilding of machinery of government, and strengthening of law and justice (RAMSI 2008; interview with RAMSI personnel, 2007). While each pillar has clear links with post-colonial ideas of good governance, the relevant technologies of governance affect the lives of individuals, especially the poor. RAMSI sees this governance as responsibilization: "RAMSI is helping the Solomon Islands Government and the people to help themselves. RAMSI's mission is to help get Solomon Islands working and growing again. RAMSI is creating the conditions for Solomon Islanders to re-assume control of their country, their lives and their future" (2008).

RAMSI's presence and its actions in shadowing government agencies and personnel, providing physical security, and reforming economic, bureaucratic, and judicial governance have, we argue, further incorporated both national government and people into the new global-aid regime. The relative peace that it has helped create – in co-operation with community leaders, local NGOs such as Women for Peace, and government officials – has facilitated the establishment in Solomon Islands of the Asian Development Bank; the European Union; foreign donor agencies; a host of NGOs such as

Caritas, Oxfam Australia, and Oxfam New Zealand; UN agencies; and the World Bank.[4]

The World Bank hopes to work in partnership with major donors, particularly AusAID, the European Union, and NZAID, to develop strategy and pilot projects for rural growth (see Figure 7.3). Microcredit may operate as a means of "changing the conduct of populations" (Duffield 2001b: 310) through, for example, the UNDP's Financial Literacy Programme, which accompanies Banking the Unbanked – the ANZ Bank's credit program.

In conjunction with donor partners, a local NGO, the People First Network, delivers this program through remote banking portals that the ANZ Bank operates via satellite phone internet sites in remote communities. The program teaches people about savings as well as microcredit business loans. It is one example of an effort to mend the social fabric by creating social capital and thereby enhancing service delivery and economic stability, while also bringing on board the "previously unbankable" – the phrase of Carolyn Badlock from the ANZ Bank (UNDP 2005). Furthermore, such a program facilitates market access, thus responsibilizing the poor by promoting solutions to poverty that provide no social safety net beyond market control. These concurrent rationalities of responsibilization and market solutions, as we showed above, allow the new global-aid regime to govern, as this chapter continues to reveal.

In Solomon Islands, microcredit seems to be a tool of human security, privileging partnerships with private and non-state actors – the ANZ Bank, Oxfam Australia, and the People First Network – and therefore allowing civil society to drive development and economic empowerment. However, we argue that this focus in a nation where four-fifths of residents live by subsistence is pushing them to market. Such an approach is a chief feature of post-conflict good governance and development in Solomon Islands.

SOLOMON ISLANDS: A GOVERNANCE STATE

Solomon Islands represents a pattern of intervention in Duffield's "governance states" (2008). As we saw above in Namibia and specifically Katutura, in these 'fragile,' sovereign, post-colonial states, international development organizations and donors operate with the national government and its people through complex development-aid arrangements (Duffield 2008). If one broadens the idea of fragile states beyond conventional security and insecurity notions to refer intentionally to developing states where at least one aspect of functions of state is in crisis, then one can see more broadly the development aid intervention of international organizations and donors as occurring within this idea of 'governance states.' The linking of security and development has made residents rather than the state the designated site of security, with social bodies sites of intervention, monitoring, and securitization. Nations in the South such as Solomon Islands are losing relevance, except as sites for reform or reconstruction within this new public–private security framework (see Duffield 2007). Donor agencies take little notice of local particularities, except as sites for reform (Hughes and Pupavac 2005).

Mitchell Dean's exploration of exceptionalism in liberal governance gives us insight into such interventions. Agents of governance can call on security crises and create states of emergency, or moments of exception (Agamben 2005), which can be "formally declared or simply announced by employing a specific language" (Dean 2007: 185). Dean, in contrast, thinks these moments increasingly common and even continuous, rather than momentary. The state of exception "is present in every normalizing power and expert knowledge by which liberal forms of governing carve out the life of the self-determining individual" (189) and "can cover not only declared or undeclared emergencies but also the entire mass of exceptions to what are construed as the normal forms of life in contemporary liberal democracy" (188).

Concurrent with the RAMSI intervention, the Australian government in 2007 declared a "national emergency" in Aboriginal[5] communities in its own Northern Territory. It introduced into Parliament bills to facilitate an emergency response in the Northern Territory, which, among other things, placed more police and the army in Aboriginal communities, introduced pornography filters on publicly funded computers and prohibited sale of pornography, restricted alcohol sales and banned kava (a form of home brew), blocked some welfare payments, and, through five-year leases, acquired townships formerly under the Native Title Act. The government took these measures in response to the territory's publication of a report on high levels of sexual abuse of children in some Aboriginal communities (Wild and Anderson 2006; and see Altman and Hinkson 2007). Anderson himself commented later: "There is no relationship between the Federal response and our recommendations. We [the writers of the report] feel betrayed and disappointed and hurt and angry and pretty pissed off at the same time" (Gellman and Dankoff 2008). This "creeping emergency" (Dean 2007: 192) facilitated authoritarian governance of indigenous Australians in an openly militaristic approach: "Using the language and strategic force of a military campaign, the Minister for Indigenous Affairs has described his government's new approach towards Aboriginal communities in the terms: 'stabilise, normalize, exit'" (Altman and Hinkson 2007).

These tactics of intervention, of stabilization and normalization, are evident too in the security mission to Solomon Islands. Many actors shape the lives of Solomon Islanders within the new global-aid regime and its exceptionalism of biopolitics and security. The Asian Development Bank's publication (ADB 2006) is a typical country assessment and demonstrates the techniques of governance that frame intervention and quantifications of poverty and underdevelopment:

> Solomon Islands is one of the least developed of ADB's Pacific developing member countries (PDMCs), ranking 128 out of 177 countries covered in the 2005 Human Development Index (HDI), slightly ahead of Papua New Guinea and Timor Leste. The country lacks an adequate social infrastructure and services and does not generate enough income-generating and employment opportunities for a fast-growing population, of which about 50% is below 25 years and 85% lives in rural areas. The annual population growth rate of 2.8% is among the highest in the world. There is little formal employment outside urban Honiara; unemployment is rising, particularly among the youth; there is a high incidence of malaria; and HIV/AIDS has emerged as an important issue. If poverty is to be reduced and the social fabric healed, there needs to be a substantial improvement in delivery of basic social services and economic growth that engages the rural population. (ADB 2006)[6]

The next line, however, speaks about the apparent difficulty in balancing these prescriptions, for unsustainable logging practices were helping economic performance. The report does little to connect economic outlook and performance indicators with provision of social service. The ADB states that it will "continue its highly focused strategy and program, and seek to maximize impact in two priority

areas – transportation and infrastructure and services; and the enabling business environment" (ADB 2006). This emphasis fits with
broader rationalities of market-based growth and development as
routes out of poverty.

The ADB's Country Strategy and Program facilitating market capacity is representative of the new global-aid regime's focus in
Solomon Islands. The assemblage of actors – including NGOs, the
national government, RAMSI, and international financial organizations – emphasizes rural growth through increased market activity.
The government's Grand Coalition for Change Policy Framework
Document pledges "a development process through a bottom-up
and holistic approach that encompasses the empowerment of the
people through effective rural advancement strategies, the pursuit of
the Millennium Development Goals, the revitalization of the economy, improving Law and Order, effective service delivery and the
devolution of powers, fuctions [sic] and decision making to the per-
iphery" (Sogavare 2006). In this reform project, human security promotes economic growth and market access, rather than addressing
economic and material needs. Pro-poor poverty reduction is not an
explicit goal; instead pursuit of the Millennium Development Goals
(P. Green 2006) and "empowerment" and "advancement strategies"
are simply part of a "transformation" (Sogavare 2006) that aims at
the market. Ideas of good governance, reform, and infrastructural
and rural development seem synonymous with poverty reduction
and development. For example, the ADB's program of reform and
intervention barely links economic growth to greater provision of
health and education, which it suggests will necessarily follow (ADB
2006; see also Sogavare 2006). Global biopolitical governance of
Solomon Islands' poor relies on the precariousness of life.

Security becomes precious in situations of instability, of precariousness. People may not speak directly about it but may rather
shape it to take certain forms. RAMSI, for example, promotes partnership with Solomon Islanders to increase security, but various parties want that security – the national government, international
organizations, the region, other nations, and individuals and their
communities. Lisa Smirl writes that the "archetype of international
securitization is the walled and gated compound" (2008: 241). In a
governance state such as Solomon Islands, this compound clearly
takes on many spatial and non-spatial forms and enacts security

through wide-ranging programs and practices. For example, Solomon Islanders face stringent visa controls to visit, stay, or fly through Australia and New Zealand, principals in the RAMSI mission.

A UNDP staffer in Honiara, talking about 'capacity building' programs – such as Banking the Unbanked, government technical and policy advice, and partnership with Oxfams Australia and New Zealand on their Young Farmers Programme – saw all these efforts as increasing security of life, livelihood, and nation (interview, 2007). These endeavours' relationship with poverty reduction, however, is not explicit. The many understandings of security, and the obscurification of the differences, are clear in a report by Oxfam Australia and New Zealand (2006). Some Solomon Islanders apparently feel frustration at the narrow focus: "While definitions of security varied among community members, the lack of economic and development opportunities dominated discussion: 'The problem in the Solomon Islands is that people don't have jobs. RAMSI may come and restore law and remove guns, but we need development.' ... A villager stressed that the ongoing level of poverty was tied to issues of governance and leadership: 'The problem they solved is law and order. We enjoy the presence of RAMSI in our community. However, we are still poor. Why we are still poor, even though RAMSI is here, is that we still have the same corrupt people in government'" (2006: 12). Surely human security should, they think, concentrate on the needs and rights of the poor.

We see further that linking security and development through the rationalities of good governance and human security has facilitated privatization of the technologies of development, or the parcelling out of development functions to a range of non-state and private actors. The new global-aid regime has seen governments and business interests from Taiwan and the European Union negotiating with Solomon Islands for direct access to its lucrative fisheries in return for direct foreign investment and development aid (Oxfam New Zealand 2006). The national *Solomon Star* mentions one major effect of RAMSI's presence: "More investors are investing here, Director of Foreign Investment Division Derick Aihari said. He said the investment trend is growing in the last few years. So far this year, Mr Aihari said 71 applications were approved. 'Yes, foreign investment here is growing,' Mr Aihari said. He said this had picked up after the arrival of RAMSI in 2003" (Mamu 2008).

New direct foreign investment, decentralization and privatization, and the complex assemblage of international and local actors thus shape securitization of development aid in Solomon Islands. Leander and van Munster (2006) argue a similar point in their study of Darfur: advanced liberal governmental practices and modes of expertise from the private sector reconfigure the social realm as a series of markets and quasi-markets. While private and public actors work for advanced liberal development, the aid structure changes: "Well, I suppose with RAMSI's presence there's a natural split, and the bi-lateral programme has become quite focused on community engagement, community activities and basic service delivery, support for basic service delivery. The RAMSI programmes on the other hand are focused on governance and fiscal and financial management and the law and justice sector. So that's become the split; obviously that's only been the case since 2003 though; prior to that the aid programme would have had a different focus and would have incorporated aspects of governance and judicial support as well as having the traditional community and provincial area support" (interview, Solomon Islands, 2007). Further complicating this stratification, however, are the myriad partnerships in and through poverty reduction. As we saw in financial literacy, such partnerships often draw individuals into poverty reduction focusing on the market. The efforts target the individual's well-being, or security, through access to resources and services, even political participation, as part of the broader biopolitical governance.

CONCLUSION

Biopolitical governance concurrently includes and excludes the poor, territorially and in reducing their own poverty. Synergetic, yet independent, technologies of exclusion and inclusion shape governance of the global poor. These technologies act alongside other rationalities and technologies of governance that we have demonstrated throughout this book, and the vast assemblage enmeshes poor populations, responsibilizing them and drawing them into market solutions and partnerships to defeat poverty. Additionally, these technologies of exclusion and inclusion, as we have revealed, are key to the new global-aid regime, particularly in the broad rationality of biopolitical governance – security.

In the case study of Solomon Islands, security offers a means to constitute the poor as a bound population at the same time as controlling them. We have identified several processes of this constitution, from spatial exclusion to concurrent advanced liberal development and territorial security that operate locally and globally. These policies draw the poor into their own solutions to poverty while excluding pro-poor responses that do not fit the new regime of global aid. Yet ongoing resistance, or everyday social-justice life-politics, secures and sustains life in the form, for example, of subsistence food production (see, for example, Gegeo and Watson-Gegeo 2002). The RAMSI security mission to Solomon Islands has evolved into a broad platform for promoting advanced liberal governance and facilitating the post-colonial governance state in the new global-aid regime. Security, defined and practised simultaneously and interdependently as human, territorial, and/or regional, has served as a multifaceted rationality of governance vis-à-vis the poor of Solomon Islands.

It is fitting to end this chapter with a reflective call for solutions to poverty and insecurity in Solomon Islands that build both on indigenous and local practices and ideas and on those from abroad. It is an appeal for Solomon Islanders and for poverty-reduction policy-makers and poverty experts to look beyond essentialist notions of tradition, or a "'return to kastom [custom]'" including subsistence alone, 'traditional' medicine, and dissolution of police – or reliance on ideas from outside alone (Fraenkel 2004: 188). Instead, Fraenkel calls for local means of addressing poverty that also acknowledge and adapt foreign ideas and practices:

> In the actual history of the Solomon Islands (as distinct from the mechanical juxtaposing-based variant), everything was hybrid. The imported institutions, even if they were at first forced inwards, were internally negotiated, and the indigenous cultures remoulded. Flexibility, as ever, was considerable. Much of the outside world came inside, but it came in ways that seemed to make good cultural sense. The challenge for the period ahead, if political ideas and reform are able to move, will be to find ways of enhancing democratic control and improving living standards that fit well on Solomons soil. (Fraenkel 2004: 188)

Such hope for local solutions echoes our own call for alternatives to global pro-poor solutions. Part of the recognition of the effects of diverse aid relations on poverty reduction in places such as Solomon Islands is the corresponding recognition of and call for social justice.

These alternatives have local and global advocates, and implementation must recognize local particularities, rather than market or security imperatives. RAMSI's ongoing and increasing enfolding of Solomon Islanders, as a singularly constituted population, into the new global-aid regime has provoked contestation and challenge. The methods of globalizing solutions to poverty in this seemingly remote and exotic part of the world under the guise of security solutions hint powerfully at the vast scope and reach of the new global-aid regime.

Conclusion

Exercises of poverty reduction and practices of global aid have been the subject of this study of governing the poor. Experts have long claimed that solutions to the problems of the poor, such as the structural-adjustment policies of the 1980s and 1990s and the poverty-reduction programs of the last decade, would generate innovative social and economic benefits. These solutions, according to their advanced liberal proponents, would revitalize civil society, foster private, public, and nongovernmental partnerships, and develop a new kind of governance that would be more economically efficient. Supporters have included national governments, international development and aid organizations, and world-wide campaigns and programs, such as Make Poverty History, Make Trade Fair, the United Nations Millennium Development Goals, and the World Bank's Operationalizing Pro-Poor Growth program.

From our perspective, our study has raised questions about these solutions to poverty and has related governmentality studies to the international domain generally and to international exercises of poverty reduction and practices of aid more specifically. In this study, we have argued that the governing of the poor occurs not through an absolute state of domination and coercion but through advanced liberal techniques, such as empowerment, responsibilization, and partnership, that emerge in different spheres and on different scales. We have demonstrated that the poor have been enmeshed as subjects and objects of citizenship schemes, community and spatial politics, colonial and apartheid rule, biopolitical forces, and security implementations. These webs of relations have, in varying degrees, cultivated new conceptions of what it means to be poor, new links between the poor and governmental authorities and authoritarianism, and new relations connecting the poor to poverty reduction and global aid plans. The ideas and arguments that we advance in *Governing the Poor* flow from our analysis of archival and public-policy documents, poverty reports, media and ethnographic accounts, field-site visits, and in-depth interviews with research and policy personnel at local, national, regional, and international levels.

Ideas of poverty spread globally through numerous authoritative channels. These channels range from specialized counselling manuals, self-help handbooks, and educational films and documentaries to world-wide government policy reports, international aid initiatives, and expert advice on the poor and solutions to poverty. Such ideas increasingly call for empowerment of the poor through their own responsible activities as a route to eradicating poverty. It is there and in other sites that poverty has become a problem with links not only to empowerment, but also to social policy, colonial reform, urbanization, security, global markets, and the Millennium Declaration and its eight goals. Through an advanced liberal and international focus on solving the problems of the poor, new international actors, imaginations, and programs have emerged and, as we argue, formed part of the new global-aid regime.

The focus of international program and policy on solving poverty has intimate connections to the new dispensation and its governmental authorities. This regime operates within and beyond nation states and is one of many global flows that embrace waves of aid organizations, groups, knowledge, information, objects, risks, and networks moving across regions in diverse and uneven ways. Through its affiliated agencies and organizations, the regime fosters poverty reduction, promotes governing technologies and programs for transforming the lives of the poor, and brings together actors and sectors within and outside the aid domain. It has support from national and international decision-makers, policy advisers and analysts, poverty experts, international programs, and international financial organizations, such as the World Bank and the International Monetary Fund. As we argue, the World Bank is one of the leaders in the drive to solve the problems of the global poor and to transform their lives on a global scale. This problem solving is to take place through various policy programs that include private enterprise, national government, and social protection and that aim to meet the requirements of individual countries through national poverty-reduction strategies. However, and as Craig and Porter (2003) and Rojas (2004) reveal, questions and concerns increasingly surface on how and to what extent such efforts lessen poverty and help the poor.

Through our analysis of poverty reports, documents, policies, ethnographic accounts, field-site visits, and in-depth interviews with research and policy personnel in nongovernmental and international organizations, we show that the new global-aid regime produces multifarious forms of global co-ordination that involve businesses, NGOs, governments, and international development-aid organizations. Of particular interest is the advent of numerous, new NGOs that are increasingly responsible for carrying out more and more activities vis-à-vis the poor. Since the dismantling of welfare states and the shifting of responsibility and risk to individuals (Brodie 2007; Dean 2007; Rose 2007), these bodies are implementing pro-poor projects and programs in particular locales and regions all over the developing world. International financial organizations, such as the World Bank, have launched many of them, and international aid and development organizations support them through their poverty-reduction and aid initiatives. As part of the new global-aid regime, these organizations cultivate new ties among participants of the South and North and encourage new market relations and new responsibilities for the poor, all of which contribute to new ways of governing them on a global scale.

In our study we argue that the new dispensation, despite its broad aims, the span of its international participants, and the numerable spaces of poverty that it beleaguers and envelops, has not reduced global poverty in any noteworthy manner. Instead, it has entangled and nurtured new kinds of relations and new understandings of poverty that are more about governing the poor through advanced liberal reforms and authoritarian agendas than about providing for more equitable and socially just solutions to their impoverishment. Consequently, exercises of poverty reduction, as a rationality of aid, involve complex forms of global organization and governing technologies that engage business, national government, and regional participants, often to the further exclusion of marginal and marginalized groups. Indeed, the new regime, as we demonstrate, draws the poor into relations of rule and power according to advanced liberal rationalities and technologies of governance as well as authoritarian liberal modes of governance. These relations of rule stand in stark opposition to the concerns of the poor.

The new dispensation, and its advanced liberal efforts, form elements within a global governmentality (Larner and Walters 2004b; Rojas 2004) that shape our knowledge of the poor and draw together an assemblage of autonomous aims represented by many participatory bodies. NGOs, national governments, and international organizations – ranging from the World Bank and UN agencies, such as the FAO, the UNDP, UNESCO, and UNICEF, to the European Union and Oxfam International – implement on their own and with partners policies and programs to assist the global poor. These collaborative efforts, which work both 'at a distance' and more immediately, introduce new ways of thinking about the poor and new solutions to poverty in the developing world. We demonstrate how, for example, NGOs and their aid projects in the developing economies of Namibia and Solomon Islands not only embody a significant local dynamic but are a creation of national and international forces. These NGOs often act as partners for large-scale aid and poverty-reduction programs. We show how this partnership trend operates in other parts of the developing world. Learning from our own field, interview, document, and policy research and in the light of work by Gould (2005b), Gould and Ojanen (2005), P. Green and Hulme (2005), and others, we argue that this trend reframes development initiatives and programs and focuses attention on the global governance of other ideas vis-à-vis the poor, such as empowerment and human security.

The governing of the poor remains at centre stage in many international aid and development programs and in pro-poor government initiatives. Exercises of poverty reduction and practices of global aid loom large in partnerships, compacts, and relations, or through a 'partnering mentality.' As forming part of the new global-aid regime, this mentality imagines the poor to be the potential recipients of stability, to receive their basic requirements, and to garner the prospective benefits of human security. We argue, however, that partnerships involving the poor and flowing from poverty-reduction efforts create new kinds of international relations that foster specific forms of integration between South and North, such as transnational capital as well as private-sector and national government relations in Namibia, Solomon Islands, and elsewhere.

In this regard, we emphasize that these forms of integration coexist with other forms of exclusion and marginalization at national, regional, and international levels. Such global partnerships to engage the poor and solve poverty are both complex and conflicting:

they are much more about generating new forms of government that involve sharing of activities by the private sector, NGOs, and international organizations and opening up of new spaces for governing the poor and for how the poor should manage themselves. Indeed, as an integral component of the new global-aid regime, a partnering mentality transpires in a field of agreements, dependencies, responsibilities, and inequalities.

The new regime cultivates new ways of thinking about the poor and their potential marketability or entrepreneurial spirit. It fosters programs of social and economic development to reduce poverty, such as microcredit, microfinance, or, more broadly, microenterprise. Private enterprise, NGOs (such as CARE International, Oxfam International, and World Vision), national governments, international financial organizations (such as the World Bank), and international development and aid organizations (such as the UNDP and USAID) are projecting control over the poor through their ongoing support of microenterprise. As we argue, these and other similar organizations operate in a global governmentality that seeks to mobilize, standardize, and govern the social conduct of the poor on a global scale, what some scholars call "mobile sovereignty" (Hardt and Negri 2000; Sassen 1996) or "transnational governmentality" (Ferguson and Gupta 2002). Even areas of conflict or crisis where states no longer advance bureaucratic control, Ferguson (2006) asserts, often experience transnational or humanitarian governance. In the conflict zones of Africa and the Pacific, for example, transnational organizations frequently conduct the daily work of providing elementary governmental and social services, a process he terms "government-by-NGO," which is a form of transnational governmentality.

Through its practices of governing the poor, the new global-aid regime promotes enterprise and independence. It includes initiatives that it deems advantageous for the poor, such as pro-poor programs. For example, it touts international projects and programs such as pro-poor tourism as alternatives to conventional tourism, an approach that focuses on generating net benefits for the poor. This approach views poverty as multidimensional and recognizes, among other things, the ability to 'unlock' opportunities for the poor (Chok et al. 2007). Pro-poor tourism comprises many participants, such as private enterprises, NGOs, development centres and institutes, government departments, aid agencies, and international organizations.

As an international organization and specialized agency of the United Nations, the World Tourism Organization launched its Sustainable Tourism – Eliminating Poverty program at the World Summit for Sustainable Development in Johannesburg in 2002. International financial organizations, such as the World Bank, support tourism projects as part of their pro-poor growth objectives. As Chok, Macbeth, and Warren (2007: 38) suggest, advocates of pro-poor tourism see the advantages that the activity can offer to developing economies and to the poor people who occupy them. Developing countries possess resources that are valuable to the tourism industry, such as wildlife, parks, and landscapes. From an advanced liberal perspective, the poor are in a position to garner the benefits of the social and cultural environments within which they live and where tourism is dependent. Such a style of thinking aims to increase local involvement in tourism and in further establishment of private enterprises. This process has characterized the new tourist sites in Namibia's conservancies; there, we reveal, pro-poor tourism and its links to international aid organizations and how they operate within a global governmentality that attempts to placate colonized and marginalized populations. Although pro-poor tourism has not been a fundamental concern to this contribution, it is an area for future research because of the strong trend towards this particular solution to poverty.

The techniques of governing the poor that are part of the new global-aid regime and its international initiatives exist alongside populations that are acutely aware of their social, political, and economic desires and goals, as well as of their own marginalization, and are willing to act and speak out. The political actions of the governed include advocacy and resistance groups that seek to counter the predominant governmentalities and advanced liberal solutions to poverty. These groups depend on dialogue and commitments to social, political, and economic transformation. They engage a diverse range of participants – including poor people, aid recipients, the urban dispossessed, slum dwellers, alternative co-operative groups, and urban, regional, and national coalitions, as well as people from nongovernmental and international organizations – and generate forums to voice their concerns for social and democratic change.

These concerns, which are open to reinterpretation and contestation, range from rising unemployment, low wages, and deteriorating health and living conditions to the suffering, dispossession, and displacement that often mark the lives of the poor. Such advocacy and resistance groups and participants are calling for and enacting changes that derive collectively from diverse understandings of social justice which focus on more inclusive political participation, recognition of diverse cultural expressions, and more equitable distribution of social and economic resources.

While the political actions of the governed are promising in various parts of the globe, much more research and advocacy are necessary to challenge not only the exercises of poverty reduction and practices of aid, but also governing relations. This book has concentrated on uncovering the ways in which broad coalitions of actors under the new global-aid regime govern the lives of the poor; it has also, however, begun an unearthing of the ways in which poor people are challenging, resisting, and subverting aspects of these regimes of rule in order to forge a social-justice life-politics that can transcend their own needs and aspirations. This process moves governmentality studies towards an ontology of change rather than a focus on power relations antagonistic to social justice. Governing relations have for too long enumerated, classified, and ranked the poor, identified them as targets of colonial, biopolitical, security, and aid programs, and reproduced social and political power relations at local, national, and international levels.

The new dispensation, and its advanced liberal programs as well as its authoritarian and colonial dimensions, is certainly not always successful in governing or mollifying marginal populations. Indeed, the challenges, contestation, and resistance that the poor forge may not be on the scale of the programs of rule of local and international organizations acting in communities; nevertheless they are present in decisions to participate in particular programs in particular ways – to use the Namibian BIG funds, for example, to pay for school rather than to participate in the market or to barter local food products in Solomon Islands rather than participate in a cash-crop economy.

On a broader scale, a social-justice life-politics takes the form of more organized challenges and resistance that move through and beyond individuals, groups, and organizations – such as anti-poverty coalitions, counter-globalization groups, debt-cancellation advocates, and local and global democracy activists – and that have the potential to disrupt the prevailing mechanisms and technologies for governing bodies, populations, and poverty. It can serve as a basis for invoking transformation that can bring the state and organizations of power to task for their modes of governing the poor and for not fulfilling their promises to reduce poverty and provide the poor with a fair standard of living and livelihood and safe access to necessary social and economic amenities. A social-justice life-politics assumes modes of action and practices that make possible other kinds of actions and practices, forces that stimulate transformation and link to other forces above and below the level of everyday actors' control. Such a life-politics is much more about producing new kinds of questions, new frames of orientation, and new ways of becoming.

Notes

1 See, for example, the headlines of a range of recent news items and calls for action by development agencies: "Climate change hits the poor hardest" (SIDA 2008); "Bangladesh cyclone hits poor hardest" (BBC News 2007); "Budget cuts hit the poor hardest" (*Oakland Tribune* 2008); and "Inflation hits the poor hardest" (*Washington Post* 2008).

2 For more on the many ways of governing individuals and populations and the programs and policies of governance, see, for example, the work of the following scholars, whose work this book discusses: Brodie 2007; Craig and Porter 2006; Dean 2007, 2010; Escobar 1995a; Ferguson and Gupta 2005; Goldman 2005a; Ilcan 2009; Isin 2000, 2002; Lacey 2007; Larner and Butler 2005; Larner and Walters 2004a; Nadesan 2008; Rojas 2004; Rose 1999, 2007; Walters 2000, 2002, 2004.

3 See, for example, Denzin and Lincoln 2005; Ong and Collier 2005; Silverman 2000.

CHAPTER ONE

1 See also, for example, Charles Dickens's *Bleak House* ([1853]1977) and the recorded 'self-definitions' of interviewees in William T. Vollmann's *Poor People* (2007: 3-102).

2 According to Shields (1997: 2), the concept of flow has links with a paradigm shift within cultural studies and sociology from the analysis of objects to processes; the notion of 'nomadism'; the breakdown of the fixity of boundaries and barriers; and the lived experience of global mass migrations and movements of refugees.

3 The quantification of poverty has shifted from Pogge's, for example, use
   of $1 per day to a figure of $2 per day, which probably more accurately
   reflects purchasing-power parity. The World Bank, the source of both
   Pogge's figure and a reference baseline for international and national comparative and absolute poverty quantifications, has updated its poverty
   measure to reflect inflationary effects but maintains the utility of a standard measure:

   When estimating poverty worldwide, the same reference poverty line has
   to be used, and expressed in a common unit across countries. Therefore,
   for the purpose of global aggregation and comparison, the World Bank
   uses reference lines set at $1.25 and $2 per day (2005 Purchasing Power
   Parity terms). Using improved price data from the latest (2005) round of
   the International Comparison Program, new poverty estimates released in
   August 2008 show that about 1.4 billion people in the developing world
   (one in four) were living on less than $1.25 a day in 2005, down from
   1.9 billion (one in two) in 1981. The new international poverty line of
   $1.25 a day at 2005 prices is the mean of the national poverty lines for
   the 10–20 poorest countries of the world. While the revised estimate is
   significantly higher than earlier estimates of less than a billion people living under $1 a day in 1993 prices, the developing world as a whole re-
   mains on track to meet the first Millennium Development Goal to halve
   extreme poverty from its 1990 levels by 2015. However, poverty is more
   pervasive than earlier estimated, and efforts to fight it will have to be re-
   doubled, especially in Sub-Saharan Africa. Also, lags in survey data availability mean that the new estimates do not yet reflect the potentially large
   impact on poor people of rising food and fuel prices since 2005.
   The research behind the new estimates is explained in a research paper
   "The Developing World Is Poorer Than We Thought, But No Less
   Successful in the Fight against Poverty" by Ravallion and Chen (2008).
   World Bank 2009 Overview http://go.worldbank.org/RQBDCTUXW0

4 The forty-four original signatory countries were Australia, Belgium,
   Bolivia, Brazil, Canada, China, Chile, Colombia, Costa Rica, Cuba,
   Czechoslovakia, Dominican Republic, Ecuador, Egypt, El Salvador,
   Ethiopia, French Committee of National Liberation, Greece, Guatemala,
   Haiti, Honduras, Iceland, India, Iran, Iraq, Liberia, Luxembourg, Mexico,
   the Netherlands, New Zealand, Nicaragua, Norway, Panama, Paraguay,
   Peru, the Philippines, Poland, South Africa, the United Kingdom, the
   Union of Soviet Socialist Republics, the United States, Uruguay, Venezuela,
   and Yugoslavia. Britain, Canada, China, the USSR, and the United States
   were the five members of the Central Committee.

5 The UNDP defines the human development index, first aggregated in 1990: "a summary composite index that measures a country's average achievements in three basic aspects of human development: health, knowledge, and a decent standard of living. Health is measured by life expectancy at birth; knowledge is measured by a combination of the adult literacy rate and the combined primary, secondary, and tertiary gross enrolment ratio; and standard of living by GDP [gross domestic product] per capita (PPP [purchasing power parity] US$)" (UNDP 2009b: no page number).

6 "In line with WFP's Strategic Objectives (SOs), the PRRO activities will have the following objectives: 'improve health and nutrition among malnourished children under 5 and pregnant and lactating women (SO3); complement medical assistance to tuberculosis, leprosy and HIV/AIDS patients (SO3); increase enrolment and attendance rates, especially for girls, at pre-primary and primary schools in the most vulnerable areas (SO4); improve household food security in targeted areas through rehabilitation of land and creation of community assets (SO2); and, strengthen government and local NGO capacity to establish and manage food assistance and hunger-reduction programmes (SO5)'" (World Food Programme 2009b).

7 Debates about the efficacy of aid abound. A recent publication critiquing a liberalization of development aid is Collier (2007). New Zealand's government recently invoked the ineffectiveness of development aid when promoting plans to reabsorb the NZAID overseas-development agency back into the Ministry for Foreign Affairs and Trade. A national newspaper reports: "The National Government plans to take more political control of a half-billion-dollar foreign aid programme, and wants to change the way the money is spent. Foreign Minister Murray McCully has ordered two reviews into NZAID. He said yesterday that the agency's $480 million annual budget would not change, but he criticised its goal of 'poverty elimination' as far too broad. Payments had become 'a handout rather than a hand up', he said. 'You could ride around in a helicopter pushing hundred-dollar notes out the door and call that poverty elimination.' Mr McCully said New Zealand's aid policy would shift from NZAID's current focus on 'poverty elimination' to one closer to the Government's policy aims, such as economic development in the Pacific" (Gower and Johnston 2009).

8 A stark example of this relationship between relief aid and rehabilitative ideas of development appears in the UNDP Private Sector Strategy, which upholds private–public partnerships as an effective and apolitical – or 'impartial' – means of ensuring development in a wide range of circumstances:

In terms of concrete partnerships with the private sector, UNDP has established a significant number of partnership projects in which one or more companies partner with UNDP and provide financial, in-kind, expert and/ or management resources to UNDP managed projects. In the period 2004–2006, UNDP engaged in more than 130 such partnership projects with around 85 companies. For example, in the countries affected by the tsunami in 2004, UNDP has worked with Coca Cola and the UN Foundation to support rehabilitation of water and sanitation systems; in Angola UNDP works with ChevronTexaco to promote small enterprise development and in China the world's largest steel company Arcelor Mittal works with UNDP on a range of environment and energy efficiency issues ... The issue of engaging the private sector in concrete partnership activities in developing countries can in some instances be viewed as a sensitive matter. UNDP is well positioned as an impartial multilateral actor that can act as a trusted intermediary, without being perceived to be associated with a particular national, financial or commercial agenda. (UNDP 2007a)

9 See, for example, Edkins (2000: 67–102) on food relief in contrast to development programs centring on agricultural reform.

10 According to Gibson-Graham: "We can discern the lineaments of the *emerging political imaginary* that we have identified with a politics of possibility in the *here* and *now*: the centrality of subjects and ethical practices of self-cultivation; the role of place as a site of becoming, and as the ground of a global politics of local transformation; the uneven spatiality and negotiability of power, which is always available to be skirted, marshaled, or redirected through ethical practices of freedom; and the everyday temporality of change and the vision of transformation as a continual struggle to change subjects, places, and conditions of life under inherited circumstances of difficulty and uncertainty" (p. xxvii).

11 Nadine Changfoot writes of these pro-poor, participatory aspects of resistance by poor people in local activism in Peterborough, Ontario, Canada. She describes the efforts by two local activist collectives, in the context of the performative aspects of what she terms neoliberal citizenship practices:
    One recent development that has emerged from poor people's resistance is the introduction of a One Space committee comprising People Putting Poverty on the Agenda, Food Not Bombs, the Peterborough Social Planning Council, and Peterborough Social Services ... In this space, poor people work to transform the patterns of communication that occur among middle-class poverty advocates and bureaucrats. People Putting Poverty on the Agenda and Food Not Bombs are insisting that: the meetings be held in a venue where poor people will feel comfortable,

rather than in the boardrooms of Social Services; poor people be able
to speak their mind on issues that concern them; the agenda and flow
of the meetings be flexible; poor people all have the same authority to
make suggestions and recommendations to the process and outcomes;
all in attendance need to understand that poor people need to express
their rage associated with poverty at the committee meetings, and that
food and music be part of the meetings. (2007: 143)
These practices echo the calls by Chambers (2007), for example, for pro-
poor paradigms to emerge from participation, creativity, and pluralism.

CHAPTER TWO

1 Suzan Ilcan delivered the 38th Sorokin Lecture at the University of
   Saskatchewan in March 2007 and examined the notion of 'privatizing
   responsibility' and its 'responsibilizing ethos.' A version appears in the
   Canadian Review of Sociology (see Ilcan 2009), and we draw on and
   expand some of these ideas in the context of the poor in this chapter.
2 Nikolas Rose 1996 considers these programs for assembling the social
   'identification projects.'
3 For more on these and related ideas, see, for example, Brodie 1996; Dean
   2007; Lemke 2002; Rojas 2002.
4 For studies documenting these and other similar changes in the Canadian
   context, see, for example, Armstrong and Armstrong 2002; Basok and
   Ilcan 2003; Brock and Banting 2001; Brodie 1996, 2008; Ilcan 2009; Isin
   and Wood 1999; McDaniel 2003; O'Connor and Ilcan 2005; Vokso 2006.
5 See Goldman 2005b for an excellent historical and contemporary analysis
   of the World Bank and its engagement in colonial and development regimes, as well as its initiatives on poverty.
6 For current, detailed analysis of these governmental plans, see Brodie
   2007; Dean 2007; Gould 2005a; Isin and Wood 1999; Larner and Walters
   2004b; Rose 2007.
7 This is not to suggest that Western liberal states have withered away. As
   Aretzaga (2003) states: "Since 1945, the number of states has more than
   quadrupled. From 1989, when the Berlin Wall fell, to 1994 there were 22
   new states created ... , and the number has increased since then."
8 Scholars working from the perspective of Deleuzian cultural analysis relate
   assemblage to imaginaries for the shifting relations and emergent conditions
   of study in globalization today. See, for example, Marcus and Saka 2006;
   Ong and Collier 2005; see also Ilcan and Phillips 2008 on the role of 'knowledge mobilities' as an assemblage of global governance networks.

9 See Dean 1999, 2007; Foucault 1984; Rose 1999; and others for more on problematization.

10 For more on these and related issues, see, for example, P. Green and Hulme 2005.

11 For example, through outsourcing and administrative decentralization by Western liberal states, some citizen groups are taking on national government duties. A case in point is the voluntary sector's role in delivering public services; see, for example, Brock and Banting 2001; Milligan and Fyfe 2005; S. Phillips 2006.

12 These responsible actors may even appear to be the ideal citizen, which generally involves practices that grant human, social, civil, and political rights and benefits for citizens within a particular territory. These practices can, however, vary across the globe (see Haddad 2006) and socially sort or categorize people as belonging or not to a particular territory or settlement (see Carrington 2006; Hindess 2000; Ilcan 2002).

13 Some critics view the decline of social government in the United States as facilitating growth of a national security and police state (see Giroux 2005).

14 In an analysis of shifting schemes and incentives in Western capitalist states, Gould (2007: 275) reminds us that individual nation states have relinquished large tracts of their strategic authority to other bodies, such as public agencies and private corporations.

15 For recent work on public-sector reform and privatization, see, for example, Armstrong and Armstrong 2002; Brodie 2008; Ilcan 2009; Isin 2008; Lippert and O'Connor 2006; McDaniel 2003; Rose 2007; Trudeau and Veronis 2009; Weir 2006.

16 For more on these initiatives and their effects, see Hilary 2005.

17 For more in-depth research on this issue, see, for example, Graefe 2006; Lawson 2007; Tickell and Peck 2003.

18 The OECD also works with governments on new developments and identified problems, such as corporate governance, the information economy, and the challenges of an ageing population. It allows governments to share policy experiences, seek answers to 'common problems,' identify 'good practice,' and co-ordinate domestic and international policies (OECD 2006).

19 *The World Development Report 2000/2001: Attacking Poverty* (World Bank 2001) argues that major reductions in all dimensions of poverty are possible – that interaction of markets, civil society, and national government institutions can harness the forces of economic integration and technological change to serve the interests of poor people and increase their share of society's prosperity.

20 See Goldman 2006 for more on the role of the IMF and World Bank.

21 Such relations between international organizations and liberal state governments, which Hindess (2004) might call 'international neo-liberalism,' implicate citizenship responsibilities and rights within, across, and beyond the
state. See Isin and Turner's (2007: 14) discussion on how diverse international arrangements implicate citizens in a web of rights and responsibilities.

22 According to Dean (2007: 70), the domain of 'culture governance' contains not only internationalists promoting a "cosmopolitan identity" but
also "neoliberals hoping it will deliver a more entrepreneurial self, and
conservatives and religious organizations as an opportunity to recruit
born-again Christians."

23 Some of these groups govern themselves in the name of enhanced 'freedom,' and this kind of governing is facilitated by a wide range of actors
within, across, and beyond the state. For research on governing beyond
the state in the context of international organizations and their neo- or
advanced liberal initiatives, see, for example, Basok and Ilcan 2006; Dean
2007; Larner and Walters 2004a.

24 For an excellent discussion of indicators, see Rosga and Satterthwaite's
2009 analysis of indicators in measuring human rights.

25 Rydin explains that indicators "make such performance the object of scrutiny and avowedly aim to influence behaviour through 'naming and sham-
ing' (that is, the publication of indicator trends) in order to 'improve'
performance" (2007: 612). She suggests that indicators have a normative
directionality that makes 'improved performance' evident: "In this way,
the behaviour of actors is 'controlled at a distance' and the objective of the
indicator is potentially rendered governable through the expedient of providing knowledge about it" (612).

26 Working closely with the UNDP, the UNCDF is an independent UN body
that makes investments in least-developed countries (LDCs) using grants
and loans. It is the only UN entity working "on the ground" exclusively in
LDCs. It currently works in 33 of the 50 LDCs and focuses its investments
on local development and "inclusive finance," with a total program port-
folio amounting to about U.S.$130 million. UNCDF investments are "de-
signed to help the LDCs reduce poverty and achieve the objectives of the
Brussels Programme of Action for the LDCs" (UNCDF 2007c).

27 The concept of group lending has developed against the background of
the Grameen Bank's apparent history of 'success.' Isabelle Guerin (2006)
alerts us to some of its negative effects for women, including the risk of
transforming social capital into 'forced co-operation' and the potentially
coercive effects of 'monitoring repayment.'

CHAPTER THREE

1 To produce this chapter, we extensively expanded and revised an article in *Globalisations* (see Ilcan and Lacey 2006). In addition to new historical information on Oxfam and its programs, the chapter also includes new interview data and analysis on its programs and policies both generally and in Namibia.

2 This chapter does not aim to challenge the individual motivations of people who work under the Oxfam umbrella.

3 For example, Amin retains a cosmopolitan sense of social and spatial connectivity and commitment to the notion of community. He argues that regeneration cannot be a local affair or a matter of local responsibility alone, but must be part of a wider political economy of decentred power and redistributive justice. He maintains that local society – at least in areas facing social and economic hardship – "deserves to be understood as part of a cosmopolitan society, not blamed for its symptoms, but empowered without expectations. There is a democracy to be preserved and a right to be and become to be respected in such areas, including the right to engage freely, the right not to agree, the right not to play community, the right not to resolve your own affairs. This is not asking for a return to the old days of dependency on the state and others, but to suggest that community empowerment alone will not remake economy and society in the hard-pressed areas, and also to ask why such places deserve only local community while others are allowed to enjoy cosmopolitan society" (2005: 630).

4 Walters discusses nineteenth-century strategies for governing poverty, which focused on thrift and self-providence and "converged on the figure of the thrifty, self-reliant individual – political economists, charities, and assorted moral reformers extolled the virtues of thrift, urging the poor to discipline themselves against the temptations of immediate self-gratification, extolling men to become prudent providers for their families" (2000: 66–7).

5 For example, the World Bank's *World Development Report 1990* relaunched poverty reduction as a primary objective (see M. Hall 2007: 6), and currently the World Bank provides enormous funding to tourism projects around the world. Goldman (2005b) reveals multiple levels at which its development initiatives operate, generate power, and effect change, including its direct engagement with hunger, poverty, and the poor over the past sixty years.

6 For more on these diverse organizations, see Denis 2003; Edkins 2000; Essex 2008; Ilcan and Phillips 2005, 2008.

7 See, for example, Baker and Simon 2002; Brodie 2002, 2007; Craig and Porter 2006; Dean 1999, 2007; Ferguson and Gupta 2005; Larner and Butler 2005.

8 For an excellent analysis of specific 'communities' that have been the object and target of government, see, for example, Cruikshank 1994, 1999; Dean 2007; Peters 2001; Trudeau 2008; Walters 2000.

9 For a parallel discussion on the field of work, see Miller and Rose 1995: 430.

10 See Miller and Rose's 1995 analyses of the domain of work and workplace organization.

11 For an insightful analysis of the roles of NGOs in this broad context, see, for example, Trudeau 2008.

12 In 1998, Simmons ranked Oxfam third, based on several criteria, among eight major groups of international NGOs, each of which controlled approximately $500 million in the $8–billion relief market. The eight were, in descending order: CARE, World Vision International, the Oxfam Federation, Médecins sans Frontières, the Save the Children Federation, Eurostep (secular European NGOs), CIDSE (Coopération internationale pour le développement et la solidarité), and APDOVE (Association of Protestant Development Organizations in Europe) (1998: 92). Despite extensive research, no such more up-to-date ranking exists.

13 For more on these and other technologies, see Brodie 2002, 2007; Craig and Porter 2006; Dean 2007; Ferguson and Gupta 2005; Larner and Butler 2005.

14 Similar programs of mobile education operate in Turkana, northwest Kenya (Oxfam International 2007f).

15 Consequently, more than 4.5 million people now suffer because of the conflict and depend on humanitarian assistance (Oxfam Canada 2008).

16 For more on aid, see, for example, Edkins (2000: 68).

17 For more on these issues, see, for example, Chesters 2004; della Porta 2007; Gindin 2002; Ilcan and Basok 2004; Lacey 2005b.

18 For more on Oxfam's online charity stores, see Yorkshireforward at http://www.yorkshireforward.com/www/view.asp?content_id=7183&parent_id=263 (accessed 17 March 2008).

19 "Fair trade differs from ethical trading in that its primary focus is on improving trading relationships rather than labour practices, it engages primarily with marginal producers, and aims to establish an alternative trading model rather than working within the confines of conventional international trading relationships ... Ethical trade – or ethical sourcing – means the assumption of responsibility by a company for the labour and

human rights practices within its supply chain" (Ethical Trade Initiative: www.ethicaltrade.org/; [accessed 28 May 2007]). This is a brief summary of a contentious semantic debate.

20 Shiva is far more forthright. She argues that Oxfam must choose: "Will it stand for trade regulated by principles of peace, justice and sustainability or will it become a weak, co-opted, voice of the dominant free trade interests? Will it put people first or trade first?" (2002: 13).

CHAPTER FOUR

1 For studies in this area, see, for example, Chhotray 2004; Owusu 2004; H. Weber 2004.

2 The Decentralization Act, for example, has devolved various functions, such as rural water supplies and health services. The "process needs more support from core ministries to enhance its implementation. Devolution of power to the regions is getting more and more important, including the transfer of budgets" (Republic of Namibia, National Planning Commission, 2005: 21).

3 For recent work on this theme, see, for example, Duffield 2001, 2005a; Ferguson 2006; Mosse and Lewis 2005.

4 At this time, the German government created a settler parliament (the Landesrat) without any representation of the colonized people. Although the body did not have legislative authority, it made recommendations on legislative and administrative matters to the emperor, the Colonial Ministry, and the governor (Steinmetz and Hell 2006).

5 According to Steinmetz and Hell, "Efforts to name and memorialize these events as genocide have met with resistance" (2006: 257). For more on these efforts, see the rest of that article.

6 In this colonial context, see Ilcan (2008) for an analysis of camp biopolitics and mobile sovereignty.

7 German colonialism in the territory now known as Namibia has evoked wide discussion in recent years, especially the attempted extermination of the Ovaherero people in 1904. Steinmetz and Hell (2006) alert us to how Germany's involvement created new discursive connections that are transforming colonial memories in both Germany and Namibia.

8 The German authorities divided the country by an imaginary line – the 'police zone.' They administered the area south of the line much more tightly than they did the north. For more on these and related issues, see, for example, Müller-Friedman 2008; Ramutsindela 2001; Steinmetz and Hell 2006.

9 Even in Namibia today, Friedman (2006) presents a post-structuralist critique of this kind of development using as a case study the Epupa project – construction of a 360-megawatt power station on the Kunene River. Formulation and design of the project have generated debate among interest groups and stakeholders, ranging from supporters to opponents who view it as way to displace local populations and force them into conditions of extreme vulnerability (2006: 2).

10 Müller-Friedman (2008: 31) argues poignantly that Namibian architecture and urban planning are practically indistinguishable from those in comparable South African cities.

11 Dzinesa and Rupiya (2005) stress anti-colonial movements, such as the Ovamboland People's Organization (OPO), under Andimba Toivo ja Toivo, which organized strikes at the Luderitz port; and the South West Africa National Union (SWANU) (2005: 201).

12 Metsola recounts a key period in SWAPO's history: "Tens of thousands of Namibians joined SWAPO in exile in the 1970s and 1980s. Namibians were also recruited on the South African side in the South West Africa Territorial Force (SWATF) and paramilitary police unit Koevoet" (2006: 1120). See Figure 4.1.

13 Olsson (2001) examines the United Nations Transitional Assistance Group (UNTAG) project of 1989–90, which aimed to introduce a "civilian component" to peacekeeping efforts by way of a "gender policy." UNTAG institutionalized gender into the SWAPO government structure, targeting women and enhancing their skills.

14 According to Ramutsindela, "the demarcation of new local government boundaries was important because of the history of territorial segregation and huge imbalances in the distribution of resources in that country. The integration of municipalities under the Local Authorities Act of 1992 was an attempt to infuse the non-racial political agenda of the Namibian state, while at the same time making efforts to develop financially sound institutions that would facilitate the distribution of resources to the entire population" (2001: 62–3).

15 Just before independence, UNESCO posted a staff member to Windhoek to work with UNDP, UNHCR, and UNICEF and to assist in identifying UNESCO's post-independence orientation (see UNESCO 2008b).

16 During conflict and war, nations may come to rely heavily on humanitarian aid. For example, and according to Duffield (2007: 72), at the end of the 1970s many Western governments not only chose to view Vietnam's invasion of Cambodia and the toppling of the genocidal Pol Pot regime as an act of violence but pushed for an international ban on humanitarian

aid and assistance for Vietnam. A number of international organizations and NGOs, including Oxfam, however, resisted this ban.

17 These kinds of phenomena, as Ferguson (2006: 100–1) argues, fit uneasily in the state-versus-civil society framework, especially as international financial organizations can impose far-reaching economic and social programs in developing states such as those in Africa.

18 See Gould (2005a, b) and Nelson (2000: 160) for more on these international organizations and their role in international development and aid.

19 The World Bank, for example, pursues advanced liberal pro-growth schemes of development that encourage participation via implementation and promotion of organizations such as the UN agencies as instruments for promoting its interests in penetrating the developing world (Crawford 2003a) and for addressing poverty through its Poverty Reduction Strategy Papers.

20 Levine also states: "A second source of increased demand for effective systems to monitor poverty has come from the global and national drive towards the Millennium Development Goals derived from the Millennium Declaration that was agreed to by all UN member states in 2000." He also recognizes that countries reporting on the MDGs face challenges, such as trying "to define poverty indicators and tailor global goals and targets to reflect the national context" (2006: 90).

21 This triadic relationship connects to global anti-poverty initiatives such as Make Poverty History. For example, in 2005 the world's leaders received a global mandate to "make poverty history" and in response to public pressure promised to increase aid, eradicate poverty, and cancel many poor countries' debts. These actions have, however, not materialized (www.makepovertyhistory.org/2007/).

22 By the year 2000, overseas development aid to Namibia had fallen from U.S.$130 per Namibian per year immediately after independence to U.S.$60. According to the Office of the United Nations Resident Coordinator, this reduction occurred because of Namibia's classification as a lower middle–income country (UNIC 2005).

23 Similarly, the Namibian government engages in participatory poverty assessments (PPAs) in an effort to achieve the MDGs. This is a tool that aims to involve poor people and their institutions in defining and analysing poverty from their own perspective. For example, three regions have completed the exercise since 2006 ("Poverty Monitoring System," National Archives of Namibia, no date). Namibia's PPAs resemble other strategies elsewhere that analyse poverty in terms of income and de facto social

exclusion – for example, as P. Green and Hulme (2005: 868) demonstrate, measures of household income, surveys of household expenditure, and government statistics.

24 USAID identifies major problems: "Even prior to the impacts of the HIV/AIDS epidemic, Namibia lacked the resources and capacity to fully address widespread poverty and extreme social and economic inequality resulting from 100 years of colonialism and apartheid. Half of the country's population live below the poverty line, survive on ten percent of national income, and is under or unemployed. The UNDP estimates the Gini coefficient measuring income disparity in Namibia as the highest in the world at 70.7 on a scale of 100 with 0 representing perfect equality … Though Namibia has relatively good infrastructure, developing job opportunities and promoting equitable economic growth is challenging due to its extremely arid environment, an under-educated and low-skilled workforce, and an economy that remains heavily reliant on the extraction and export of primary resources with little value added" (USAID 2008a)

25 Before a country can qualify for assistance, MCC examines its performance on 'independent' and 'transparent' policy indicators. For more on these and other issues, see MCC 2008.

26 According to Brigitte Weidlich in the *Namibian* (Windhoek, 7 April 2008): "This tenth package of development support for Namibia is covering six years instead of the usual five-year period in order to dovetail with the third National Development Plan (NDP3), which runs for the same period. According to EU Ambassador Dr Elisabeth Pape, some N$420,2 million will go to Namibia's Education and Training Sector Improvement Plan (ETSIP), which will cost N$2,4 billion over the next five years."

27 In February 2008, six Namibian dollars was equivalent to one Canadian dollar.

28 This assistance represented just under one-third of EU aid. However, this share has increased to about 50 per cent, as many member states have phased out bilateral aid to Namibia since expiry of its "as if LDC" (least-developed country) status in 2002; see European Commission 2008: www.ec.europa.eu/development/geographical/regionscountries/countries/namibia.htm (accessed 10 April 2008).

29 See Englebert (1997) for a very useful discussion of these and other issues.

30 In Namibia, UNESCO began with a representative, who also served as the regional communication adviser for southern Africa, and a secretary, and its office worked to establish joint relationships with the Namibian government on development in culture, education, and science.

31 On this field, see, for example, Barry 2004; Dean 2010; Escobar 1995b;
    Ferguson 2006; Goldman 2005a; Ilcan 2006; Ilcan and L. Phillips 2010;
    Lacey 2007; Larner and Walters 2004b; Rojas 2004.

32 For more information on Vision 2030, see www.tech.na/vision2030.htm

33 Furthermore, the Global Environment Facility (GEF) currently funds two
    projects that the World Bank runs, and it is preparing a third (World
    Bank 2008d).

CHAPTER FIVE

1 On racialized spatial practices in Namibia, see Müller-Friedman (2008).

2 Walters (forthcoming) offers critical insights into terms such as biopolitics and biopower. He suggests that scholars must note how they "com-
   bine with other forms of power and other specifications of the subject.
   Foucault once noted how the 'welfare state problem' involved the 'tricky
   adjustment' between a pastoral power exercised over living individuals
   and a political power wielded over legal subjects (Foucault 1988: 67)."
   For Walters, this tricky adjustment relates not just to the welfare state; it
   is also evident in "the birth of the humanitarian border" (forthcoming:
   14).

3 In Namibia today, where white settlers make up about 8 per cent of the
   population, commercial land under freehold title comprises about 6,300
   farms, which belong to 4,128 white farmers. According to Moyo (2003):
   "This freehold title land covers 44% of available land and 70% of the
   most productive agricultural land, while only 2.2 million hectares of the
   commercial farmlands belong to black farmers. By contrast, communal
   lands comprise 138,000 households with an area of 33.5 million hectares, which is only 41% of the land available" (2003: 41).

4 Dean suggests that sovereignty itself can be "'dispersed' like other power
   relations onto individuals, parents, families, health experts." Delegation is
   "caught within a network of forms of expertise … in as much as it is within the remit of legislatures, courts, judges and politicians" (2007: 93).

5 In the history of indigenous peoples within lands of colonization, for example, Dean observes that "there is hardly a form of the liberal government of the state that does not rest upon domination, coercion, violence
   or the threat and symbolics of violence. It is impossible to examine the
   constitutional legitimacy of the founding of states such as the United
   States, Canada, New Zealand and Australia, for example, without confronting the violent appropriation of land and extirpation of its inhabitants that this entailed" (2007: 95).

6 In 1960 the OPO became a movement of national liberation – SWAPO (see chapter 4 above) – working for an independent and democratic land, free from colonial oppression (see National Union of Namibian Workers 2008)

7 In the light of Deleuze and Guatarri (1994), Grosz (2005: 38) focuses on the unpredictability and singularity of events.

8 Human Rights Day, on 10 December, recalls the ethnic violence that took place on that day in 1959.

9 In 1962, South Africa's Odendaal Commission recommended partition of 40 per cent of SouthWest Africa into eleven bantustans (homelands) and confinement of blacks to these 'reserves' (Asante and Asombang 1989).

10 Many protests since have responded to policing of blacks in Katutura – for example, the Namibia National Students Organization's protest of 12 June 1988.

11 In May 1967, the General Assembly, following its 1966 decision to terminate South Africa's mandate, established the United Nations Council for South West Africa to administer the territory, with a commissioner to assist the eleven member states. The council met first on 16 August 1967, and in 1990 it concluded its business shortly after independence (UN 1990: 951).

12 In 1966, the General Assembly's twenty-four-member Special Committee on the Situation with regard to the Implementation of the Declaration on the Granting of Independence to Colonial Countries and Peoples received complaints from petitioners from South West Africa. The petitioners "strongly believed in the right of self-determination and independence for the people of South West Africa." They noted the suppression and exploitation, despite many UN resolutions. "South Africa was continuing its military development in the territory, contrary to the terms of the Mandate, including an air base, a military base and a training camp. Furthermore, the Chief Native Commissioner of South West Africa had stated that since the Afrikaners had won that territory by bloodshed, the only way Africans would regain it was by bloodshed. Reports in the press had also indicated that a military pact was thought to exist between South Africa, Portugal, and the illegal régime of Southern Rhodesia" (UN 1966: 596).

13 See Ilcan (2002) for an analysis of settlement and resettlement practices.

14 For more on tourist travels to and in Katutura, see www.namibian.org/travel/adventure/face.htm

15 See F. Friedman (2000) on the social and spatial organization of Windhoek today.

16 ELCIN has 660,000 members, over 200 pastors, and about 1,000 church workers (FELM 2008).

17 Although most residents had some form of work, independence made freedom of movement a right. Consequently, migrants mainly from northern

rural Namibia sought, and continue to seek, employment in Windhoek and other urban centres. Most end up in shacks in Katutura. According to Frayne (2004: 490–1), in addition to rapid population growth, rural–urban migration is increasing unemployment, which stands at about 40 per cent. Furthermore, Windhoek's economy has not expanded sufficiently to create enough jobs over the last decade.

18 On some of the ideas at this event, see, for example, New Era/All Africa Global Media via COMTEX (2008).

19 The NGO Sister Namibia, which aims to 'empower' girls and women in the struggle for gender equity and equality through media work, capacity building, research, documentation, networking, and collective action, developed a new vision for KCR with other NGOs in Namibia, especially in Windhoek (see www.drfn.org.na/awareness2.htm; accessed 25 June 2008).

20 As well as supporting media in certain parts of Namibia, UNESCO assisted community outlets, such as KCR (see UNESCO 2008b: 8).

21 Homeless International, a voluntary association formed in 1992, has worked with the Namibia Housing Action Group (NHAG). It has been assisting low-income housing groups since the late 1990s. "NHAG later restructured to become the support NGO for the newly created Shack Dwellers Federation of Namibia (SDFN). Residents in informal settlements in Namibia have been organising savings groups since 1987, but it was not until 1998 that the savings groups came together as a nationwide network to form SDFN" (Homeless International 2008). By the end of 2005, the SDFN boasted savings groups in all thirteen regions of Namibia, "with a total of around 300 different saving schemes and 15,000 households actively saving. SDFN has been able to save more than £250,000 and go on to accomplish an extraordinary number of feats for such a newly united federation" (Homeless International 2008).

22 On good-governance initiatives elsewhere, see, for example, Anders (2005: 37) and Ong (2006b).

23 For example, Nadesan (2008: 190), drawing on Valverde and Mopas (2004), argues that risk management requires extensive surveillance and can foster "targeted governance" of risky spaces, relations, and populations.

24 The national NGO NANASO works with other NGOs to address HIV/AIDS in Namibia. Many other NGOs also focus on HIV/AIDS in the country and specifically in Katutura.

25 For more on this NGO, see www.terredeshommes.it/english/about.php

26 This centre, with its home in Augsburg College, has been co-ordinating education in southern Africa since 1990. It began with short-term

programs and in 1994 set up an undergraduate semester program in Windhoek.

27 Namibia has transformed basic education since independence. For example, in partnership with the Ministry of Education since 1999, the Academy for Educational Development (AED) has aimed to alter classroom practices and student learning. It has trained almost 3,000 teachers and teacher educators on how to assess "learner performance," which is resulting in new teaching strategies and model lesson plans. "To measure the effectiveness of classroom instruction, new baseline standards of teacher performance based on the observation of 170 classrooms have been established. The value and replicability of these changes in classroom practice are best seen by the Ministry of Education's decision to expand the program from its initial pilot of 14 schools to over 900 schools covering the majority of Namibia's primary school teachers and students"; AED 2008 at www.one.aed.org/CentersandExperts/upload/GlobalEd_Bro_forweb.pdf (accessed 26 June 2008).

CHAPTER SIX

1 CARE Canada operates the 'click and sponsor' program as one of many marketing campaigns for development aid. For agencies such as Christian Children's Fund and World Vision, however, child sponsorship is the leading means of raising money (see, for example, Christian Children's Fund 2008; World Vision 2008).

2 For more on this idea, see, for example, Béland 2007a, 2007b; Bland 1973; Bugra and Keyder 2006; Fox Piven et al. 2002; Procacci 1989; Reid 2005; Schild 2000; Watson 2006.

3 See, for example, Foucault's discussion of pastoral care as a mode of governing both the individual and the 'flock' (2007: 128–9). Compare this analysis to that of later modes of governing in the 'post-pastoral' state (352–5).

4 See also Lee and Zhu (2006) on neoliberal housing reform in China; von Mahs (2005) on homeless policies in Berlin and Los Angeles; and Britain's Homeless Link (2004) on partnership and coalition work.

5 The many reports of success rely on accounts by either or both business and NGO partners.

6 The phrase 'new architecture of aid' – Farrington and Lomax (2001) – has featured in critical evaluations of aid regimes from the 1990s on.

7 One recent initiative is a Sino–German 'friendship' hospital. Shanghai's Tongji University, Siemens, and German hospital operator Asklepios

Kliniken have established a facility under a public–private partnership in the Shanghai International Medical Zone. Tongji University will train Chinese medical students in collaboration with Hanover's Medical University and Berlin's Charité Hospital (ChinaCSR.com 2007).

8 In their review of 'how to' literature on partnerships, Wildridge et al. use the term 'partnership imperative' to describe the proliferation of such arrangements in the United Kingdom: "Within the public, private and voluntary sectors, the need for partnership working, often cross-sectoral working or working beyond the boundaries, is recognized as a vital component of success ... As the focus moves away from the centralized government provision of public services, cross-sectoral partnerships involved in service delivery are becoming more common" (2004: 3).

9 The definition of fragile states is contentious and often relates to civil or outside conflict. Britain's DFID (2005) on fragile states is an example of broader notions: "where the government cannot or will not deliver core functions to the majority of its people, including the poor. The most important functions of the state for poverty reduction are territorial control, safety and security, capacity to manage public resources, delivery of basic services, and the ability to protect and support the ways in which the poorest people sustain themselves. DFID does not limit its definition of fragile states to those affected by conflict" (DFID 2005: 7). For conceptual debates and definitions and for 'state failure,' see, for example, Gross 1996; Jackson 1987; Milliken and Krause 2002; Zartman 1995.

10 On difficulties and issues in comparing aid donors, see, for example, Nowels (2006). As a percentage of gross domestic product, official U.S. overseas development assistance falls behind that of the European Union and Japan, according to figures for 2007–8.

CHAPTER SEVEN

1 Dinnen writes that the nation's half-million or so inhabitants speak more than eighty languages. Most people live on the six largest islands: Choiseul, Guadalcanal, Makira, Malaita, New Georgia, and Santa Isabel. Honiara, the capital, is on Guadalcanal (Dinnen 2003a).

2 Clive Moore describes adoption of the phrase *helpem fren* – "helping the government and the people to help themselves" (2007: 147).

3 Nga Hoe Tuputupu-mai-tawhiti is the Maori name for NZAID. Russell Glenn uses it as a subtitle for a section in Glenn (2007). We seek to convey the sense of aid coming to Solomon Islands, whether from New Zealand or from elsewhere.

4 No gross data exist on flows of development aid to Solomon Islands.
5 Following Gellman and Dankoff (2008), we note that the name Aboriginal
   and Torres Strait Islanders recognizes the geographical diversity of
   Australia's traditional owners. We use the term 'Aboriginal' to signify traditional owners of the lands, who are indigenous and non-white.
6 See also UNDP (2009b) and United Nations Statistics Division (2007).

Works Cited

Abrahamsen, R. 2004. "The power of partnerships in global governance." *Third World Quarterly* 25(8): 1453–67

Abrahamson, P. 2004. "Liquid modernity: Bauman on contemporary welfare society." *Acta Sociologica* 47(2): 171–9

Academy for Educational Development (AED) 2008. www.one.aed.org/CentersandExperts/upload/GlobalEd_Bro_forweb.pdf (accessed 26 June 2008)

Adongo, J., and M. Deen-Swarray. 2006. "Poverty alleviation in rural Namibia through improved access to financial services." NEPRU Working Paper No. 109. Windhoek: Namibian Economic Policy Research Unit

Affleck, A., and M. Mellor. 2006. "Community development finance: a neo-market solution to social exclusion." *Journal of Social Politics* 35(2):303–319

Africa News Update. 2007. "Namibia: poor should help themselves." 13 June. www.afrika.no/Detailed/14350.html (accessed 25 June 2008)

Agamben, G. 1998. *Homo Sacer: Sovereign Power and Bare Life.* Stanford, Calif.: Stanford University Press

– 2005. *State of Exception.* Trans. K. Attell. Chicago: University of Chicago Press

Agier, M. 2002. "Between war and city: towards an urban anthropology of refugee camps." *Ethnography* 3(3): 317–41

Aikman, S. 2003. "Mobile education in Darfur, Western Sudan." Oxfam International Enewsletter 11 Dec. www.oxfam.org/eng/story_Sudan_educ.htm (accessed 1 Dec. 2003)

Aitken, R. 2010. "Ambiguous incorporations: microfinance and global governmentality." *Global Networks* 10 (2): 223–43

Alasia, S. 2007. "Rainbows across the mountains: the first post-RAMSI general elections in Solomon Islands, April 2006, and the policies of the second Sogavare government." *Journal of Pacific History* 42(2): 165–86

Altman, J., and M. Hinkson (eds.) 2007. *Coercive Reconciliation: Stabilise, Normalise, Exit Aboriginal Australia.* Melbourne: Arena Publications

Amin, A. 2005. "Local community on trial." *Economy and Society* 34(4): 612–33

Amin, A., and N. Thrift 1992. "Neo-Marshallian nodes in global networks." *International Journal of Urban and Regional Research* 16: 571–87

Amstel, R. 2003. "Patterns of exclusion: sanitizing space, criminalizing homelessness." *Social Justice* 30(1): 195–221

Anders, G. 2005. "Good governance as technology: towards an ethnography of the Bretton Woods institutions." In D. Mosse and D. Lewis (eds.), *The Aid Effect.* London: Pluto Press: 37–60

Appadurai, A. 2001a. "Deep democracy: urban governmentality and the horizon of politics." *Environment and Urbanization* 13(2): 23–44

– 2001b. "Grassroots globalization and the research imagination." In A. Appadurai (ed.), *Globalization.* Durham, NC: Duke University Press: 1–21

– 2006. *Fear of Small Numbers: An Essay on the Geography of Anger.* Durham, NC: Duke University Press

Aretzaga, B. 2003. "Maddening states." *Annual Review of Anthropology.* 32:393–410

Armstrong, P., and Armstrong, H. 2002. "Women, privatization, and health care reform: the Ontario case." In Pat Armstrong et al. (eds.)., *Exposing Privatization: Women and Health Care Reform in Canada.* Aurora, Ont.: Garamond Press, 163–215

Aronowitz, S., and H. Gautney 2003. "The debate about globalization: an introduction." In S. Aronowitz and H. Gautney (eds.), *Implicating Empire: Globalization and Resistance in the 21st Century World Order.* New York: Basic Books: xi-xxx

Asante, S.K.B., and W.W. Asombang. 1989. "An independent Namibia? the future facing SWAPO." *Third World Quarterly* 11(3): 1–19

Asia–Pacific Defense FORUM Staff. 2008. "Pacific Partnership Mission: Solomon Islands." *Asia-Pacific Defense FORUM* (2nd quarter): 24–7

Asian Development Bank (ADB). 2006. "Country strategy and program update 2007–2009: Solomon Islands." www.adb.org/Documents/CSPs/SOL/2006/csp0200.asp (accessed 21 July 2008)

Aslanbeigui, N., and G. Summerfield. 2001. "Risk, gender, and development in the 21st century." *International Journal of Politics, Culture and Society.* 15(1): 7–26

AusAID 2007. "Aid activities in Solomon Islands: RAMSI economic governance and broad based growth." www.ausaid.gov.au/country/cbrief.cfm?DCon=5714_5074_8646_2331_4632&CountryID=16&Region=SouthAsia (accessed 21 March 2008)

Ayodele, T., F. Cudjoe, T.A. Nolutshungu, and C.K. Sunwabe. 2005. "African perspectives on aid: foreign assistance will not pull Africa out of poverty." *Cato Institute Economic Development Bulletin No. 2*

Bach, J., and D. Stark. 2004. "Link, search, interact: the co-evolution of NGOs and interactive technology." *Theory, Culture and Society* 21: 101–17

Bach, S., and G. Della Rocca. 2001. "The new public management in Europe." In C. Dell'Argina, G. Della Rocca, and B. Keller (eds.), *Strategic Choices in Reforming Public Service Employment: An International Handbook* (New York: Palgrave): 24–47

Backer, D., and D. Carroll. 2001. "NGOs and constructive engagement: promoting civil society, good governance and the rule of law in Liberia." *International Politics* 38(1): 1–26

Bäckstrand, K., and E. Lövbrand. 2006. "Planting trees to mitigate climate change: contested discourses of ecological modernization, green governmentality and civic environmentalism." *Global Environmental Politics* 6(1): 50–75

Baker, M. 2002. "Strengthening families through government programmes: before the era of partnerships." Local Partnerships and Governance Research Group: Research Paper Number 1, University of Auckland

Baker, T., and J. Simon. 2002. "Embracing risk." In T. Baker and J. Simon (eds.), *Embracing Risk: The Changing Culture of Insurance and Responsibility.* Chicago: University of Chicago Press: 1–25

Bandyopadhyay, S., M.N. Humavindu, P. Shyamsundar, and L. Wang. 2004. "Do households gain from community-based natural resource management? an evaluation of community conservancies in Namibia." Policy Research Working Paper 3337. Washington, DC: World Bank Group

Banks, G. 2008. "Understanding resource conflicts in Papua New Guinea." *Asia Pacific Viewpoint* 49(1): 23–34

Barnes, J.I., J. Macgregore, and L.C. Weaver. 2002. "Economic efficiency and incentives for change within Namibia's community wildlife use initiatives." *World Development* 30(4): 667–81

Basaran, T. 2008. "Security, law, borders: spaces of exclusion." *International Political Sociology* 2(4): 339–54

Basok, T., and S. Ilcan. 2006. "In the name of human rights: global organizations and participating citizens." *Citizenship Studies* 10(3): 309–72

- 2003. "The voluntary sector and the depoliticization of civil society: implications for social justice." *International Journal of Canadian Studies*. 28: 111–29

Bauer, G. 1998. *Labor and Democracy in Namibia, 1971–1996*. Athens: Ohio University Press

- 2001. "Namibia in the first decade of independence: how democratic?" *Journal of Southern African Studies* 27(1): 33–55

Bauman, Z. 2001. *Community: Seeking Safety in an Insecure World*. Cambridge: Polity

- 2006. *Liquid Fear*. Cambridge: Polity

BBC News. 2007. "Bangladesh cyclone hits poor hardest." www.news.bbc.co.uk/go/rss/-/2/hi/south_asia/7100879.stm (accessed 7 Aug. 2008)

Becker, B. 2005. *Speaking Out: Namibians Share Their Perspectives on Independence*. Windhoek: Out of Africa Publishers

Becker, H. 2007. "Making tradition: an historical perspective on gender in Namibia." In S. LaFont and D. Hubbard (eds.), *Unravelling Taboos: Gender and Sexuality in Namibia*. Windhoek: Legal Assistance Centre: 22–38

- 2005. "'Let me come to tell you': Loide Shikongo, the King, and poetic license in colonial Ovamboland." *History and Anthropology* 16(2): 235–58

Béland, D. 2007a. "Neo-liberalism and social policy: the politics of ownership." *Policy Studies* 28(2): 91–107

- 2007b. "The social exclusion discourse: ideas and policy change." *Policy and Politics* 35(1): 123–39

Bellamy, A.J., and M. McDonald. 2002. "The utility of human security: which humans? What security? A reply to Thomas and Tow." *Security Dialogue* 33(3): 373–7

Bellamy, A.J., and P. Williams (eds.). 2005. *Peace Operations and Global Order*. London: Routledge

Bello, W. 2002a. "The Oxfam debate: from controversy to common strategy." *South Bulletin* 36: 13–16

- 2002b. "What's wrong with the Oxfam trade campaign." *Global Policy Forum*. 26 April. www.focusweb.org/publications/2002/whats-wrong-with-the-oxfam-trade-campaign.html (accessed 28 July 2003)

Beneria, L. 2001. "Shifting the risk: new employment patterns, informalization, and women's work." *International Journal of Politics, Culture and Society* 15(1): 27–53

Bennett, J. 2002. "Roots of conflict in Solomon Islands: though much is taken, much abides: legacies of tradition and colonialism." State Society and Governance in Melanesia Discussion Paper 02/5. State Society and Governance in Melanesia Project. Canberra, Research School of Pacific and Asian Studies, Australian National University: 1–16

Bland, D.E. 1973. "Population and liberalism." *Journal of the History of Ideas* 34(1): 113–22

Blaser, M., H. Feit, and G. McRae. 2004. "Indigenous peoples and development processes: new terrains of struggle." In M. Blaser, H. Feit, and G. McRae (eds.), *In the Way of Development*. London: Zed Books: 1–25

Bond, P. 2002. "Moderates wilt but radical South Africans struggle on." *ZNet Daily Commentaries*. 17 April. www.zmag.org/sustainers/content/2002-04/17bond.cfm (accessed 9 Sept. 2003)

– 2006a. "Global governance campaigning and MDGs: from top-down to bottom-up anti-poverty work." *Third World Quarterly* 27(2): 339–54

– 2006b. *Looting Africa: The Economics of Exploitation*. London: Zed Books

Bondi, L. 2005. "The changing landscape of voluntary sector counselling in Scotland." Institute of Geography, School of Geosciences, University of Edinburgh. hdl.handle.net/1842/823 (accessed 11 March 2007)

Borch, C. 2005. "Systemic power: Luhmann, Foucault, and analytics of power." *Acta Sociologica* 48(2): 155–66

Bornstein, E. 2003. *The Spirit of Development: Protestant NGOs, Morality and Economics in Zimbabwe*. New York: Routledge

Bosworth, M. 2007. "Creating the responsible prisoner: federal admission and orientation packs." *Punishment and Society* 9(1): 67–85

Bourdieu, P. 1992. "The practice of reflexive sociology (The Paris Workshop)." In P. Bourdieu and L.J.D. Wacquant (eds.), *An Invitation to Reflexive Sociology*. Chicago: University of Chicago Press: 217–60

Bowker, G., and S.L. Star. 2000. *Sorting Things Out: Classification and Its Consequences*. Cambridge, Mass.: MIT Press

Braidotti, R. 1994. *Nomadic Subjects: Embodiment and Sexual Difference in Contemporary Feminist Theory*. New York: Columbia University Press

– 2006. *Transpositions: On Nomadic Ethics*. Cambridge: Polity

Brauman, R. 2004. "From philanthropy to humanitarianism: remarks and an interview." *South Atlantic Quarterly* 103(2/3): 397–417

Brenner, N., and N. Theodore. 2002. "Cities and the geographies of 'actually existing neoliberalism.'" In N. Brenner and N. Theodore (eds.), *Spaces of Neoliberalism: Urban Restructuring in North America and Western Europe*. Malden, Mass.: Blackwell Publishers: 2–32

Brinkerhoff, D.W. 2007. "Introduction – governance challenges in fragile states: re-establishing security, rebuilding effectiveness, and reconstituting legitimacy." In D.W. Brinkerhoff (ed.), *Governance in Post-Conflict Societies: Rebuilding Fragile States*. London: Routledge: 1–22

Brinkerhoff, J.M. 2002. *Partnership for International Development: Rhetoric or Results?* Boulder, Col.: Lynne Rienner

Brinkerhoff, J.M., and A.A. Goldsmith. 2005. "Institutional dualism and international development: a revisionist interpretation of good governance." *Administration and Society* 37(2): 199–224

Brock, K., and K. Banting. 2001. "The nonprofit sector and government in a new century: an introduction." In K. Brock and K. Banting (eds.), *The Nonprofit Sector and Government in a New Century*. Montreal: McGill-Queen's University Press: 1–20

Brodie, J. 1996. "Restructuring and the new citizenship." In Isabella Bakker (ed.), *Rethinking Restructuring: Gender and Change in Canada*. Toronto: University of Toronto Press: 126–41

– 2002. "Citizenship and solidarity: reflections on the Canadian way." *Citizenship Studies* 6(4): 377–94

– 2007. "Reforming social justice and neoliberal times." *Studies in Social Justice* 1(2): 93–107

– 2008. "The social in social citizenship." In E. Isin (ed.), *Recasting the Social in Citizenship*. Toronto: University of Toronto Press: 20–44

Brody, L. 2003. "Coffee quality: Oxfam United States stirring up Kraft worldwide." www.maketradefair.com (accessed 22 July 2003)

Brydon, D., and W. Coleman. 2007. "Globalization, autonomy, and community." In D. Brydon and W. Coleman (eds.), *Renegotiating Community: Interdisciplinary Perspectives, Global Contexts*. Vancouver: UBC Press: 1–28

Buğra, A., and Ç. Keyder 2006. "The Turkish welfare regime in transformation." *Journal of European Social Policy* 16(3): 211–28

Bulmer, M. 1995. "Some observations on the history of large philanthropic foundations in Britain and the United States." *Voluntas: International Journal of Voluntary and Nonprofit Organizations* 6(3): 275–91

Burchell, G. 1996. "Liberal government and techniques of the self." In A. Barry, T. Osbourne, and N. Rose (eds.), *Foucault and Political Reason: Liberalism, Neoliberalism, and Rationalities of Government*. Chicago: University of Chicago Press: 19–36

Butler, J. 1993. *Bodies That Matter: On the Discursive Limits of "Sex"*. London: Routledge

– 1997. *The Psychic Life of Power: Theories of Subjection*. Stanford, Calif.: Stanford University Press

Capoor, I. 2005. Square pegs in round holes: Redefining public–private partnership. *Development* 48(4): 137–42

CARE Canada. 2008. Homepage. www.care.ca/care_e.asp (accessed 12 Feb. 2008)

Carrington, K. 2006. "Law and order on the border in the neo-colonial antipodes." In Sharon Pickering and Leanne Weber (eds.), *Borders, Mobilities, and Technologies of Control*. Dordrecht, the Netherlands: Springer: 179–206

Carroll, W.K. 2003. "Undoing the end of history: Canada-centered reflections on the challenge of globalization." In *Global Shaping and Its Alternatives*. Toronto: Garamond Press: 33–55

Castells, M. 1996. *The Information Age, vol. 1, The Rise of the Network Society*. Oxford: Blackwell.

CDP (Committee for Development Policy). 2004. "Poverty reduction and good governance: report of the Committee for Development Policy on the sixth session (29 March–2 April 2004)." New York: United Nations Department of Economic and Social Affairs

Chambers, R. 1983. *Rural Development: Putting the Last First*. London: Langman

– 2001. "The World Development Report: concepts, content and a chapter 12." *Journal of International Development* 13(3): 299–306

Chandler, D. 2001. "The road to military humanitarianism: how the human rights NGOs shaped a new humanitarian agenda." *Human Rights Quarterly* 23: 678–700

– 2003. "New rights for old? Cosmopolitan citizenship and the critique of state sovereignty." *Political Studies* 51(2): 332–49

Changfoot, N. 2007. "Local activism and neoliberalism: performing neoliberal citizenship as resistance." *Studies in Political Economy* 80: 129–49

Chase-Dunn, C., Y. Kawano, and B.D. Brewer. 2000. "Trade globalization since 1795: waves of integration in the world-system." *American Sociological Review* 65: 77–95

Chesters, G. 2004. "Global complexity and global civil society." *Voluntas: International Journal of Voluntary and Nonprofit Organizations* 15(4): 323–42

Chhotray, V. 2004. "The negation of politics in participatory development projects, Kurnool, Andhra Pradesh." *Development and Change* 35(2): 327–52

ChinaCSR. 2007. "Public–private partnership aids Sino-German friend-ship hospital." www.chinacsr.com/2007/05/28/1359-public-private-partnership-aids-sino-germ (accessed 27 Feb. 2008)

Chiware, E.R.T. 2007. "Designing and implementing business information services in the SMME sector in a developing country: the case for Namibia." IFLA Journal 33: 136–44

Chok, S., J. Macbeth, and C. Warren. 2007. "Tourism as a tool for poverty alleviation: a critical analysis of 'pro-poor tourism' and implications for sustainability." Current Issues in Tourism 10(2–3): 144–65

Christian Children's Fund. 2008. Homepage. www.christianchildrensfund.org/ (accessed 12 Feb. 2008)

CIDA (Canadian International Development Agency). 2007. "CIDA Update – January 2005." www.acdi-cida.gc.ca/CIDAWEB/acdicida.nsf/En/STE-42484832-H5K (accessed 17 Oct. 2007)

Cling, J.-P., M. Razafindrakoto, and F. Roubaud. 2003. "Poverty Reduction Strategy Papers: old wine in new bottles?" In J.-P. Cling, M. Razafindrakoto, and F. Roubaud (eds.), New International Poverty Reduction Strategies. London: Routledge: 180–202

Coates, D. 2006. "Welfare state change: towards a Third Way?" Perspectives on Politics 4(1): 212–13

Coe, N., and T. Bunnell. 2003. "'Spatializing' knowledge communities: to-wards a conceptualization of transnational innovation networks." Global Networks 3(4): 437–56

Collier, P. 2007. The Bottom Billion: Why the Poorest Countries Are Failing and What Can Be Done About It. Oxford: Oxford University Press

Consultative Group to Assist the Poorest (CGAP). 2006. "Access for all: building inclusive financial systems." Washington, DC: World Bank

Cooke, B. 2003. "A new continuity with colonial administration: partici-pation in development management." Third World Quarterly 24(1): 47–61

Cooke, B., and U. Kothari (eds.). 2001. Participation: The New Tyranny? London: Zed Books

Cornwall, A. 1998. "Gender, participation and the politics of difference." In I. Guijt and M. Shah (eds.), The Myth of Community: Gender Issues in Participatory Development. London: Intermediate Technology Publications: 46–57

Cornwall, A., and K. Brock. 2005. "What do buzzwords do for develop-ment policy? a critical look at 'participation', 'empowerment', and 'pov-erty reduction'." Third World Quarterly 26(7): 1043–60

Corsi, M., F. Botti, T. Rondinella, and G. Zacchia. 2006. "Women and microfinance in Mediterranean countries." *Development* 49(2): 67–74

Craig, D., and D. Porter. 2003. "Poverty Reduction Strategy Papers: a new convergence world." *Development* 31(1): 53–69

– 2005. "The Third Way and the Third World: poverty reduction and social inclusion strategies in the rise of inclusive liberalism." *Review of International Political Economy* 12(2): 226–63

– 2006. *Development beyond Neo-Liberalism: Governance, Poverty Reduction and Political Economy*. London: Routledge

Crawford, G. 2003a. "Partnership or power? deconstructing the 'Partnership for Governance Reform' in Indonesia." *Third World Quarterly* 24(1): 139–59

– 2003b. "Promoting democracy from without – learning from within (part I)." *Democratization* 10(1): 77–98

Cruikshank, B. 1993. "Revolutions within: self-government and self-esteem." *Economy and Society* 22(3): 327–44

– 1994. "The will to empower: technologies of citizenship and the war on poverty." *Socialist Review* 23(4): 29–55

– 1999. *The Will to Empower: Democratic Citizens and Other Subjects*. Ithaca, NY: Cornell University Press

Crush, J. 1995. "Introduction: imagining development." In J. Crush (ed.), *Power of Development*. London: Routledge: 1–24

Davis, M. 2006. *Planet of Slums*. London: Verso

DCLG (Department for Communities and Local Government). 2006a. Strong and prosperous communities – a summary. www.communities.gov.uk/publications/localgovernment/strongprosperous (accessed 12 Feb. 2008)

– 2006b. "Strong and prosperous communities: the Local Government White Paper." www.communities.gov.uk/documents/localgovernment/pdf/152456 (accessed 12 Feb. 2008)

Deacon, B., E. Ollila, M. Koivusalo, and P. Stubbs. 2003. *Global Social Governance*. Helsinki: Ministry for Foreign Affairs of Finland, Department for International Development Cooperation

Dean, M. 1991. *The Constitution of Poverty: Toward a Theory of Liberal Governance*. London: Routledge

– 1999. *Governmentality: Power and Rule in Modern Society*. London: Sage

– 2002. "Liberal government and authoritarianism." *Economy and Society* 31(1): 37–61

– 2007. *Governing Societies: Political Perspectives on Domestic and International Law*. Berkshire, England: Open University Press/McGraw Hill

- 2010. *Governmentality: Power and Rule in Modern Society.* 2nd ed. London: Sage

Dean, M., and B. Hindess (eds.). 1998. *Governing Australia: Studies in Contemporary Rationalities of Government.* Cambridge: Cambridge University Press: 210–26

Dearden, S. 2004. "An assessment of the EU's Namibia Country Strategy Papers." EU Development Policy Discussion Paper. Brussels: European Commission

Deleuze, G. 1988. *Bergsonism.* Trans. H. Tomlinson and H. Habberjam. Boston: Zone Books

Deleuze, G., and F. Guattari. 1987. *A Thousand Plateaus: Capitalism and Schizophrenia.* Trans. B. Massumi. London: Continuum

Deleuze, G., and Parnet, C. 1987. *Dialogues.* Trans. H. Thomlinson and B. Habberjam. New York: Columbia University Press

Della Porta, D. 2007. "The global justice movement: an introduction." In D. della Porta (ed.), *The Global Justice Movement: Cross-National and Transnational Perspectives.* Boulder, Col.: Paradigm Publishers: 1–28

Dell'Aringa, C. 2001. "Reforming public sector labor relations." In C. Dell'Aringa, G. Della Rocca, and B. Keller (eds.), *Strategic Choices in Reforming Public Service Employment: An International Handbook.* Basingstoke, England: Palgrave Publishers: 1–23

Denis, A. 2003. *Women and Globalization in the Economic North and South: Global Shaping and Its Alternatives.* Canada: Kumerian Press, Inc.

Denzin, N., and Y. Lincoln (eds.). 2005. *Handbook of Qualitative Research.* London: Sage Publications

DFID (Department for International Development). 2005. "Why we need to work more effectively in fragile states." www.dfid.gov.uk/pubs/files/fragilestates-paper.pdf (accessed 16 March 2008)

- 2007. "Transforming rural livelihoods in India." www.dfid.gov.uk/pubs/files/Transforming-RL-India.pdf (accessed 16 March 2008)

Dickens, C. 1977 [1853]. *Bleak House.* Ed. G. Ford and S. Monod. New York: W.W.Norton

Diken, B., and C.B. Laustsen. 2005. *The Culture of Exception: Sociology Facing the Camp.* Abingdon, Oxon.: Routledge

Dillon, M., and J. Reid. 2001. "Global liberal governance: biopolitics, security and war." *Millennium: Journal of International Studies* 30(1): 44–66

- 2009. *The Liberal Way of War: Killing to Make a Life Live.* Abingdon, Oxon.: Routledge

Dinnen, S. 2002. "Political chronicles – winners and losers: politics and disorder in the Solomon Islands 2000–2002." *Journal of Pacific History* 37(3): 285–98

– 2003a. "Guns, money and politics: disorder in the Solomon Islands." In
R. May (ed.), *"Arc of Instability"? Melanesia in the Early 2000s.*
Christchurch: Macmillan Brown Centre for Pacific Studies and State
Society and Governance in Melanesia Project: 27–41

– 2003b. "Restorative justice in the Pacific Islands: an introduction." In
S. Dinnen, A. Jowitt, and T. Cain (eds.), *A Kind of Mending: Restorative
Justice in the Pacific Islands.* Canberra: Pandanus: 1–34

– 2007. "A comment on state-building in Solomon Islands." *Journal of
Pacific History* 42(2): 255–63

Dobrowolsky, A., and J. Jenson. 2004. "Shifting representations of citizenship:
Canadian politics of 'women' and 'children.'" *Social Politics* 11: 154–80

Donoghue, M. 2007. "The early economic writings of William Thomas
Thornton." *History of Political Economy* 39(2): 209–52

Donzelot, J. 1988. "The promotion of the social." *Economy and Society*
17(3): 395–427

Duffield, M. 2001a. *Global Governance and the New Wars: The Merging
of Development and Security.* London: Zed Books

– 2001b. "Governing the borderlands: decoding the power of aid."
Disasters 25(4): 308–20

– 2005. "Social reconstruction: the reuniting of aid and politics."
Development 48(3): 16–24

– 2007. *Development, Security and Unending War.* London: Polity

– 2008. "Global civil war: the non-insured, international containment and
post-interventionary society." *Journal of Refugee Studies* 21(2): 145–65

Duneier, M. 1999. *Sidewalk.* New York: Farrar, Straus and Giroux

Dureau, C. 2001. "Recounting and remembering 'First Contact' on Simbo." In
J.M. Mageo (ed.), *Cultural Memory: Reconfiguring History and Identity in
the Postcolonial Pacific.* Honolulu: University of Hawai'i Press: 130–63

Dzinesa, G., and M. Rupiya. 2005. "Promoting national reconciliation and
regional integration: the Namibian Defence Force from 1990–2005." In
*Evolutions and Revolutions: A Contemporary History of Militaries in
Southern Africa.* Pretoria: Institute for Security Studies: 199–234

Eade, D., and S. Williams. 1995. *The Oxfam Handbook of Relief and
Development.* Oxford: Oxfam

EAIF. 2007. EAIF *Six-monthly Report April 2007.* London: DFID

Economist. 2006. "Microcredit in India: microsharks." 19 Aug.

Edkins, J. 2000. *Whose Hunger? Concepts of Famine, Practices of Aid.*
Minneapolis: University of Minnesota Press

– 2007. "Missing persons: Manhattan, September 2001." In E. Dauphinee
and C. Masters (eds.), *The Logics of Biopower and the War on Terror:
Living, Dying, Surviving.* New York: Palgrave: 25–42

Elden, S. 2002. "The war of races and the constitution of the state: Foucault's 'Il faut défendre la société' and the politics of calculation." *Boundary* 2(29): 125–51

Emerging Africa Infrastructure Fund (EAIF). 2007. www.emergingafric-afund.com/about-us.aspx (accessed 3 Sept. 2007)

Englebert, P. 1997. "The contemporary African state: neither African nor state." *Third World Quarterly* 18(4): 767–75

Escobar, A. 1995a. *Encountering Development: The Making and Unmaking of the Third World.* Princeton, NJ: Princeton University Press

– 1995b. "Imagining a post-development era." In J. Crush (ed.), *Power of Development.* London: Routledge: 205–22

– 2005. "Economics and the space of modernity." *Cultural Studies* 19(2): 139–75

Essex, J. 2008. "The neoliberalization of development: trade capacity building and security at the US Agency for International Development." *Antipode* 40 (2): 229–51

Etzioni, A. 2006. "Sovereignty as responsibility." *Orbis* 50 (1): 71–85

European Commission. 2008. "Mission and role." www.ec.europa.eu/development/about/mission_en.cfm (accessed 9 April 2008)

Falkner, D. 2003. "Taking citizenship seriously: social capital and criminal justice in a changing world." *Criminal Justice* 3(3): 287–315

Farrington, J., and J. Lomax. 2001. "Rural development and the 'new architecture of aid': convergence and constraints." *Development Policy Review* 19(4): 533–44

Faux, J. 2004. "Without consent: global capital mobility and democracy." *Dissent* 51(1): 43–50

Fay, S.B. 1944. UNRRA. *Current History* 7: 8–12

FELM. 2008. www.mission.fi/in_english/global_mission/regions/namibia/ (accessed 20 July 2008)

Ferguson, J. 1994. *The Anti-Politics Machine: "Development," Depoliticization and Bureaucratic Power in Lesotho.* Cambridge: Cambridge University Press

– 2002. "Global disconnect: abjection and the aftermath of modernism." In J.X. Inda and R. Rosaldo (eds.), *The Anthropology of Globalization.* Oxford: Blackwell Publishers: 136–56

– 2006. *Global Shadows: Africa in the Neoliberal World Order.* Durham, NC: Duke University Press

Ferguson, J., and A. Gupta. 2002. "Spatializing states: toward an ethnography of neoliberal governmentality." *American Ethnologist* 29(4): 981–1002

– 2005. "Spatializing states: toward an ethnography of globalization." In J.X. Inda (ed.), *Anthropologies of Modernity: Foucault, Governmentality, and Life Politics.* Malden, Mass.: Blackwell Publishers: 105–34

Flint, J. 2006. "Maintaining an arm's length? housing, community governance and the management of 'problematic' populations." *Housing Studies* 21(2): 171–86

Flynn, P. 2007. "Microfinance: the newest financial technology of the Washington Consensus." *Challenge* 50(2): 110–21

Folke, S., and H. Nielsen. 2006. *Aid Impact and Poverty Reduction.* New York: Palgrave

Forrest, J.B. 1994. "Namibia – the first postapartheid democracy." *Journal of Democracy* 5(3): 88–100

Foucault, M. 1972. *Archaeology of Knowledge.* Trans. A.M. Sheridan Smith. London: Tavistock Publications

– 1978. *The History of Sexuality: An Introduction.* Trans. R. Hurley. Harmondsworth: Penguin

– 1979. *Discipline and Punish.* Vintage Books: New York

– 1984. "Polemics, politics, and problematizations." In P. Rabinow (ed.), *The Foucault Reader.* New York: Pantheon

– 1988. "The ethic of the care for the self as a practice of freedom." In J. Bernauer and D. Rasmussen (eds.), *The Final Foucault.* Cambridge Mass.: MIT Press: 1–20

– 1989. *The Archaeology of Knowledge.* London: Routledge

– 1990. *The Use of Pleasure: The History of Sexuality.* Vol. 2. New York: Vintage Books

– 1993. *About the Beginning of the Hermeunetics of the Self (Transcription of Two Lectures in Dartmouth on November 17 and 24, 1980).* Ed. M. Blasius. *Political Theory* 21 (2): 198–227

– 1994. "Nietzsche, genealogy, history." In P. Rabinow and N. Rose (eds.), *The Essential Foucault: Selections from Essential Works of Foucault, 1954–1984.* New York: New Press: 370–6

– 2001a. *The Hermeneutics of the Subject: Lectures at the Collège de France, 1981–82.* Ed. F. Gros and trans. G. Burchell. New York: Picador.

– 2001b. "The subject and power." In *The Essential Works 1954–1984, Vol. 3: Power.* London: Allen Lane

– 2003a. *The Essential Foucault: Selections from Essential Works of Foucault, 1954–1984.* Ed. P. Rabinow and N. Rose. New York: New Press

– 2003b. *Society Must Be Defended (Lectures at the Collège de France 1975–1976).* Ed. M. Bertani and A. Fontana and trans. D. Macey. New York: Picador

– 2007. *Security, Territory, Population* (Lectures at the Collège de France, 1977–1978). Ed. M. Senellart and trans. G. Burchell. New York: Palgrave MacMillian

Fouinat, F. 2006. "A comprehensive framework for human security." In R. Picciotto and R. Weaving (eds.), *Security and Development: Investing in Peace and Prosperity*. London: Routledge: 71–80

Fox Piven, F., J. Acker, M. Hallock, and S. Morgen (eds.). 2002. *Work, Welfare, and Politics: Confronting Poverty in the Wake of Welfare Reform*. Eugene: University of Oregon Press

Fraenkel, J. 2004. *The Manipulation of Custom: From Uprising to Intervention in the Solomon Islands*. Wellington: Victoria University Press

Fraser, N. 1997. *Justice Interruptus: Critical Reflections on "Postsocialist" Condition*. New York: Routledge

– 2008. "Abnormal justice." *Critical Inquiry* 34: 393–422

– 2009. *Scales of Justice: Reimagining Political Space in a Globalizing World*. New York: Columbia University Press

Fraser, N., and A. Honneth. 2003. *Redistribution or Recognition? A Political-Philosophical Exchange*. London: Verso

Frayne, B. 2004. "Migration and urban survival strategies in Windhoek, Namibia." *Geoforum* 35: 489–505

Frayne, B., and W. Pendleton. 2001. "Home is where the heart is: Namibians on cross-border migration and regional integration." *African Studies* 60 (2): 205–24

Friedman, F. 2000. "Deconstructing Windhoek: the urban morphology of a post-apartheid city." Department Planning Unit Working Paper No. 111. London: University College London

Friedman, J.T. 2006. "On the post-structuralist critique of development: a view from north-west Namibia." *Development Southern African* 23(5): 587–603

Frye, N. 2005. "Repositioning the third sector: From 'shadowy enclave' to 'centre stage.' *Antipode* 37(3): 536–57

Fudge, J., and Vosko, L. 2001. "Gender, segmentation and the standard employment relationship in Canadian labour law, legislation and policy." *Economic and Industrial Democracy* 22: 271–310

Fuller, S. 2005. "Public sector employment and gender wage inequalities in British Columbia: assessing the effects of a shrinking public sector." *Canadian Journal of Sociology* 30(4): 405–39

Gabriel, B., and S. Ilcan (eds.). 2004. *Post-Modernism and the Ethical Subject*. Montreal: McGill-Queen's University Press

Garland, D. 1996. "The limits of the sovereign state: strategies of crime
control in contemporary society." *British Journal of Criminology* 36(4):
445–71

GAVI Alliance 2008. "Innovative partnership." www.gavialliance.org/
about/in_partnership/index.php (accessed 16 Feb. 2008)

Gegeo, D.W., and K.A. Watson-Gegeo. 2002. "Whose knowledge? epis-
temological collisions in Solomon Islands community development."
Contemporary Pacific 14(2): 377–409

Gellman, M., and J. Dankoff. 2008. "Australian government intervenes in
Aboriginal communities." *Toward Freedom*. www.towardfreedom.com/
home/content/view/1221/69/ (accessed 2 Jan. 2009)

Gewald, J.B. 2001. '*We Thought We Could Be Free ...*' *Socio-Cultural
Aspects of Herero History*. Cologne: Rüdiger Köppe Verlag

Ghosh Banerjee, S., and D.A. Rondinelli. 2003. "Does foreign aid promote
privatization? empirical evidence from developing countries." *World
Development* 31(9): 1527–48

Gibson-Graham, J.K. 2006. *A Post-Capitalist Politics*. Minneapolis:
University of Minnesota Press

Gindin, S. 2002. "Anti-capitalism and the terrain of social justice."
Monthly Review 53(9): 1–14

Giroux, H. 2005. "The terror of neoliberalism: rethinking the significance
of cultural politics." *College Literature* 32(1): 1–19

Glenn, R. 2007. *Counterinsurgency in a Test Tube: Analyzing the Success
of the Regional Assistance Mission to Solomon Islands*. Santa Monica,
Calif.: RAND Corporation

Glennie, J. 2006. "The myth of charity: a 2005 reality check."
Globalizations 3(2): 258–60

Goldman, M. 1998. "Inventing the commons: theories and practices of the
commons' professional." In M. Goldman (ed.), *Privatizing Nature:
Political Struggles for the Global Commons*. New Brunswick, NJ:
Rutgers University Press: 1–19

– 2005a. *Imperial Nature: The World Bank and Struggles for Social
Justice in the Age of Globalization*. New Haven, Conn.: Yale University
Press.

– 2005b. "Tracing the roots/routes of World Bank power." *International
Journal of Sociology and Social Policy* 25(1/2): 10–29

– 2006. "How 'Water for All!' policy became hegemonic: the power of the
World Bank and its transnational policy networks." Presentation for
Science, Knowledge Communities and Environmental Governance:

Global–Local Linkages Conference, Center for Global Change and
Governance, Rutgers University, 4–5 May

Gonzales, M.C. 2000. "Re-educating Namibia: the early years of radical
education reform, 1990–1995." *Africa Today* 47(1): 104–24

Gough, J., A. Eisenschitz, and A. McCulloch. 2006. *Spaces of Social
Exclusion*. London: Routledge

Gould, J. 2005a. "Conclusion: the politics of consultation." In J. Gould
(ed.), *The New Conditionality: The Politics of Poverty Reduction
Strategies*. London: Zed Books: 135–60

– 2005b. "Poverty, politics and states of partnership." In J. Gould (ed.),
The New Conditionality: The Politics of Poverty Reduction Strategies.
London: Zed Books: 1–16

– 2005c. "Timing, scale and style: capacity as governmentality in
Tanzania." In D. Mosse and D. Lewis (eds.), *The Aid Effect*. London:
Pluto Press: 61–84

– 2007. "[Dis]assembling development." In J. Gould and L. Siitonen
(eds.), *Anomalies of Aid: A Festschrift for Juhani Koponen*. Helsinki:
Institute of Development Studies (Interkont Books 15): 269–95

Gould, J., and J. Ojanen. 2005. "Tanzania: merging in the circle." In
J. Gould (ed.), *The New Conditionality: The Politics of Poverty
Reduction Strategies* London: Zed Books: 17–65

Gower, P., and M. Johnston. 2009. "Govt wants more say on $480m for-
eign aid." *New Zealand Herald* (3 March) www.nzherald.co.nz/nz/
news/article.cfm?c_id=1&objectid=10559626 (accessed 23 May 2009)

Graefe, P. 2006. "The social economy and the American model: relating new
social policy directions to the old." *Global Social Policy* 6(2): 197–219

Grameen Foundation 2007. Homepage. www.grameenfoundation.org/
what_we_do/microfinance_in_action/faqs/ (accessed 17 Oct. 2007)

Green, M. 2006. "Representing poverty and attacking representations:
perspectives on poverty from social anthropology." *Journal of
Development Studies* 42(7): 1108–29

Green, P. 2006. "State crime beyond borders." In Sharon Pickering and
Leanne Weber (eds.), *Borders, Mobilities, and Technologies of Control*.
Dordrecht, the Netherlands: Springer: 149–66

Green, P., and D. Hulme. 2005. "From correlates and characteristics to
causes: thinking about poverty from a chronic poverty perspective."
World Development 33(6): 867–80

Gross, J.-G. 1996. "Toward a taxonomy of failed states in the New World
Order: decaying Somalia, Liberia, Rwanda, and Haiti." *Third World
Quarterly* 17(3): 455–72

Grosz, E. 2005. *Time Travels: Feminism, Nature, Power*. Durham, NC: Duke University Press

Guerin, I. 2006. "Women and money: lessons from Senegal." *Development and Change* 37(3): 549–70

Gupta, A., and J. Ferguson (eds.). 1999. *Culture, Power, Place: Explorations in Critical Anthropology*. Durham, NC: Duke University Press

Haarmann, C., and D. Haarmann. 2007. "From survival to decent employment: basic income security in Namibia." *International Journal of Basic Income Research* 2(1): 1–7

Haddad, M.A. 2006. "Civic responsibility and patterns of voluntary participation around the world." *Comparative Political Studies* 39(10): 1220–42

Hall, M. (ed.). 2007. *Pro-Poor Tourism: Who Benefits – Perspectives on Tourism and Poverty Reduction*. Clevedon: Channel View Publications

Hall, M.H., and P.B. Reed. 1998. "Shifting the burden: how much can government download to the non-profit sector?" *Canadian Public Administration* 41: 1–20

Hamber, B. 2002. "'Ere their story die': truth, justice and reconciliation in South Africa." *Race and Class* 44(1): 61–79

Hameiri, S. 2007. "The trouble with RAMSI: re-examining the roots of conflict in Solomon Islands." *Contemporary Pacific* 19(2): 409–41

Haque, M.S. 2004. "Governance based on partnership with NGOs: implications for development and empowerment in rural Bangladesh." *International Review of Administrative Sciences* 70(2): 271–90

Hardt, M., and A. Negri. 2000. *Empire*. Cambridge, Mass.: Harvard University Press

Harrington, M. 1962. *The Other America*. New York: Macmillan

Hartmann, W., J. Silvester, and P. Hayes (eds.). 2001. *The Colonising Camera: Photographs in the Making of Namibian History*. Cape Town: Cape Town University Press

Harvey, D. 2005. *Spaces of Neoliberalization: Towards a Theory of Uneven Geographical Development* (Hettner Lecture 2004). Stuttgart: Franz Steiner Verlag

Hattori, T. 2003. "Giving as a mechanism of consent: international aid organizations and the ethical hegemony of capitalism." *International Relations* 17(2): 153–73

Hay, J. 2003. "Unaided virtues: the (neo)liberalization of the domestic sphere and the new architecture of community." In J. Bratich, J. Packer, and C. McCarthy (eds.), *Foucault, Cultural Studies, and Governmentality*. Albany: State University of New York: 165–206

Hiatt, S.R., and W.P. Woodworth. 2006. "Alleviating poverty through microfinance: village banking outcomes in Central America." *Social Science Journal* 43: 471–7

Hilary, J. 2005. "DFID, UK and public services privatization: time for change." *Global Social Policy* 5(2): 134–6

Hilhorst, D. 2003. *The Real World of NGOs: Discourses, Diversity and Development*. London: Zed Books

Hindess, B. 1998. "Neoliberalism and the national economy." In M. Dean and B. Hindess (eds.), *Governing Australia: Studies in Contemporary Rationalities of Government*. Cambridge: Cambridge University Press: 210–26

– 2000. "Citizenship in the international management of populations." *American Behavioural Scientist* 43(9): 1486–97

– 2001. "The liberal government of unfreedom." *Alternatives: Global, Local, Political* 26(2): 93–111

– 2002. "Neoliberal citizenship." *Citizenship Studies* 6(2): 127–43

– 2004. "Liberalism – what's in a name?" In W. Larner and W. Walters (eds.), *Global Governmentality*. London : Routledge: 23–39

Homeless International. 2008. "Namibia." www.homeless-international. org/standard_1.aspx?id=0:384&id=0:276&id=0:262 (accessed 18 July 2008)

Homeless Link. 2004. "Regional housing and planning consultation briefing response." www.homeless.org.uk/briefings/briefing.2004-12-06. 3377663376 (accessed 27 Feb. 2008)

Howard, J. 2003. Transcript of Prime Minister John Howard's address to the Sydney Institute, Sydney, 1 July. www.pm.gov.au/news/speeches/ speech323.html (accessed 11 March 2007)

HRSDC (Human Resources and Social Development Canada). 2007. "The new homelessness partnering strategy." www.homelessness.gc.ca/about_ us/index_e.asp (accessed 20 Feb. 2008)

Hughes, C., and V. Pupavac. 2005. "Framing post-conflict societies: international pathologisation of Cambodia and the post-Yugoslav states." *Third World Quarterly* 26(6): 873–89

IDB (Inter-American Development Bank). 2007. "Development banks are in a competitive market." www.iadb.org/idbamerica/index.cfm?thisid= 4109 (accessed 17 Oct. 2007)

Ilcan, S. 2002. *Longing in Belonging: The Cultural Politics of Settlement*. New York: Praeger

– 2006. "Global governing organizations: order-building and waste management." *Current Sociology* 54(6): 851–72

– 2008. "Camp biopolitics and mobile sovereignty in colonial Namibia." Presentation to the Security and Exclusion Conference, Centre for Studies in Social Justice. University of Windsor. 23 Oct.

– 2009. "Privatizing responsibility: public sector reform under neoliberal government." *Canadian Review of Sociology* 46(3): 207–34

Ilcan, S., and T. Basok. 2004. "Community government: voluntary agencies, social justice, and the responsibilization of citizens." *Citizenship Studies* 8(2): 129–44

Ilcan, S., and A. Lacey. 2005. "Practices of globalization and aid: the 'new aid regime' of Oxfam Canada and CARE Canada." Presentation to the Global Studies Association (GSA) conference. University of Tennessee, Knoxville, April

– 2006. "Governing through empowerment: Oxfam's global trade and reform campaigns." *Globalizations* 3(2): 207–25

Ilcan, S., D. O'Connor, and M. Oliver. 2003. "Contract governance and the Canadian public sector." *Relations Industrielle/Industrial Relations* 58(4): 620–43

Ilcan, S., M. Oliver, and D. O'Connor. 2007. "Spaces of governance: gender and public sector restructuring in Canada." *Gender, Place and Culture* 14(10): 75–92

Ilcan, S., and L. Phillips. 2003. "Making food count: expert knowledge and global technologies of government." *Canadian Review of Sociology and Anthropology.* 40(4): 441–62

– 2005. "Circulations of insecurity: globalizing food standards in historical perspective. In J. Bingen and L. Busch (eds.), *Agricultural Standards: The Shape of the Gobal Food and Fiber System.* Dordrecht, the Netherlands: Kluwer, 51–72

– 2008. "Governing through global networks: knowledge mobilities and participatory development." *Current Sociology* 56(6): 711–34

– 2010. "Developmentalities and calculative practices: the Millennium Development Goals." *Antipode* 42(4): 844–74

Inter-American Development Bank. See IDB.

International Strategy for Disaster Reduction 2007. www.unisdr.org/eng/public_aware/world_camp/2006–2007/iddr/2007-iddr-activities-f.html (accessed 2 July 2008)

Isin, E.F. 2000. "Governing cities without government." In E. Isin (ed.), *Democracy, Citizenship and the Global City.* London: Routledge: 148–68

– 2002. *Being Political: Genealogies of Citizenship.* Minneapolis: Minnesota Press

– 2007. "Theorizing acts of citizenship." In E.F Isin and G. Nielsen (eds.), *Acts of Citizenship*. London: Palgrave Macmillan: 15–43

Isin, E.F., and G. Nielsen (eds.). 2007. *Acts of Citizenship*. London: Palgrave Macmillan

Isin, E.F., and K. Rygiel. 2007. "Abject spaces: frontiers, zones, camps." In E. Dauphinee and C. Masters (eds.), *The Logics of Biopower and the War on Terror: Living, Dying, Surviving*. New York: Palgrave: 181–204

Isin, E.F., and B. Turner. 2007. "Investigating citizenship: an agenda for citizenship studies." *Citizenship Studies* 11(1): 5–17

Isin, E.F., and P. Wood. 1999. *Citizenship and Identity*. London: Sage Publications

Jackson, R.H. 1987. "Quasi-states, dual regimes, and neoclassical theory: international jurisprudence and the Third World." *International Organization* 41(4): 519–49

Jameson, F., and M. Miyoshi (eds.). 1998. *The Cultures of Globalization*. Durham, NC: Duke University Press

Jennings, M. 2001. "Development is very political in Tanzania: Oxfam and the Chunya Integrated Development Programme." In O. Barrow and M. Jennings (eds.), *The Charitable Impulse: NGOs and Development in East and North-East Africa*. Bloomfields, Conn.: Kumarian Press

Jessup, P.C. 1944. "UNRRA, sample of world organization." *Foreign Affairs* 22: 362–73

Johnson, L., and C. Shearing. 2003. *Governing Security*. London: Routledge

Jolly, M. 2007. "Imagining Oceania: indigenous and foreign representations of a sea of islands." *Contemporary Pacific* 19(2): 508–45

Kabutaulaka, T.T. 2001. "Beyond ethnicity: the political economy of the Guadalcanal crisis in Solomon Islands." State Society and Governance in Melanesia Working Paper 01/1. State Society and Governance in Melanesia Project. Canberra, Research School of Pacific and Asian Studies, Australian National University: 1–24

– 2002. "A weak state and the Solomon Islands peace process." East West Centre Pacific Islands Development Series Working Paper 14. Manoa, East West Centre, University of Hawaii: 1–34

—2005. "Australian foreign policy and the RAMSI intervention in Solomon Islands." *Contemporary Pacific* 17(2): 283–99

– 2007. "Political reviews: Solomon Islands." *Contemporary Pacific* 19(2): 597–605

– 2008. "Dancing, dying, crawling, crying: stories of continuity and change in the Polynesian community of Tikopia." *Solomon Star* 12 Feb.

www.solomonstarnews.com/index.php?option=com_content&task=
view&id=379&Itemid=26&change=71&changeown= (accessed 15 Aug.
2008)

Kamat, S. 2004. "The privatization of public interest: theorizing NGO discourse in a neoliberal era." *Review of International Political Economy*
11(1): 155–76

Kameeta, Z., C. Haarmann, D. Haarmann, and H. Jauch 2007.
"Promoting employment and decent work for all: towards a good practice model in Namibia." Presentation to the United Nations Commission
for Social Development, 45th Session, 7–16 Feb. 2007. Windhoek

Keating, M. 2003. "Social inclusion, devolution and policy divergence."
Political Quarterly 74(4): 429–38

Kerkvliet, B.J. 2005. *The Power of Everyday Politics: How Vietnamese
Peasants Transformed National Policy.* Ithaca, NY: Cornell University Press

Kidd, A. 2002. "The 'liberal state': civil society and social welfare in nineteenth-century England." *Journal of Historical Sociology* 15(1): 114–19

Kilby, P. 2007. "The Australian aid program: dealing with poverty?"
Australian Journal of International Affairs 61(1): 114–29

Koenig-Archibug, M. 2003. "Mapping global governance." Background
paper for the concluding discussion of Workshop 11 – The Governance
of Global Issues: Effectiveness, Accountability, and Constitutionaliza-
tion, 2003 ECPR Joint Sessions, Edinburgh

Kössler, R. 2007. "Facing a fragmented past: memory, culture and politics
in Namibia." *Journal of Southern African Studies* 33(2): 361–82

Lacey, A. 2005a. "Networked communities: social centres and activist
spaces in contemporary Britain." *Space and Culture: The International
Journal of Social Spaces* 8(3): 286–301

– 2005b. "Spaces of justice: the social divine of global anti-capital activists' sites of resistance." *Canadian Review of Sociology and
Anthropology* 42(4): 403–20

– 2007. "Forging spaces of justice." In S. Shukaitis and D. Graeber (eds.),
*Constituent Imagination: Militant Investigations, Collective
Theorization.* Edinburgh: AK Press: 242–8

Lacey, A., and S. Ilcan. 2006. "Volunteer labour, responsible citizenship,
and international NGOs." *International Journal of Comparative
Sociology* 47(1): 35–53

Lakoff, A. 2005. "The private life of numbers: pharmaceutical marketing
in post-welfare Argentina." In A. Ong and S. Collier (eds.), *Global
Assemblages: Technology, Politics, and Ethics as Anthropological
Problems.* Malden, Mass.: Blackwell: 194–213

Lancet. 2005. "Bill Gates: a 21st century Robin Hood?" 365(9463): 911–12

Land, I. 2005. "Bread and arsenic: citizenship from the bottom up in Georgian London." *Journal of Social History* 39(1): 89–110

Larner, W. 2000. "Privatization, governance and identity: the United Kingdom and New Zealand compared." *Policy and Politics* 28(3): 361–77

– 2002. "The political rationality of 'new regionalism': toward a genealogy of the region." *Theory and Society* 31: 391–432

– 2004. "Global benchmarking: participating 'at a distance' in the globalizing economy." In W. Larner and W. Walters (eds.), *Global Governmentality: Governing International Spaces*. Milton Park, England: Routledge: 212–32

Larner, W., and M. Butler. 2005. "Governmentalities of local partnerships: the rise of the 'partnering state' in New Zealand." *Studies in Political Economy* 75: 79–101

Larner, W., and R. Le Heron. 2005. "Neoliberalising spaces and subjectivities: reinventing New Zealand universities." *Organization* 12(6): 843–62

Larner, W., and W. Walters (eds.). 2004a. *Global Governmentality: Governing International Spaces*. London: Routledge

– 2004b. Introduction. In Larner and Walters (2004a): 1–20

LaRRI 2008. Homepage. www.larri.com.na/index.htm (accessed 20 July 2008)

Larsen, J.E. 2004. "The politics of marginal space." In J. Andersen and B. Siim (eds.), *The Politics of Inclusion and Empowerment: Gender, Class, and Citizenship*. New York: Palgrave Macmillan: 202–23

Latour, B. 1993. *We Have Never Been Modern*. Cambridge, Mass.: Harvard University Press

Lawson, A. 2007. "Geographies of care and responsibility." *Annals of the Association of American Geographers* 97(1): 1–11

Lazar, S. 2006. "El Alto, Ciudad Rebelde: organisational bases for revolt." *Bulletin of Latin American Research* 25(2): 183–99

– 2007. "Education for credit: microcredit NGOs as citizenship projects." Paper presented at the Annual Conference of the Norwegian Association for Development Research, Oslo, 23–24 Oct.

Leader, N., and P. Colenso. 2005. "Aid instruments in fragile states." www. oecd (accessed 12 Aug. 2007)

Leander, A., and R. van Munster. 2007. "Private security contractors in Darfur: reflecting and reinforcing neo-liberal governmentality." *International Relations* 21(2): 201–16

LeBeau, D., and E.M. Ipinge. 2004. "Namibia's progress towards gender equality: post-Beijing policies and programmes." In D. LeBeau, E.M. Ipinge, J. Hunter, and G.J. Spence (eds.), *Beijing + 10: The Way Forward – An Introduction to Gender Issues in Namibia*. Windhoek: Namibia Institute for Democracy

Lee, J., and Y.-P. Zhu. 2006. "Urban governance, neoliberalism and housing reform in China." *Pacific Review* 19(1): 39–61

Legal Assistance Centre (LAC). 2006. *Our Land They Took: San Land Rights Under Threat in Namibia*. Windhoek: Legal Assistance Centre

– n.d. "What does the Legal Assistance Centre do?" Pamphlet. Windhoek: Legal Assistance Centre

Leitner, H., and E. Sheppard. 1998. "Economic uncertainty, interurban competition and the efficacy of entrepreneurialism." In T. Hall and P. Hubbard (eds.), *The Entrepreneurial City*. Chichester, England: Wiley: 285–308

Lemke, T. 2002. "Foucault, governmentality, and critique." *Rethinking Marxism* 14: 49–64

Levine, S. 2006. "Measuring progress towards global poverty goals: challenges and lessons from southern Africa." *African Statistical Journal* 3: 89–110

Leys, C., and S. Brown. 2005. *Histories of Namibia: Living through the Liberation Struggle*. London: Merlin Press

Liew, J. 2006. "Banking the unbanked in Fiji: the ANZ Bank and UNDP Partnership Model." World Bank Global Conference on Access to Finance: Building Inclusive Financial Systems, Washington, DC, 30–31 May. www.microfinance-pasifika.org/Documents/Publications/Banking_the_unbnaked_in_Fiji_WB_Paper_16_05_06.pdf (accessed 12 Aug. 2007)

Lippert, R., and D. O'Connor. 2003. "Security assemblages: airport security, flexible work, and liberal governance." *Alternatives* 28(3): 331–58

– 2006. "Security intelligence networks and the transformation of private security." *Policing and Society* 16(1): 49–65

Lister, S., and W. Nyamugasira. 2003. "Design contradictions in the new architecture of aid? reflections from Uganda on the roles of civil society organizations." *Development Policy Review* 21(1): 93–106

Low, A., A. Tjongarero, A. Low, and B. Nambundunga. 2001. "Donor support to human resource capacity building in Namibia: experience of resident technical assistance support for workplace learning and assessment of alternative options." *Journal of International Development* 13: 269–85

Lucarelli, B. 2005. "Microcredit: a cautionary tale." *Journal of Contemporary Asia* 35: 78–87

Lyon-Callo, V. 2004. *Inequality, Poverty, and Neoliberal Governance: Activist Ethnography in the Homeless Sheltering Industry.* Toronto: Broadview

MacDonald, L. 2001. "NGOs and the discourse of participatory development in Costa Rica." In H.Veltmeyer and A. O'Malley (eds.), *Transcending Neoliberalism: Community-Based Development in Latin America.* Bloomfield, Conn.: Kumarian Press: 123–53

Mamu, M. 2008. "More investors are coming here." *Solomon Star* 19 Aug. www.solomonstarnews.com/index.php?option=com_content&task=view&id=2949&Itemid=26 (accessed 19 Aug. 2008)

Manathunga, C. 2007. "Supervision as mentoring: the role of power and boundary crossing." *Studies in Continuing Education* 29(2): 207–21

Martinez Lucio, M., and R. MacKenzie. 2004. "'Unstable boundaries?' evaluating the 'new regulation' within employment relations." *Economy and Society* 33(1): 77–97

Marshall, T.H. (1983[1950]). "Citizenship and social class." In D. Held (ed.), *States and Societies.* Basil Blackwell: Oxford: 248–60

Matthews, S. 2008. "The role of the privileged in responding to poverty: perspectives emerging from the post-development debate." *Third World Quarterly* 29(6): 1035–49

May, J., P. Cloke, and S. Johnsen. 2005. "Re-phasing neoliberalism: new Labour and Britain's crisis of street homelessness." *Antipode* 37(4): 703–30

Mbembe, A. 2003. "Necropolitics." Trans. L. Meintjes. *Public Culture* 15(1): 11–40

– 2008. "Aesthetics of superfluity." In S. Nuttall and A. Mbembe (eds.), *Johannesburg: The Elusive Metropolis.* Durham, NC: Duke University Press: 37–67

MCC (Millennium Challenge Corporation). 2008. "About MCC." www.mcc.gov/about/index.php (accessed 9 April 2008)

McConnell, T. 2000. "Personal narratives of political history: social memory and silence in Namibia." *Dialectical Anthropology* 25: 27–59

McDaniel, S. 2003. "Social cohesion and gender: reflections on tendencies and tensions." *Canadian Journal of Sociology* 28(1): 43–50

McErvale, J., and N. Maclellan. 2007. "The Social Empowerment and Education Program (SEEP), Fiji. Run by the Ecumenical Centre for Research, Education and Advocacy. Supported by Oxfam Australia. A case study for the AusAID *Building Demand for Better Governance* initiative." www.oxfam.org.au/resources/filestore/originals/OAus-SocialEmpowermentFiji-1205.pdf (accessed 12 Aug. 2009)

McGrath, S., and K. King. 2004. "Knowledge-based aid: a four agency comparative study." *International Journal of Educational Development* 24(2): 167–81

Mehra, R., and G.R. Gupta. 2006. "Gender mainstreaming: making it happen." www.siteresources.worldbank.org/INTGENDER/Resources/Mehra GuptaGenderMainstreamingMakingItHappen.pdf (accessed 12 July 2007)

Melber, H. 2005. "Namibia's post-colonial socio-economic (non-)transformation: business as usual." *Quartal* 3(4): 306–21

Mertes, T. 2004. Introduction. In T. Mertes (ed.), *A Movement of Movements: Is Another World Really Possible?* London: Verso: vii-xii

Metsola, L. 2006. "Reintegration of ex-combatants and former fighters: a lens into state formation and citizenship in Namibia." *Third World Quarterly* 27(6): 1119–35

Meyer, H. 2002. "Educational partnerships and democratic education in Namibia." *Africa Today* 113–31

Microcredit Summit Campaign. 2007. Homepage. www.microcredit summit.org/summit/previous.htm (accessed 15 Oct. 2007)

Millennium Challenge Corporation. See MCC.

Miller, P. 1992. "Accounting and objectivity: the invention of calculating selves and calculable spaces." *Annals of Scholarship* 9(1/2): 61–86

– 1995. "Production, identity, and democracy." *Theory and Society* 24: 427–67

Miller, P., and N. Rose. 2008. *Governing the Present: Administering Economic, Social and Personal Life.* Cambridge: Polity

Milligan, C., and N. Fyfe. 2005. "Preserving space for volunteers: exploring the links between voluntary welfare organisations, volunteering and citizenship." *Urban Studies* 42: 417–33

Milliken, J., and K. Krause 2002. "State failure, state collapse, and state reconstruction: concepts, lessons, and strategies." *Development and Change* 33(5): 753–74

Missingham, B. 2002. "The village of the poor confronts the state: a geography of protest in the assembly of the poor." *Urban Studies* 39(9): 1647–63

Mitlin, D. 2003. "A fund to secure land for shelter: supporting strategies of the organized poor." *Environment and Urbanization* 15(1): 181–92

– 2008. "With and beyond the state – co-production as a route to political influence, power and transformation for grassroots organizations." *Environment and Urbanization* 20(2): 339–60

Mitlin, D., and D. Satterthwaite. 2007. "Strategies for grassroots control of international aid." *Environment and Urbanization* 19(2): 483–500

Mkapa, B.W. 2004. "Cancun's false promise: a view from the South." *Foreign Affairs* 83(3): 33–135

Molyneux, M. 2001. "Ethnography and global processes." *Ethnography* 2(2): 273–82

Molz, J. 2005. "Getting a 'flexible eye': round-the-world travel and scales of cosmopolitan citizenship." *Citizenship Studies* 9(5): 517–31

Moore, C. 2004. *Happy Isles in Crisis: The Historical Causes for a Failing State in Solomon Islands, 1998–2004.* Canberra: Asia Pacific Press

– 2007. "External intervention: the Solomon Islands beyond RAMSI." In M.A. Brown (ed.), *Security and Development in the Pacific Islands: Social Resilience in Emerging States.* Boulder, Col.: Lynne Reinner Publishers: 169–96

Morgan, R. 1991. "State pensions as an income safety net in Namibia." *Food Policy* 16(5): 351–9

Morison, J. 2000. "The government–voluntary sector compacts: governance, governmentality, and civil society." *Journal of Law and Society* 27(1): 98–132

Mosse, D. 2005a. *Cultivating Development: An Ethnography of Aid Policy and Practice.* London: Pluto Press

– 2005b. "Global governance and the ethnography of international aid." In Mosse and Lewis (2005): 1–36

Mosse, D., and D. Lewis (eds.). 2005. *The Aid Effect: Giving and Governing in International Development.* London: Pluto Press

Moyo, S. 2003. *Human Development Report 2004. Socio-Economic Dominance of Ethnic and Racial Groups – the African Experience.* Prepared for the UNDP, Human Development Report Office

Mramba, B.P. 2005. "Tanzania: 'smart' partnerships." *Finance and Development* 42(3) www.imf.org/external/pubs/ft/fandd/2005/09/mramba.htm (accessed 30 Oct. 2007)

Muller, A., and D. Mitlin. 2007. "Securing inclusion: strategies for community empowerment and state redistribution." *Environment and Urbanization* 19(2): 425–39

Müller-Friedman, F. 2008. "Toward a (post) apartheid architecture? a view from Namibia." *Planning Perspectives* 23(1): 29–48

Munck, R. 2005. *Globalization and Social Exclusion: A Transformationalist Perspective.* Bloomfield, Conn.: Kumarian Press

Murdoch, J. 2004. "Putting discourse in its place: planning, sustainability and the urban capacity study." *Area* 36(1): 50–8NACSO (Namibian

Association of CBNRM Support Organizations). 2007. "Namibia's Communal Conservancies: A Review of Progress in 2006." Windhoek: NACSO

Nadesan, M.H. 2008. *Governmentality, Biopower and Everyday Life.* London: Routledge

Namibia Red Cross. 2009. *Annual General Meeting.*

Namibia Travel. 2008. "Windhoek Township tour." Namibia: Cardboard Box Travel Shop: www.namibian.org/travel/adventure/windhoek-township.html (accessed 10 April 2008)

The *Namibian.* 2008. Windhoek, 7 April. www.allafrica.com/stories/200804070970.html) (accessed 10 April 2008)

Namibian Development Trust (NDT). 2004–6. NDT *Report January 2004– December 2006.* Windhoek

NANGOF. 2008. "Overview of partnerships." www.nangof.iway.na/ Namibia Red Cross (accessed 24 June 2008)

National Planning Commission (Republic of Namibia). 2006. *Poverty Bulletin: Addressing Rural Poverty* 1(2). Windhoek: National Archives of Namibia

National Union of Namibian Workers. 2008. Homepage. www.nunw.org. na/swapo.htm (accessed 22 July 2008)

Neal, A.W. 2006. "Foucault in Guantanamo: towards an archaeology of the exception." *Security Dialogue* 37(1): 31–46

Nelson, P. 2000. "Globalization, NGO advocacy and international financial policy – unlearning lessons from lobbying the World Bank?" *Oxfam America Working Paper 6.* Washington, DC: Oxfam America

New Era/All Africa Global Media via COMTEX. 2008. "Genocide reparations group plans long march." 30 May

NGOConnect.Net. 2008. "NGOConnect.Net: sharing resources and knowledge among the global NGO community." www.ngoconnect.net/ home (accessed 13 Dec. 2008)

Nguyen, V.-K. 2005. "Antiretroviral globalism, biopolitics, and therapeutic citizenship." In A. Ong and S.J. Collier (eds.), *Global Assemblages: Technology, Politics, and Ethics as Anthropological Problems.* Malden, Mass.: Blackwell: 124–44

Nietzsche, F.W. 1999. *On the Genealogy of Morals: A Polemic by Way of Clarification and Supplement to My Last Book, Beyond Good and Evil.* Trans. D. Smith; contributor D. Smith. Oxford: Oxford University Press

Nowels, L. 2006. *Foreign Aid: Understanding Data Used to Compare Donors. CRS Report to Congress.* www.fas.org/sgp/crs/row/RS22032. pdf (accessed 23 Sept. 2007)

Nunn, A. 2007. "The capacity building programme for English local gov-
    ernment: evaluating mechanisms for delivering improvement support to
    local authorities." *Local Government Studies* 33(3): 465–84

Nyers, P. 2006. *Rethinking Refugees: Beyond States of Emergency.* New
    York: Routledge

– 2007. "Community without status: non-status migrants and cities of
    refuge." In D. Brydon and W. Coleman (eds.), *Renegotiating Community:
    Interdisciplinary Perspectives, Global Contexts.* Vancouver: UBC Press:
    123–40

NZAID. 2007. "Making a difference in Solomon Islands." www.nzaid.govt.
    nz/programmes/c-solomon-islands.html (accessed 12 Aug. 2007)

– 2009. "Where NZAID works: Solomon Islands." www.nzaid.govt.nz/
    programmes/c-solomon-islands.html (accessed 13 Dec. 2009)

Oakland Tribune. 2008. "Budget cuts hit the poor hardest." www.findarticles.
    com/p/articles/mi_qn4176/is_20080216/ai_n24315066 (accessed 7 Aug.
    2008)

O'Connor, D., and S. Ilcan. 2005. "The folding of liberal government: con-
    tract governance and the transformation of the public service in
    Canada." *Alternatives: Global, Local, Political* 30(1): 1–23

O'Connor, D., R. Lippert, D. Spencer, and L. Smylie. 2008. "Seeing private
    security like a state." *Criminology and Criminal Justice* 8(2): 203–26

O'Donnell, M., C. Allan, and D. Peetz. 2001. "The new public management and
    workplace change." *Economic and Labour Relations Review* 12: 85–103

Office of the United States Trade Representative. 2007. *2007 Compre-
    hensive Report on U.S. Trade and Investment Policy toward Sub-Saharan
    Africa and Implementation of the African Growth and Opportunity Act.*
    www.usaid.gov/locations/sub-saharan_africa/initiatives/2007_agoa_ustr_
    report.pdf (accessed 30 Oct. 2007)

Ogbaharya, D.G. 2006. "A capability theory of CBNRM: the case of
    Namibia's communal conservancy program." Paper presented at the
    International Conference of the Human Development and Capability
    Association, Groningen, the Netherlands, 29 Aug.–1 Sept.

Olds, K., and N. Thrift. 2005. "Cultures on the brink: reengineering the
    soul of capitalism – on a global scale." In A. Ong and S. Collier (eds.),
    *Global Assemblages: Technology, Politics, and Ethics as Anthropological
    Problems.* Malden, Mass.: Blackwell: 270–90

Olsson, L. 2001. "Gender mainstreaming in practice: the United Nations
    transitional assistance group in Namibia." *International Peacekeeping*
    8(2): 97–110

O'Malley, P. 2004. *Risk, Uncertainty and Government*. London: GlassHouse Press

Ong, A. 1999. *Flexible Citizenship: The Cultural Logics of Transnationality*. Durham, NC: Duke University Press

– 2005. "Ecologies of expertise: assembling flows, managing citizenship." In A. Ong and S. Collier (eds.), *Global Assemblages*. Malden, Mass.: Blackwell Publishers: 337–53

– 2006a. "Mutations in citizenship." *Theory, Culture and Society* 32(2–3): 499–531

– 2006b. *Neoliberalism as Exception: Mutations in Citizenship and Sovereignty*. Durham, NC: Duke University Press

Organization for Economic Cooperation and Development (OECD). 2006. "Promoting pro-poor growth: key policy messages." www.oecd.org/dataoecd/0/61/37852580.pdf (accessed 18 Oct. 2007)

– 2007. "Poverty reduction." www.oecd.org/department/0,3355,en_2649_34621_1_1_1_1_1,00.html (accessed 18 Oct. 2007)

Orissa Poverty Reduction Mission. 2007. "Tender call: expression of interest for human resource strategy for Orissa Poverty Reduction Mission (TRIPTI Project)." www.orissapanchayat.gov.in/English/download/EOI_HR_Strategy.pdf (accessed 30 Nov. 2007)

Owens, J. 2008. "Blood ties and tongue ties: the role of children in shifting the boundaries of Namibia's German-speaking community." *Journal of the History of Childhood and Youth* 1(2): 232–49

Owusu, C. 2004. "An international NGO staff reflections on power, procedures and relationships." In L. Groves and R. Hinton (eds.), *Inclusive Aid: Changing Power and Relationships in International Development*. London: Earthscan: 108–22

Oxaal, Z. 1997. "Gender and empowerment: definitions, approaches and implications for policy." Working Paper. Brighton, England: Institute of Development Studies

Oxfam Australia and New Zealand. 2006. "Bridging the gap between state and society: new directions for the Solomon Islands." www.oxfam.org.au/www.oxfam.org.nz (accessed 1 May 2007)

Oxfam Canada. 2002a. "Let's harness trade for development: why Oxfam opposes FTAA." www.oxfam.ca/news/Peoples_Summit/Opposes_FTAA.htm (accessed 28 July 2003)

– 2002b. "Media misreads Oxfam report – no break with movement." www.oxfam.ca/news/MakeTradeFair/Media_reply.htm (accessed 22 July 2003)

- 2003a. "Aid agencies target WTO agriculture talks – world hunger in the balance." www.oxfam.ca/news/MakeTradeFair/WTOAgTalksBrief.htm (accessed 9 May 2003)
- 2003b. "Squeezed to the last drop." www.oxfam.ca/News/MakeTrade Fair/Kraftaction2.htm (accessed 9 May 2003)
- 2006. "The right to basic social services – Namibia: improving basic healthcare for the San people." www.oxfam.ca/what_we_do/thm02_ BasicNecessary.htm (accessed 5 Sept. 2006)
- 2007a. "No sweat: ethical purchasing policies gain support." www. oxfam.ca/what-we-do/campaigns/no-sweat/ethical-purchasing-policies-gain-support/?searchterm=sweatshop (accessed 12 July 2007)
- 2007b. "Oxfam Canada annual report." 2007. www.oxfam.ca/news-and-publications/publications-and-reports/oxfam-canada-annual-report-2007/file (accessed 23 March 2008)
- 2008. "Emergencies." oxfam.ca/what-we-do/emergencies (accessed 23 March 2008)
Oxfam GB. 2002a. "About Oxfam: a short history of Oxfam." www. oxfam.org.uk/atwork/history/oxhist1.htm (accessed 7 Aug. 2003)
- 2002b. "Before October 5th: the origins of Oxfam." www.oxfam.org. uk/atwork/history/oxhist1.htm (accessed 7 Aug. 2003)
- 2005. "Programme impact report: Oxfam GB's work with partners and allies around the world." www.oxfam.org.uk/what_we_do/issues/ evaluation/impact_report_2005.htm (accessed 28 March 2007)
- 2007a. "Incense: the sweet smell of success." www.oxfam.org.uk/what_ we_do/fairtrade/parables/incense/index.htm (accessed 12 July 2007)
- 2007b. "Oxfam: shop on-line and on the High Street." www.oxfam.org. uk/shop/index.html (accessed 28 June 2007)
- 2007c. "Why is fair trade important?" www.oxfam.org.uk/what_we_ do/fairtrade/why_ft.htm (accessed 2 July 2007)
Oxfam Gender Team. 1994. "Women linking for change: Oxfam's women's linking project." Focus on Gender 2(3): 29–33
Oxfam International. 2001a. "Oxfam: code of conduct." www.oxfam.org/ eng/ (accessed 9 May 2003)
- 2001b. "Stichting Oxfam International Constitution." www.oxfam.org/ eng/ (accessed 9 May 2003)
- 2001c. "Strategic Plan." www.oxfam.org/eng/about_strat_balance.htm (accessed 6 May 2003)
- 2002a. "Five aims of Oxfam International – a rights-based approach." www.oxfam.org/eng/campaigns_aims.htm (accessed 9 May 2003)

– 2002b. "Mugged: poverty in your coffee cup (Make Trade Fair)." www.oxfam.org/eng/ (accessed 9 May 2003)

– 2002c. "Oxfam's response to Walden Bello." www.oxfam.org/eng/ (accessed 28 July 2003)

– 2002d. "Rigged rules and double standards: trade, globalisation and the fight against poverty." www.maketradefair.com/assets/english/Report_English.pdf (accessed 28 May 2003)

– 2002e. "What we do." www.oxfam.org/eng/about_what.htm (accessed 9 May 2003)

– 2003a. "EU hypocrisy unmasked: why EU trade policy hurts development." www.oxfam.org/eng/ (accessed 9 May 2003)

– 2003b. "Partners: internal policy paper." www.oxfam.org/eng/campaigns_part.htm (accessed 9 May 2003)

– 2003c. "Strategic plan: beyond business as usual." www.oxfam.org/eng/about_strat_business.htm (accessed 9 May 2003)

– 2003d. "The emperor's new clothes: why rich countries want WTO investment agreement." www.oxfam.org/eng/ (accessed 9 May 2003)

– 2003e. "Walk the talk: a call to action to restore coffee farmers' livelihoods." www.oxfam.org/eng/ (accessed 9 May 2003)

– 2004. Homepage. www.oxfam.org/eng/index.htm (accessed 2 June 2004)

– 2005a. "About us." www.oxfam.org/eng/about.htm (accessed 29 June 2005)

– 2005b. "Global campaign for education briefing paper." www.oxfam.org/eng/pdfs/gce_030911_no_%20progress.pdf (accessed 14 June 2005)

– 2005c. "Kicking down the door: how upcoming WTO talks threaten farmers in poor countries." www.maketradefair.com/en/assets/english/kickingreport.pdf (accessed 2 May 2005)

– 2005d. "Making trade work for development in 2005: what the EU should do." www.maketradefair.com/en/assets/english/eu2005.pdf (accessed 14 June 2005)

– 2005e. "Oxfam International annual report 2005." www.oxfam.org/en/files/annual_report_2005.pdf (accessed 31 Aug. 2006)

– 2005f. "Oxfam International's mission statement." www.oxfam.org/en/about/mission (accessed 20 June 2007)

– 2005g. "Oxfam International submission to World Bank review of conditionality, May 2005." www.siteresources.worldbank.org/PROJECTS/578280-1119562936151/20554736/World%20Bank%20cond%20submission.pdf (accessed 31 Aug. 2006)

– 2005h. "Oxfam's Make Trade Fair campaign." www.oxfam.org/en/
policy/briefingnotes/OI_mtf_wsf_2005_final_eng (accessed 20 June
2007)

– 2005i. "Paying the price: why rich countries must invest now in a war
on poverty." www.oxfam.org/pub.htm (accessed 12 May 2005)

– 2005j. "What happened in Hong Kong? Initial analysis of the WTO
Ministerial, December 2005." www.oxfam.org/pub.htm (accessed
8 Sept. 2006)

– 2006. "Oxfam International campaigns: global call to action against
poverty." www.oxfam.org/en/programs/campaigns/endpoverty/index.
htm (accessed 27 Aug. 2006)

– 2007a. "Children in Kalma sing to keep healthy." www.oxfam.org/en/
programs/emergencies/sudan/kalma_singing (accessed 12 July 2007)

– 2007b. "Oxfam: about us – who we are." www.oxfam.org/en/about/
who/ (accessed 20 June 2007)

– 2007c. "Oxfam celebrates win-win outcome for Ethiopian coffee."
Oxfam press release, 21 June. www.oxfam.org/en/news/2007/
pr070621_win-win-outcome-for-ethiopian-coffee-farmers-and-starbucks.
html (accessed 23 March 2008)

– 2007d. "Oxfam International Strategic Plan 2007–2012." www.oxfam.
org/en/files/oi_strategic_plan_2007.pdf (accessed 14 July 2007)

– 2007e. "Oxfam/Make Trade Fair – celebrities dumping photos." www.
maketradefair.com/work/celebs/ (accessed 12 July 2007)

– 2007f. "Press release – 25 July 2006: Current approaches to food crises
are failing Africa's poor." www.oxfam.org/en/news/pressreleases2006/
pr060724_africa_food_crisis (accessed 12 July 2007)

– 2007g. "Signing away the future: how trade and investment agreements
between rich and poor countries undermine development." www.oxfam.
org/en/policy/briefingpapers/bp101_regional_trade_agreements_0703
(accessed 12 July 2007)

– 2007h. "Sudan crisis, situation update, July 2007." www.oxfam.org/en/
programs/emergencies/sudan/update_0707 (accessed 12 July 2007)

– 2008a. "Oxfam International humanitarian policy on food aid." www.
oxfam.ca/what-we-do/emergencies/oxfam-international-humanitarian-
policy-notes/oi_hum_policy_foodaid.pdf (accessed 23 March 2008)

– 2008b. "Oxfam International strategic plan." www.oxfam.org/en/about/
accountability/strategic_plan (accessed 17 March 2008)

Oxfam New Zealand. 2006. *Fishing for a Future: The Advantages and
Drawbacks of a Comprehensive Fisheries Agreement between the Pacific
and European Union.* Auckland: Oxfam NZ

Peck, J. 1998. "Workfare: a geopolitical etymology." *Environment and Planning D: Society and Space* 16: 133–61

Pendleton, W.C. 1996. *Katutura: A Place Where We Stay: Life in a Post-Apartheid Township in Namibia.* Athens: Ohio University Center for International Studies

Perrons, D., and S. Skyers. 2003. "Empowerment through participation? conceptual explorations and a case study." *International Journal of Urban and Regional Research* 27(2): 265–85

Peters, M. 2001. "Education, enterprise culture and the entrepreneurial self: a Foucauldian perspective." *Journal of Educational Enquiry* 2(2): 58–71

Phillipps, L. 2000. "Taxing the market citizen: fiscal policy and inequality in an age of privatization." *Law and Contemporary Problems* 63: 111–32

Phillips, J. 2006. "Agencement/assemblage." *Theory, Culture and Society* 23(2–3): 108–9

Phillips, L., and S. Ilcan. 2004. "Capacity-building: the neoliberal governance of development." *Canadian Journal of Development Studies* 25(3): 393–409

– 2003. "'A world free from hunger': global imagination and governance in the age of scientific management." *Sociologia Ruralis* 43(4): 434–53

Phillips, R., J.M. Maria Hagan, and N. Rodriguez. 2006. "Brutal borders? examining the treatment of deportees during arrest and detention." *Social Forces* 85(1): 93–109

Phillips, S. 2006. "The intersection of governance and citizenship in Canada: not quite the third way." IRPP *Policy Matters* 4(4): 1–31

Piven, F.F., and R.A. Cloward. 1971. *Regulating the Poor: The Functions of Public Welfare.* New York: Vintage

– 1977. *Poor Peoples' Movements.* New York: Pantheon Books

Pogge, T. 2007. Introduction. In T. Pogge (ed.), *Freedom from Poverty as a Human Right: Who Owes What to the Very Poor?* Oxford: UNESCO/ Oxford University Press: 1–10

– 2008. *World Poverty and Human Rights: Cosmopolitan Responsibilities and Reforms* 2nd ed. Cambridge: Polity Press

Pollard, A.A. 2000. "Resolving conflict in Solomon Islands: the Women for Peace approach." *Development Bulletin* 53: 44–6

Poovey, M. 1995. *Making a Social Body.* Chicago: University of Chicago Press

Porter, D., and D. Craig. 2004. "The Third Way and the Third World: poverty reduction and social inclusion in the rise of inclusive liberalism." *Review of International Political Economy* 11(2): 387–423

Procacci, G. 1989. "Sociology and its poor." *Politics and Society* 17(2): 115–62

– 1991. "Social economy and the government of poverty." In G. Burchell, C. Gordon, and P. Miller (eds.), *The Foucault Effect: Studies in Governmentality: With Two Lectures by and an Interview with Michel Foucault.* Chicago: University of Chicago Press: 151–69

– 2007. "Genealogies of poverty: from inclusion towards exclusion." *Development* 50(2): 26–30

Public–Private Infrastructure Advisory Facility (PPIAF). 2007. Homepage. www.ppiaf.org/ (accessed 17 Oct. 2007)

Pupavac, V. 2005. "Human security and the rise of global therapeutic governance." *CSD* 5(2): 161–82

Raghuram, P., C. Madge, and P. Noxolo. 2009. "Rethinking responsibility and care for a postcolonial world." *Geoforum* 40: 5–13

RAMSI. 2008a. "RAMSI's mandate." www.ramsi.org/node/6 (accessed 16 July 2008)

– 2008b. "RAMSI's work." www.ramsi.org/node/2 (accessed 31 March 2008)

Ramutsindela, M.F. 2001. "Down the post-colonial road: reconstructing the post-apartheid state in South Africa." *Political Geography* 20(1): 57–84

Randeria, S. 2003. "Between cunning states and unaccountable international institutions: social movements and rights of local communities to common property resources." *European Journal of Sociology* 43(1): 27–60

Ranjo-Libang, G. 1994. "Of borders, bridges and sisterhood: reflections on the Women's Linking Project." *Focus on Gender* 2(3): 37–44

Rankin, K.N. 2001. "Governing development: neoliberalism, microcredit, and rational economic woman." *Economy and Society* 30: 18–37.

Rathgeber, E. 2005. "Gender and development as a fugitive concept." *Canadian Journal of Development Studies* 26(1): 579–91

Redfield, P. 2005. "Foucault in the tropics: displacing the panopticon." In J. Inda (ed.), *Anthropologies of Modernity.* Oxford: Blackwell Publishing: 50–82

Reid, B. 2005. "Poverty alleviation and participatory development in the Philippines." *Journal of Contemporary Asia* 35(1): 29–52

Republic of Namibia, National Planning Commission. 2005. *Volume 1: Summary Report – Review and Mainstreaming of Gender, HIV/AIDS, Environment and Sustainable Development into the National Poverty*

Reduction Action Programme (NPRAP) for Namibia. April. Windhoek. National Archives of Namibia. PB/3415

Reuters. 2008. "Rising food prices." www.in.reuters.com/article/health/ idINN0443141420080804 (accessed 12 Aug. 2008)

Reuters Newsagency. 2006. "Bono backs 'Red' brand with bold anti-AIDS goal (Friday, January 26, 2006)." Reprinted in the *New Zealand Herald*. nzherald.co.nz/section/6/story.cfm?c_id=6&objectid=10365607 (accessed 18 Aug. 2007)

Riis, J.A. [1891] 1997. *How the Other Half Lives: Studies among the Tenements of New York*. Introduction and notes by L. Sante. New York: Penguin

Roberts, D. 2006. "Review essay: human security or human insecurity? Moving the debate forward." *Security Dialogue* 37: 249–61

Roberts, M.J.D. 2004. *Making English Morals: Voluntary Association and Moral Reform in England, 1787–1886*. Cambridge: Cambridge University Press

Rojas, C. 2002. *Civilization and Violence: Regimes of Representation in Nineteenth Century Colombia*. Minneapolis: University of Minnesota Press

– 2004. "Governing through the social: representations of poverty and global governmentality." In W. Larner and W. Walters (eds.), *Global Governmentality: Governing International Spaces*. London: Routledge: 97–115

Roosevelt, F.D. 1943. Address of the President in connection with the signing of the agreement setting up the United Nations' Relief and Rehabilitation Administration in the East Room November 9 1943. Franklin D. Roosevelt Library, New York. Reprinted at European Navigator – the history of a united Europe on the internet. www.ena.lu (accessed 22 May 2009)

Rose, N. 1993. "Government, authority and expertise in advanced liberalism." *Economy and Society* 22(3): 283–300

– 1996. "The death of the social? re-figuring the territory of government." *Economy and Society* 25(3): 327–56

– 1999. *Powers of Freedom*. Cambridge: Cambridge University Press

– 2000. "Community, citizenship and the third way." *American Behavorist* 43(9): 1395–1411

– 2002. "At risk of madness." In J. Simon and T. Baker (eds.), *Embracing Risk: The Changing Culture of Insurance and Responsibility*. Chicago: University of Chicago

- 2007. *The Biopolitics of Life Itself: Biomedicine, Power, and Subjectivity in the Twenty-First Century*. Princeton, NJ: Princeton University Press Press: 209–37

Rose, N., and P. Miller. 1992. "Political power beyond the state: problematics of government." *British Journal of Sociology* 43(2): 172–205

Rose, N., and C. Novas. 2005. "Biological citizenship." In A. Ong and S. Collier (eds.), *Global Assemblages*. Malden, Mass.: Blackwell Publishers: 439–63

Rose, N., P. O'Malley, and M. Valverde. 2006. "Governmentality." *Annual Review of Law and Social Science* 2(1): 83–104

Rosga, A., and M. Satterthwaite. 2009. "The trust in indicators: measuring human rights." *Berkeley Journal of International Law* 27(2): 253–315

Rydin, Y. 2007. "Indicators as a governmental technology? the lessons of community-based sustainability indicator projects." *Environment and Planning D: Society and Space* 25: 610–24

Sachs, J. 2005. *The End of Poverty: Economic Possibilities for Our Time*. London: Penguin Books

Samoff, J. 2004. "From funding projects to supporting sectors? observation on the aid relationship in Burkina Faso." *International Journal of Educational Development* 24(4): 397–427

Sassen, S. 1996. *Losing Control? Sovereignty in an Age of Globalization*. New York: Columbia University Press

- 2003. "Globalization or denationalization." *Review of International Political Economy* 10(1): 1–22

Scheyvens, R. 2007. "Exploring the tourism–poverty nexus." *Current Issues in Tourism* 10: 231–54

Schild, V. 2000. "Neo-liberalism's new gendered market citizens: the 'civilizing' dimension of social programmes in Chile." *Citizenship Studies* 4(3): 275–305

Schuster, L. 2005. "A sledgehammer to crack a nut: deportation, detention and dispersal in Europe." *Social Policy and Administration* 39(6): 606–21

Schwartz, J. 2000. *Fighting Poverty with Virtue: Moral Reform and America's Urban Poor, 1825–2000*. Bloomington: Indiana University Press

Scott, D. 2005. "Colonial governmentality." In J. Inda (ed.), *Anthropologies of Modernity*. Oxford: Blackwell Publishing: 23–49

Seddon, T., S. Billett, and A. Clemans. 2004. "Politics of social partnerships: a framework for theorizing." *Journal of Education Policy* 19(2): 123–42

Seglow, J. 2005. "The ethics of immigration." *Political Studies Review* 3: 317–34

– 2006. "Immigration justice and borders: towards a global agreement." *Contemporary Politics* 12(3): 233–46

Shamsul Haque, S. 2004. "Governance based on partnership with NGOs: implications for development and empowerment in rural Bangladesh." *International Review of Administrative Sciences* 70(2): 271–90

Shephard, B. 2008. "'Becoming planning minded': the theory and practice of relief 1940–1945." *Journal of Contemporary History* 43(3): 405–19

Shields, R. 1997. "Flow as a new paradigm." *Space and Culture* 1(1): 1–7

Shiva, V. 2002. "Oxfam's free trade recipe: export at any cost." *South Bulletin* 36: 10–13

SIDA (Swedish International Development Cooperation Agency). 2008. "Climate change hits the poor hardest." www.sida.se/sida/jsp/sida. jsp?d=1375&a=25299&language=en_US (accessed 7 Aug. 2008)

Silverman, D. 2000. "Analyzing talk and text." In N. Denzin and Y. Lincoln (eds.), *Handbook of Qualitative Research*. London: Sage Publications: 821–34

Silvester, J., P. Hayes, and W. Hartmann. 2001. "'This ideal conquest': photography and colonialism in Namibian history." In W. Hartmann, J. Silvester, and P. Hayes, *The Colonising Camera: Photographs in the Making of Namibian History*. Cape Town: University of Cape Town Press: 10–19

Simmons, P.J. 1998. "Learning to live with NGOs." *Foreign Policy* 112: 82–96

Simon, J. 2002. "Taking risks: extreme sports and the embrace of risk in advanced liberal societies." In J. Simon and T. Baker (eds.), *Embracing Risk: The Changing Culture of Insurance and Responsibility*. Chicago: University of Chicago Press: 177–208

Sklair, L. 1999. "Global system theory and the *Fortune* Global 500." *International Journal of Politics, Culture, and Society* 12(3): 435–50

Smirl, L. 2008. "Building the other, constructing ourselves: spatial dimensions of international humanitarian response." *International Political Sociology* 2: 236–53

Sofield, T. 2006. "Solomon Islands: unity in diversity – the end of a dream?" In D. Rumley, V.L. Forbes, and C. Griffen (eds.), *Australia's Arc of Instability: The Political and Cultural Dynamics of Regional Security*. Dordrecht: Springer: 71–98

Sogavare, M. 2006. "Speech to launch the policy framework doment [sic] of the Grand Coalition for Change Government." www.parliament.gov. sb/files (accessed 21 April 2007)

The *Star*. 2008. "14,833 urban poor registered, RM33m spent on courses."
    www.thestar.com.my/metro/story.asp?fil e=/2008/8/5/southneast/
    1726353&s=southneast (accessed 7 Aug. 2008)

Stasiulis, D. 2008. "The migration–citizenship nexus." In E. Isin (ed.),
    Recasting the Social in Citizenship. Toronto: University of Toronto
    Press: 134–61

Stasiulis, D., and A. Bakan. 2003. *Negotiating Citizenship: Migrant Women
    in Canada and the Global System*. New York: Palgrave MacMillan

Steinmetz, G., and J. Hell. 2006. "Colonialism's visual archive: Germany
    and Namibia." *Public Culture* 18(1): 147–83

Stinson, J. 2004. "Privatization of public services: what does it mean for
    women?" *Women and Environments International* 64–5: 5–8

Stone, D.L. 2008. "Global public policy, transnational policy communities,
    and their networks." *Policy Studies Journal* 36(1): 19–38

Strange, C., and A. Bashford. 2003. "Isolation and exclusion in the mod-
    ern world: an introductory essay." In C. Strange and A. Bashford (eds.),
    Isolation: Places and Practices of Exclusion. New York: Routledge:
    1–19

Strathern, M. (ed.). 2000. *Audit Cultures: Anthropological Studies in
    Accountability, Ethics, and the Academy*. London : Routledge

Stubbs, P. 2003. "International non-state actors and social development
    policy." *Global Social Policy* 3(3): 319–48

Sumberg, T.A. 1945. "The financial experience of UNRRA." *American
    Journal of International Law* 39: 698–712

Sumner, A. 2006. "In search of the post-Washington (dis)consensus: the
    missing content of PRSPS." *Third World Quarterly* 27(8): 1401–12

Tabureguci, D. 2007. "Business: financial literacy – key to economic pros-
    perity: WWF joins ANZ, UNDP in rural communities." www.islands
    business.com/island_business/ (accessed 21 Oct. 2007)

Teichman, J. 2004. "The World Bank and policy reform in Mexico and
    Argentina." *Latin American Politics and Society* 46(1): 39–74

Third Sector. 2007. "First on-line charity shop launched by Oxfam."
    14 Sept. www.thirdsector.co.uk/News/DailyBulletin/738188/First-online-
    charity-shop-launched-Oxfam/70F14042BF10BB1273AAE7F1A48FEF
    0F/ (accessed 17 March 2008)

Thomas, B. 1807. "A letter to the Honourable and Right Reverend the
    Lord Bishop of Durham, President of the Society for Bettering the
    Condition of the Poor: on the principle and detail of the measures now
    under consideration of Parliament for promoting and encouraging in-
    dustry and the relief and regulation of the poor." London: J. Hatchard

Thomas, C. 2000. *Global Governance, Development and Human Security: The Challenge of Poverty and Inequality.* London: Pluto Press

– 2001. "Global governance, development and human security: exploring the links." *Third World Quarterly* 22(2): 167–8

– 2006. "Review: Woman of the World: Mary McGeachy and International Cooperation by Mary Kinnear." *Canadian Woman Studies* 25(3/4): 205–7

Tickell, A., and J. Peck. 2003. "Making global rules: globalization or neo-liberalization?" In J. Peck and H. Wai-chung Yeung (eds.), *Remaking the Global Economy: Economic–Geographic Perspectives.* London: Sage: 163–81

Time. 1945a. "The faces of UNRRA." 31 Dec.

– 1945b. "What of UNRRA?" 14 May

Tobias, R.L. 2006. "A message to the American business community." www.usaid.gov/our_work/global_partnerships/gda/pdf/0000032447.pdf (accessed 23 Oct. 2007)

Townsend, J., G. Porter, and E. Mawdsley. 2004. "Creating spaces of resistance: development NGOs and their clients in Ghana, India and Mexico." *Antipode* 36(5): 871–99

Trudeau, D. 2008. "Junior partner or empowered community? the role of non-profit social service providers amidst state restructuring in the US." *Urban Studies* 45(13): 2805–27

Trudeau, D., and L. Veronis. 2009. "Enacting state restructuring: NGOs as 'translation mechanisms.'" *Environment and Planning D: Society and Space* 27: 1117–34

Tsing, A.L. 2005. *Friction: An Ethnography of Global Connection.* Princeton, NJ: Princeton University Press

Tvedten, I., and S. Nangulah. 1999. "Social relations of poverty: a case-study from Owambo, Namibia." Report 362.5 TVE. Chr. Michelsen Institute, Development Studies and Human Rights, Bergen, Norway

UNESCO. 2008a. "UNESCO history Namibia." www.portal.unesco.org/en/ ev.php-URL_ID=13224&URL_DO=DO_TOPIC&URL_SECTION= 201.html (accessed 10 April 2008)

– 2008b. "UNESCO–NAMIBIA cooperation." www.unesdoc.unesco.org/ images/0011/001159/115944Eo.pdf (accessed 2 July 2008)

Ungerson, C., and S. Yeandle (eds.). 2007. *Cash for Care in Developed Welfare States.* London: Palgrave Macmillan

UN Country Team. 2005. "Namibia and the MDGs." Windhoek: Office of the United Nations Resident Coordinator of the UN System's Operational Activities for Development in Namibia

UNICEF. 1991. "A situation analysis of children and women in Namibia." Namibian Institute for Social and Economic Research, University of Namibia, and UNICEF. Windhoek. March. Obtained through the National Archives of Namibia

– 2008. Home page. www.unicef.org/infobycountry/namibia_2202.html (accessed 2 July 2008)

UNICEF New Zealand. 2008. "Global parents." www.unicef.org.nz/donate/global-parents/ (accessed 28 March 2008)

United Nations. 1947. *Yearbook of the United Nations*. Lake Success, NY: Department of Public Information, United States

– 1950. *Yearbook of the United Nations*. Lake Success, NY: Department of Public Information, United States

– 1959. *Yearbook of the United Nations*. Lake Success, NY: Department of Public Information, United States

– 1960. *Yearbook of the United Nations*. Lake Success, NY: Department of Public Information, United States

– 1965. *Yearbook of the United Nations*. Lake Success, NY: Department of Public Information, United States

– 1966. *Yearbook of the United Nations*. Lake Success, NY: Department of Public Information, United States

– 1968. *Yearbook of the United Nations*. Lake Success, NY: Department of Public Information, United States

– 1970. *Yearbook of the United Nations*. Lake Success, NY: Department of Public Information, United States

– 1980. *Yearbook of the United Nations*. Lake Success, NY: Department of Public Information, United States

– 1988. *Yearbook of the United Nations*. Lake Success, NY: Department of Public Information, United States

– 1989. *Yearbook of the United Nations*. Lake Success, NY: Department of Public Information, United States

– 1990. *Yearbook of the United Nations*. Lake Success, NY: Department of Public Information, United States

– 1993. *Yearbook of the United Nations*. Lake Success, NY: Department of Public Information, United States

– 2000. *Yearbook of the United Nations*. Lake Success, NY: Department of Public Information, United States

– 2002. *Yearbook of the United Nations*. Lake Success, NY: Department of Public Information, United States

– 2007. *Yearbook of the United Nations*. Lake Success, NY: Department of Public Information, United States

– 2008. *Yearbook of the United Nations*. Lake Success, NY: Department of Public Information, United States

United Nations. 1993. *The Global Partnership for Environment and Development: A Guide to Agenda 21* (Post Rio Edition). New York: United Nations

– 2002. *Common Country Assessment – Solomon Islands*. Suva, Fiji: Office of the United Nations Resident Coordinator

United Nations Capital Development Fund (UNCDF). 2003. "Media matters: perspectives on advancing governance and development from the Global Forum for Media and Development." www.uncdf.org/english/local_development/uploads/thematic/MEDIAMATTERS_AR.pdf (accessed 25 Feb. 2007)

– 2007a. "International forum to build inclusive financial sectors held at UN headquarters: International Year of Microcredit unites financial sector leaders, senior government officials, corporate CEOs, and microfinance clients." www.uncdf.org/english/microfinance/pubs/newsletter/pages/2005_11/news_forum.php (accessed 17 Oct. 2007)

– 2007b. Interview with UNCDF Executive Secretary Richard Weingarten. www.uncdf.org/english/news_and_events/newsfiles/20070803_RW interview.php (accessed 15 Oct. 2007)

– 2007c. "UNCDF: Investing in the LDCs." www.uncdf.org/english/microfinance/ (accessed 15 Oct. 2007)

United Nations Development Programme (UNDP). 2005. "Launch of the report: unleashing entrepreneurship – making business work for the poor." www.undp.org/cpsd/countrylaunches/Pacific%20Islands%20workshopreport%20%201%20.pdf (accessed 21 March 2008)

– 2007a. "Microfinance: UNDP on-line essentials." www.undp.org/eo/essentials/microfinance.htm (accessed 15 Oct. 2007)

– 2007b. "Solomon Islands human development index: going beyond income. Human Development Reports 2007/2008." www.hdrstats.undp.org/countries/country_fact_sheets/cty_fs_SLB.html (accessed 20 Dec. 2007)

– 2007c. "UNDP private sector strategy promoting inclusive market development." www.undp.org/partners/business/resources/strategy_paper_ps_undp.pdf (accessed 6 May 2009)

– 2008. "Human Development Report country fact sheets: Solomon Islands." www.hdrstats.undp.org/countries/country_fact_sheets/cty_fs_SLB.html (accessed 5 Aug. 2008)

– 2009a. "Millennium Development Goals: Goal 1: eradicate extreme poverty and hunger." www.undp.org/mdg/goal1.shtml (accessed 16 March 2009)

– 2009b. "What is the human development index (HDI)?" www.hdr.undp.
  org/en/statistics/indices/hdi/question,68,en.html (accessed 11 Feb. 2009)

United Nations Food and Agricultural Organization (FAO). 2007a.
  "Entrepreneurs don't grow on trees." FAO On-line Newsroom. www.
  fao.org/newsroom/en/field/2007/1000487/index.html (accessed 15 Oct.
  2007)

– 2007b. "FAO introduces on-line learning centre for rural finance: launch
  of UN International Year of Microcredit 2005." FAO On-line
  Newsroom. www.fao.org/newsroom/en/news/2004/51590/index.html
  (accessed 15 Oct. 2007)

United Nations International Strategy for Disaster Reduction. 2008.
  Homepage. www.unisdr.org/eng/public_aware/world_camp/2006-2007/
  iddr/2007-iddr.htm (accessed 23 July 2008)

United Nations News. 2007. UN News Centre. www.un.org/news/dh/
  infocus/gs/hlp.asp (accessed 13 Jan. 2008)

United Nations Statistics Division. 2007. "Environment statistics country
  snapshot: Solomon Islands." www.unstats.un.org/unsd/environment/
  envpdf/Country%20Snapshots_apr2007/Solomon%20Islands.pdf (accessed 5 Aug. 2008)

– 2008. "Millennium Development Goals indicators." www.mdgs.un.org/
  unsd/mdg/Data.aspx (accessed 11 March 2008)

United Nations Transition Assistance Group (UNTAG). 2008. www.un.org/
  Depts/dpko/dpko/co_mission/untagM.htm (accessed 13 Dec. 2008)

United Nations Volunteers (UNV). 2007a. "Citizenship training to help
  strengthen decentralization process in Burkina Faso." July 2005. www.
  unv.org/en/news-features/news/doc/citizenship-training-to-help.html
  (accessed 1 May 2007)

– 2007b. "Proactively embracing volunteerism." By A. de Raad. 13 Jan.
  www.unv.org/en/publications/on-volunteerism/doc/proactively-embracing-
  volunteerism.html (accessed 1 May 2007)

– 2007c. UNV Homepage. www.unv.org/en/publications.html (accessed
  1 May 2007)

UNRRA – European Regional Office. 1946. Fifty Facts about UNRRA.
  London: HMSO: 1–24

Urry, J. 2000. "Mobile sociology." British Journal of Sociology 51(1):
  185–203

– 2007. Mobilities. Oxford: Polity Press

USAID. 2004a. The East and Central Africa Global Competitiveness Trade
  Hub: National AGOA Strategy Report. pdf.usaid.gov/pdf_docs/ (accessed 11 March 2008)

– 2004b. "Message from USAID Administrator Andrew S. Natsios. Fifty years of food for peace: bringing hope to the hungry 1954–2004. www. usaid.gov/our_work/humanitarian_assistance/ffp/50th (accessed 11 March 2008

– 2005a. "Capable partners overview." www.usaid.gov/our_work/cross-cutting_programs/private_voluntary_cooperation/cap.html (accessed 25 Feb. 2008)

– 2005b. "Policy: nine principles of development and reconstruction assistance." www.usaid.gov/policy/2005_nineprinciples.html (accessed 25 Feb. 2008)

– 2006a. "Policy framework for bilateral foreign aid: implementing transformational diplomacy through development." www.usaid.gov/policy/policy_framework_jan06.html (accessed 13 Dec. 2008)

– 2006b. "President Bush speaks about the success of GDA and public–private alliances." www.usaid.gov/our_work/global_partnerships/gda/ (accessed 25 Feb. 2008)

– 2006c. "USAID, Tanzania forge new partnerships under President Bush's Africa education initiative." www.usaid.gov/press/releases/2006/pro 60523_2.html (accessed 12 Feb. 2008)

– 2007a. "Conditions of registration for international organizations (non-U.S. organizations)." www.usaid.gov/our_work/cross-cutting_programs/ private_voluntary_cooperation/conditions_ipvos.pdf (accessed 25 Feb. 2008)

– 2007b. "2007 VOLAG: report of voluntary agencies." www.usaid.gov/ our_work/cross-cutting_programs/private_voluntary_cooperation/ volag07.pdf (accessed 17 Dec. 2007)

– 2008a. "Private capital fuels international development." www.usaid. gov/our_work/global_partnerships/gda/pdf/gda_privsec_resourceflows. pdf (accessed 18 March 2008)

– 2008b. "USAID: Latin America and the Caribbean." www.usaid.gov/ locations/latin_america_caribbean/LAC_Overview.pdf (accessed 16 Jan. 2009)

2008c. "USAID history." www.usaid.gov/about_usaid/usaidhist.html (accessed 25 Feb. 2008)

– USAID Namibia. 2007. Website. www.usaid.gov/na/s01.htm (accessed 20 Sept. 2007)

– 2008a. "Program overview." www.usaid.gov/na/overview.htm#69 (accessed 7 April 2008)

– 2008b. "USAID news." www.usaid.gov/na/news21.htm (accessed 24 July 2008)

U.S. Department of State/US Agency for International Development (USDS/USAID). 2007. *Strategic Plan: Fiscal Years 2007–2012*

Valverde, M., and M. Mopas. 2004. "Insecurity and the dream of targeted governance." In W. Larner and W. Walters (eds.), *Global Governmentality: Governing International Spaces*. New York: Routledge: 233–50

Van Donge, J.K. 2005. "Land reform in Namibia: issues of equity and poverty." ISS/UNDP Land, Poverty and Public Action Policy Paper No. 8

Van Rooy, G., B. Roberts, C. Schier, J. Swartz, and S. Levine, 2006. "Income poverty and inequality in Namibia." Discussion Paper No. 1. Jan. Multi-Disciplinary Research and Consultancy Centre, University of Namibia, Windhoek

Vantaa City Museum. 2008. Homepage. www.vantaa.fi/en/i_perusdoku mentti.asp?path=1;135;137;2620;218;58993;1858;29614;75003;75073 (accessed 9 July 2008)

Veltmeyer, H., and J. Petras 2002. "The social dynamics of Brazil's rural landless workers movement: ten hypotheses on successful leadership." *Canadian Review of Sociology and Anthropology* 39(1): 79–96

Vigne, R. 1987. "The politics of exile." *Third World Quarterly* 9(1): 85–107

Vision 2030. 2007. Vision 2030 webpage. www.tech.na/vision2030.htm (accessed 14 Sept. 2007)

Vollmann, W.T. 2007. *Poor People*. New York: Harper Collins

Von Mahs, J. 2005. "The sociospatial exclusion of single homeless people in Berlin and Los Angeles." *American Behavioral Scientist* 48(8): 928–60

Vosko, L., ed. 2006. *Precarious Employment: Understanding Labour Market Insecurity in Canada*. Montreal: McGill-Queen's University Press

Wacquant, L. 2003. "Toward a dictatorship over the poor? notes on the penalization of poverty in Brazil." *Punishment and Society* 5: 197

Walby, S. 2003. "The myth of the nation-state: theorizing society and polities in a global era." *Sociology* 37(3): 529–46

Walker, A., and L. Foster. 2006. "Caught between virtue and ideological necessity – a century of pensions policy in the UK." *Review of Political Economy* 18(3): 427–48

Walters, W. 1994. "The discovery of 'unemployment': new forms for the government of poverty. *Economy and Society* 23(3): 265–90

– 2000. *Unemployment and Government: Genealogies of the Social*. Cambridge: Cambridge University Press

– 2002. "Social capital and political sociology: re-imagining politics?" *Sociology* 36(2): 377–97

– 2004. "Some critical notes on 'governance.'" *Studies in Political Economy* 73: 25–42

– Forthcoming. "Foucault and frontiers: notes on the birth of the humanitarian border." In U. Brockling, S. Krassman, and T. Lemke (eds.), *Governmentality: Current Issues and Future Challenges*. London: Routledge

Walters, W., and J. Haahr. 2005. *Governing Europe: Discourse, Governmentality and European Integration*. London: Routledge

Washington Post. 2008. "Inflation hits the poor hardest." www.washing tonpost.com/wp-yn/content/article/2008/03/20/AR2008032003517. html (accessed 7 Aug. 2008)

Watson, P. 2006. "Unequalizing citizenship: the politics of Poland's health care." *Sociology* 40(6): 1079–96

Weber, H. 2004. "The 'new economy' and social risk: banking on the poor?" *Review of International Political Economy* 11(2): 356–86

Weber, T. 2006. "Bono bets on Red to battle AIDS." BBC News. www. news.bbc.co.uk/2/hi/business/4650024.stm (accessed 18 Aug. 2007)

Weir, L. 2006. *Pregnancy, Risk and Biopolitics*. New York: Routledge

Wild, R., and P. Anderson. 2007. *Ampe Akelyernemane Meke Mekarle/ Little Children Are Sacred*. Report to the Northern Territory Government. www.fahcsia.gov.au/nter/ (accessed 2 Jan. 2009)

Wildridge, V., S. Childs, L. Cawthra, and B. Madge. 2004. "How to create successful partnerships – a review of the literature." *Health Information and Library Journal* (21): 3–19

Wilson, D. 2006. "Biometrics, borders and the ideal suspect." In S. Pickering and L. Weber (eds.), *Borders, Mobilities, and Technologies of Control*. Dordrecht, the Netherlands: Springer: 87–109

Women's e-News. 2008. "States fight poverty." www.womensenews.org/ article.cfm?aid=3700 (accessed 11 Aug. 2008)

World Bank. 2001. "The World Development Report 2000/2001: attacking poverty." www.web.worldbank.org/WBSITE/EXTERNAL/ TOPICS/EXTPOVERTY/0,,contentMDK:20194762~pagePK:148956~ piPK:216618~theSitePK:336992,00.html (accessed 20 Sept. 2007)

– 2003. "The Poverty Reduction Strategy initiative: an independent evaluation of the World Bank's support through 2003." http://lnweb90. worldbank.org/oed/oeddoclib.nsf/24cc3bb1f94ae11c85256808006a004 6/6b5669f816a60aaf85256ec1006346ac/$FILE/PRSP_Evaluation.pdf (accessed 20 Sept. 2007)

– 2004. "Addressing the challenges of globalization: an independent evaluation of the World Bank's approach to global programs." www.

worldbank.org/ieg/gppp/documents/gppp_advisory_committee_report.
pdf (accessed 20 Sept. 2007)

– 2005. "Pro-poor growth in the 1990s. On behalf of the Operationalizing Pro-Poor Growth Research Program." siteresources.worldbank.
org/INTPGI/Resources/342674-1119450037681/Pro-poor_growth_in_
the_1990s.pdf (accessed 20 Sept. 2007)

– 2006. "Project Information Document (PID): Concept Stage Report
No.: AB1485." www-wds.worldbank.org/servlet/WDSContentServer/
WDSP/IB/2006/03/17/000104615_20060317161637/Rendered/PDF/
OrissaoRPRPoPIDoMaro16006.pdf (accessed 19 March 2006)

– 2007. "Solomon Islands." www.web.worldbank.org/WBSITE/
EXTERNAL/COUNTRIES/EASTASIAPACIFICEXT/PACIFICISLANDS
EXTN/0,,contentMDK:20217357~menuPK:457015~pagePK:1497618~
piPK:217854~theSitePK:441883,00.html (accessed 20 Dec. 2007)

– 2008a. "About us: partners." www.web.worldbank.org/WBSITE/
EXTERNAL/EXTABOUTUS/;[?] (accessed 15 Feb. 2008)

– 2008b. "Comprehensive development framework." www.web.world
bank.org/WBSITE/EXTERNAL/PROJECTS/STRATEGIES/CDF/0,,page
PK:60447~theSitePK:140576,00.html (accessed 28 March 2008)

– 2008c. "Country brief – Namibia." www.web.worldbank.org/WBSITE/
EXTERNAL/COUNTRIES/AFRICAEXT/NAMIBIAEXTN/0,,menuPK:
382303~pagePK:141132~piPK:141107~theSitePK:382293,00.html (accessed 7 April 2008)

– 2008d. Homepage. www.web.worldbank.org/WBSITE/EXTERNAL/
COUNTRIES/AFRICAEXT/NAMIBIAEXTN/0,,menuPK:382299~page
PK:141159~piPK:141110~theSitePK:382293,00.html (accessed
21 April 2008)

– 2008e. "International Development Association." www.web.worldbank.
org/WBSITE/EXTERNAL/EXTABOUTUS/IDA/0,,contentMDK:200512
70~menuPK:83991~pagePK:83988~piPK:84004~theSitePK:73154,00.
html (accessed 20 July 2008)

– 2008f. "The country-based development model and scaling up PREM."
Poverty Reduction Group Newsletter 2. www.siteresources.worldbank.
org/INTPRS1/Resources/383606-1170086079630/ScalingUp_Newsletter
_02.pdf (accessed 26 March 2008)

– 2009a. "Poverty: overview." www.go.worldbank.org/RQBDCTUXW0
(accessed 21 April 2009)

– 2009b . "PovertyNet." www.go.worldbank.org/F8H6CGITI0 (accessed
21 April 2009)

World Bank Group. 2007. *Pacific Islands REF Report #32261-EAP.doc* www.siteresources.worldbank.org/INTPACIFICISLANDS/Resources/ G-SOLOMON.pdf (accessed 20 Dec. 2007)

World Food Programme. 2009a. "World Food Programme: operations – post-conflict relief and rehabilitation in Guinea-Bissau." www.wfp.org/ content/post-conflict-relief-and-rehabilitation-guinea-bissau (accessed 20 May 2009)

– 2009b. "World Food Programme: operations – relief and rehabilitation (PRROs)." http://www.wfp.org/operations/relief (accessed 20 May 2009)

World Vision. 2008. "Urgent global food crisis." www.site.worldvision. org/#help_now/3 (accessed 12 Aug. 2008)

World Vision International. 2004. "Who we are." www.wvi.org/wvi/ about_us/who_we_are.htm (accessed 24 May 2004)

Yanacopulos, H. 2005. "The strategies that bind: NGO coalitions and their influence." *Global Networks* 5(1): 93–110

Yannis, A. 2001. "Humanitarian politics in collapsed states." In O. Barrow and M. Jennings (eds.), *The Charitable Impulse: NGOs and Development in East and North-East Africa*. Bloomfield, Conn.: Kumarian Press: 45–62

Yapa, L. 1996 "What causes poverty? a postmodern view." *Annals of the Association of American Geographers* 86(4): 707–28

Young, I.M. 1990. *Justice and the Politics of Difference*. Princeton, NJ: Princeton University Press

Zartman, I.W. (ed.). 1995. *Collapsed States: The Disintegration and Restoration of Legitimate Authority*. Boulder, Col.: Lynne Rienner

ZERI. 2006. The 2006 Annual Report

Zureik, E., and M.B. Salter. 2005. "Global surveillance and policing: borders, security, identity – introduction." In E. Zureik and M.B. Salter (eds.), *Global Surveillance and Policing: Borders, Security, Identity*. Cullompton, England: Willan

Index

Page numbers in *italic* refer to figures.